UMMA, AT THE EDGE OF MEMORY

A Memoir

SUNNY PAK

Published by Lunchie Press

Published by Lunchie Press

ISBN: 9798218776404 (Paperback)

First Edition

Written by Sun Yong Pak, writing as Sunny Pak

Editor: Kimberley Lim

Cover Design and Illustration: Kyoko Takahashi

Graphic Design: Pamela Olecki

For Umma

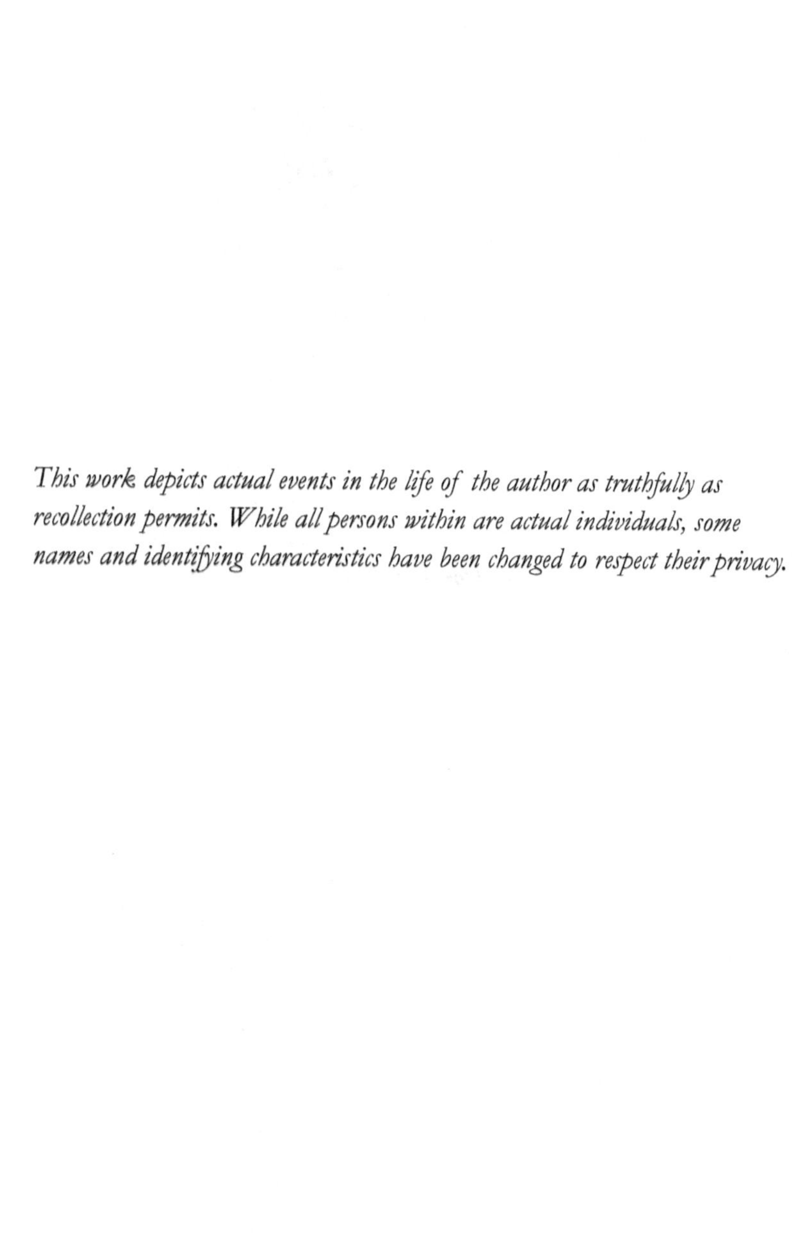

This work depicts actual events in the life of the author as truthfully as recollection permits. While all persons within are actual individuals, some names and identifying characteristics have been changed to respect their privacy.

1

I was three when we immigrated to the U.S. My mom, Johnny, and I were born in Seoul, South Korea, and my father was born in North Korea, which, my mom and I always half-joked, should have explained everything about him. Like most South Korean immigrants of the 1970s, my parents came to the U.S. after the immigration ban lifted in 1965, leaving their poverty-racked ancestral country that was split in half to pursue a life they hoped would make them whole.

My mom's younger sister, Aunt Min Jee, had already been living in Redwood Shores in Northern California for seven years after marrying a captain in the U.S. Army in Seoul. In subsequent years, Aunt Min Jee and Uncle Terry helped my grandmother and six other siblings immigrate to the U.S. My parents were the only ones with small children at the time, so it took them longer to organize and eventually settle in the Bay Area suburb where everyone else was—Redwood City. Aunt Young Soon was the eldest (and surliest), then my mom, followed by Aunt Min Jee, Aunt Soo Jin, Uncle Young Soo, Aunt Yun Hee, Aunt Seo Yun, and finally Aunt Chan Mi. Uncle Terry, Aunt Min Jee's white husband from Oklahoma, helped his in-laws settle into a brand-new country and anglicized our names, converting my father's Korean name from Chan Min to Charles, my brother's name from Chong In to John (but we called him Johnny), and my name from Sun Yong to Shirley, after one of Uncle Terry's best friends. He thought I should have been flattered by that gesture, but it felt like an ungainly interloper of an identity; I was no Shirley. My mom's name was untouched, but instead of Yong Cha, it became Yong—shorter and easier for the non-Korean to pronounce.

My mother pronounced Shirley "Shodey." When I was fourteen, my mom took me to get a perm at Fantastic Sam's right around the corner from the Richard Nixon Library. Ten minutes after my mom checked in with the front desk, the receptionist shouted, "Shorty?! Is there a Shorty here?" I didn't know who she was referring to until I saw my mom perk up in her seat next to mine and nudge me, "Shodey-a, she calling you."

We spent the first couple of years in a small apartment in the suburbs of Redwood City, thirty miles south of San Francisco. The American Dream for my mom was to work a white-collar job at a large company in the Bay Area, as she had in South Korea working as an IBM data processing supervisor for the U.S. Army. Uncle Terry helped my mom get a job as a data processor at Allstate in Menlo Park by updating her résumé and writing a letter of recommendation on official U.S. Army letterhead. She was elated because she didn't want to be relegated to the new-immigrant world of manual labor. On my mom's first day at work, her coworkers took her out to lunch to get Reuben sandwiches, "one of the first American meals I had, and it was so dee-lish-uss-u," she said. My mom was OCD-level efficient and liked her chores done early, so she packed her lunches a day in advance. She dreaded alienating her coworkers for any reason, especially with the pungent fermentation of Korean food, so she packed dull, spartan, American lunches that consisted of droopy iceberg lettuce salads with mushy tomatoes and shredded carrots in plastic Tupperware, with the Italian dressing already poured over it just to make the lettuce extra soggy when she ate it the next day. She didn't want to use another container for the dressing no matter how small—it was more to wash.

Back in South Korea, my father had completed one year of college before he started working full time as the assistant general manager at the Chosun Hotel in Seoul, a high-profile hotel that hosted political elites, celebrities, royalty, statesmen, opera singers, and dignitaries—and as a result of listening to, observing, and mimicking such people, his English was very good. He also watched a lot of American TV shows to pick up on inflection and proper pronunciation. My father knew it was an amazing opportunity to work at the Chosun Hotel in a position of quasi-unlimited authority while getting to manage up to fifty people. It was where he met and took photos with Bob Hope and the Swedish actress Anita Ekberg who starred in *Northeast of Seoul,* after one of the final scenes. It was also where he learned to wear suits every day to work so others wouldn't dare ask him to do any manual labor. My father received the respect and admiration he always wanted and demanded, so he was hell-bent on finding the same glory in the States. Entrepreneurship was his definition of power.

After a few years of living in Redwood City, my dad heard of what would become the first in a long line of get-rich-quick business ventures in the service industry in Southern California. He made my mom request to be relocated to one of Allstate's regional offices in Southern California, even though she loved working in the main corporate office where there was a certain cachet associated with being physically close to the core group; she also enjoyed living near her mother and siblings. She adored the exclusive affluence of the Bay Area even if we observed it from afar; my parents were fine being wealthy-adjacent. We studied the west coast elite—frequently outfitted in clothes from Nordstrom, Banana Republic, and Esprit—get in and out of their brand-new Mercedes-Benzes or vintage Volvos and learned through osmosis the absurd ennui that they embodied. They brushed off and obscured their wealth to appear less oozing of it, yet would have decimated any threats to it.

My mom fought with my dad about uprooting us from Northern California, but Dad promised her that we'd become rich from running a fast-food franchise, a fantasy buttressed by his lifelong gambling addiction. He took outlandish risks and relied on the women in his life to work for him and be his safety net. My mom was forced to give in. When the relocation was approved, we moved to Arcadia, a city in Los Angeles County.

My parents rented a bungalow on West Huntington Drive on a cul-de-sac in a small mixed-income, mostly white community. I was six years old and loved our neighborhood that was filled with other children my age who shared a love of roller-skating and chasing feral cats. Johnny, who was one and a half years older than me, and I shared a bedroom with matching white twin bed frames and pink floral-print comforters. My parents bought quintessential children's furniture of the seventies: white chest of drawers made of finished wood with round knob handles and chunky claw feet, with a large mirror attached to the spine. My parents liked that our bungalow looked more like the houses they saw on TV, and that it wasn't at the top of a flight of apartment stairs. Wanting to complete the look of the

American Family, my dad came home one day with a mutt we named Chong. Chong was perfect to Johnny and me, but he constantly shat on our living room rugs because my parents didn't understand that he needed to be walked several times a day. So one day my dad took Chong to a neighborhood playground and left him there. Johnny and I couldn't believe our eyes as we screamed at him from the back seat of the car. We cried for weeks looking for Chong, but my father said he had found a new home. I never believed him, nor forgave him for abandoning my dog.

Within a few months of moving, my father started complaining about some generalized abdominal pain. At first, he thought he was eating too much spicy food, so he stopped eating kimchi and spicy stews. But the pain persisted and got worse until he couldn't walk. My dad's gastroenterologist told him he had a small malignant tumor in his stomach, but it was treatable as it was in its early stages and hadn't spread. According to his doctor, his pack-a-day smoking habit, Korean barbecue consumption, and stress levels had contributed to his tiny cancerous tumor. Johnny and I were too young to understand the seriousness of the situation and were thrilled that he had to stay in the hospital for a week after his surgery, because the peace at home was a respite from my parents' constant fighting.

I don't remember exactly when my father started beating my mom, but I'm sure it preceded the time my memory formed. I'm also not sure whether I was the only six-year-old who prayed for their parents to divorce. Our household was never without the hint of potential—the potential for hostility and violence. The earth beneath our feet rumbled with warnings.

There were moments of happiness during birthday celebrations and major holidays, albeit seldom and brief like a comet flashing by. The desire for peace was primordial; even as young children Johnny and I craved it. After my parents fought, we'd ask for only my mom's confirmation that things would be back to normal: "Are you mad at Dad?" Her answer was the only barometer of wrath we cared about because she never hit us, and we loved her more. If she said no, we enthusiastically decompressed; if she said yes, we lived a few more days anticipating war. Johnny and I were addicted to her "no," the coping mechanism for our early childhood traumas; "no" was a torrent of relief washing over us.

My parents usually fought about money. My mom would become livid when my dad gambled her hard-earned money or when he made risky, impetuous business decisions. My father threatened to hurt my mom when she talked back, as she usually did with her penetrating wit that took his breath away. She was congenitally stubborn and wouldn't be bullied by a fool. So, my father beat her. Johnny and I rarely saw the beatings; we mostly heard them. I had an early contempt for my father whose violence against my mom carried over into his parenting duties. He demanded respect from Johnny and me with the same intimidation, and when we didn't comply, he hit us too. But never with the same hell-bent conviction he saved for my mom.

My father wasn't the type of abuser who beat up his wife every day, the way Farrah Fawcett's character was abused for innocuous reasons like dropping something on the floor in *The Burning Bed.* That show was cheesy even for 1984 because it imprinted in me a caricature of how abusers reacted to the abused when they stood up for themselves, when they used their voice. But it also created an awareness that the bullying, harassment, and emotional and physical abuses happening in our family were not ordinary things. Our family was not normal. And I was both surprised and not surprised that my father didn't react with the slightest resistance when he watched the show with me.

"Didn't you notice I quit smoking?" my dad asked me a month after his operation as we were packing our belongings to move from Arcadia to Virginia. We had only lived in Arcadia for a little over a year, but my dad was spooked by cancer and needed another business distraction far away. I had only noticed because my headaches went away when he stopped smoking in the car. I associated my father's smoking with headaches, which naturally made me equate him with grating irritants.

"I didn't know, Dad. Congratulations," I mumbled indifferently, a dented kid.

We traveled across country in our beige van. My mom prepared days in advance for our five-day trip because she wanted to save money on fast food and needed to eat Korean food at least once a day. Large Tupperware containers filled with sweet black beans, kimchi, seasoned spinach and soybean sprout side dishes, roasted seaweed, and white rice packed our two coolers to the brim. My mom stuffed thermoses of cold barley tea inside her purse in case they spilled in the back seat. I didn't look forward to our Korean meals on the road because I craved "Junior Whoppers," as my mom called the Whopper Jr., french fries, and a small Coke from Burger King. For every six hours of driving, we'd stop at a rest stop to use the bathroom, stretch, and eat our meals.

"Spit it in my hand." My mom put her hand under my

mouth as I was pulling out a single black bean that I had sucked on first for the sweetness.

"I already spit it out," I responded, slightly disgusted by my own string of saliva on the gnawed bean.

"Here, give it to me." My mom grabbed the shiny black bean in her hand and held it, while wiping the snot from my nose with her other hand. Then she knelt down to grab all the other black beans I had spat out that were scattered on the grass near our picnic table in the middle of god-knows-where Arizona. Her obsession with tidiness and order compelled her to dispose of the beans in the trash immediately. I thought my mom was a badass for not being disgusted by my spit. It was like the time she cleared our bathtub drain in Arcadia by pulling out my dark hair covered in slime from the pipes, barehanded. I nearly threw up when I saw the dank chunks of black, oily debris clinging to my hair, but my mom was undaunted; she'd seen and smelled worse. "Aigoo, you need to cut your hair! This is too much work for Mommy," she shrieked in a high-pitched squeal. I was afraid of my mom's temper, but I was both unsettled and relieved that we could depend on her to do the gross things we would never do. These gestures proved that my mom would do anything for Johnny and me. I'd have to close my eyes for a second when the heartbreak winded me knowing she prioritized us in every situation.

"Johnny-a, Sun Yong-a, ojumul sado gada." It was normal for my mom to slip back and forth between "Shodey" and "Sun Yong." She told Johnny and me to pee, but I didn't need to go so I jumped into the back of the van. Within twenty minutes of being back on the road, I had to go. I was too nervous to ask my dad to stop so I held my bladder for twenty more agonizing minutes. The thing about having to pee so desperately is that the urge eventually stops after holding it for too long. But the diuretic qualities of the barley tea were more powerful than my body's involuntary actions, and I started to wet my shorts.

"I have to pee!" I shouted.

My parents yelled over each other. "We gave you a chance back there, why didn't you go?! Aiisshh, you make so much trouble, napun gijibae!" Bad girl. For having to pee. There was no rest stop in sight for miles so my dad pulled over onto somebody's property whose front lawn was covered in healthy shrubs. I ran into one and squatted while my mom stood in front of me. "Make sure you shake all the ojum out. Hurry up!"

I was too young to understand and appreciate the awesomeness of driving cross-country: the expansive landscapes, red rocks, green mountains, brown hills, tall forests, dusty-pink sunsets, miles and miles of barren roads. But I did notice my parents weren't fighting on these infertile roads; nature had a calming effect outside the confines of our daily rigmarole. My mom used to always complain that my father never took us on vacations; if there was any travel in our household, it was usually my father going out on his own on golf trips with friends or seeing his mistresses. But this transcontinental drive through invisible time zones and shifting biomes was keeping their squabbling at bay. Nature shut them up.

For four days we ate fruit or prepackaged pastries from gas stations for breakfast, my mom's Korean food for lunch, and McDonald's or Burger King for dinner, before crashing at motels for the night. My parents were deliriously exhausted while Johnny and I screamed, played, and fought in the back of our creepy van. As we drove through Tennessee, my dad unintentionally cut off two white men on a quiet highway. They immediately caught up to mirror us on our left and yelled, "Fuck you, chinks!" Then they sped up, cut us off, and slammed on their brakes.

My dad stopped the van, got out, walked to the back and swung open the back doors. Johnny and I hung off our seats to see that he had grabbed his monkey wrench from the toolbox and was hard-charging toward their car. As my dad thundered toward the white racists' car, it actually looked like he was moving in slow motion because, through my side of the window, I saw the formation of the face of war he used on us: lower jaw jutting out, bottom teeth exposed while biting his upper lip—a look of intimidation that actually just accentuated his underbite. This threatening look worked on the racists who shouted, "Oh shit, he has a machete or some shit! Go!" They took off immediately. My father swaggered back, placed the monkey wrench away neatly in the toolbox, and got back in the van, cursing in Korean. My mom, Johnny, and I sat in silence.

"You must be proud of your Korean heritage!" my father emphasized in half Korean and half English. "Never let people humiliate you!" he added while calling the racists "dong saekie," which literally translated to "asshole of shit." But with all the clattery consonants of the Korean language, it sounded more violent and debasing. This was my first encounter with blatant racism in late-1970s America, a hatred for us because of our external Korean-ness—something we couldn't change or hide from because we were reminded of it every day. It was the only time I was satisfied by my father's hostility.

2

I was seven years old when we moved into a large apartment above the restaurant my parents had bought through a family friend in Newport News, Virginia, called Gate 4. It was near the Newport News Marine Terminal's main roll-on/roll-off facility for equipment and cargo like vehicles, on the north side of the James River. Our apartment was filthy, old, and repugnant, and it came with free rent, so that made up my father's mind. My mom had panic attacks living in our "upstairs hell," as she referred to the apartment. The hardwood floors were slick with grime and grease from the previous tenants. They were so bad even after multiple sweepings, moppings, and buffings that my mom told us to keep our shoes on in the house, something no Asian mother dared to do. The bathtubs and toilets were indelibly stained with use and rust, marking us with the funk and fetid stench of mold, age, and rot. Johnny and I were spoiled kids and were used to immaculate homes that my mother kept.

My mom was never diagnosed with OCD, but all the signs pointed to it: when she saw a speck of dust or piece of lint on a counter surface or floor, she swiftly and nimbly swooped down to pick it up like a hawk catching its prey; when a book or trinket was out of place, she scurried over to line it up in straight lines or at sharp right angles. At least once a day I'd catch my mom taking one step forward with her left foot, then tap her right foot back and forth three times, then finally proceed to walk. Tapping only three times seemed so arbitrary to me, yet perhaps it comforted her with its unevenness.

Whenever she left the house, she made sure the stovetop knobs were off by twisting each of them in the off position at least twenty times until one of the knobs actually came loose and fell off from her overzealousness. And she'd be damned to walk on sidewalk cracks. She leapt over them while doing her compulsive back-and-forth tap walk. I always found it peculiar even at a young age, but in my self-absorbed, puerile mind, it was amusing.

At Gate 4, my parents made hamburgers and french fries and served beer to drunk marine terminal workers and sailors. It was an instant success. There were two pool tables near the back of the restaurant, and at the front a juke box played Eddie Money, The Rolling Stones, and Hall & Oates on constant rotation. Johnny and I spent our afternoons after school playing arcade games like Pac-Man and Space Invaders in the corner next to the restrooms that smelled of urine, bleach, hair spray, and beer. We were restaurant kids, kept nearby, because our parents couldn't afford sitters. The restaurant was open from 8 a.m. to 1 a.m., so my parents were always there working their asses off, and consequently, fighting about everything.

My dad was in charge of hiring and firing, accepting money, grilling, and kicking out drunk customers at closing time. He always had a grill scraper in his hand to remove layers of grease from cooking frozen meat patties all day. My mom kept the kitchen area in the back organized and clean. She was the accountant and sous chef, utilizing her Korean food prep skills by deftly slicing, dicing, and mincing vegetables. My mom was excellent at math and could count a bundle of small bills rapidly and rabidly. Because of her OCD tendencies, she counted the daily revenue at least three times in case she missed something. OCD did not create distress or impair her daily functioning, but it was enough to slow her down. "Long times ago, I use abacus. You know how much harder that was than calculator?" my mom told me in the kitchen, holding a stack of bills with both hands. The blur of bills riffled by as she flicked each one with her right thumb, which she'd pause to lick in between flicking. She looked like a casino pit boss shuffling through cards, moving on to the next deck of cash while simultaneously answering the phone, greeting customers, and serving food.

"What's an abacus?" I asked in awe of her efficiency and accuracy.

"It's too hard for you. You're too young to understand. Your younger generation has it much easier. Money is very important. Mommy and Daddy have to work hard to make lots of money to buy you things. This is all for you and Johnny," my mom said intently, counting the dollar bills and placing the bundles in manila envelopes she'd seal with leftover cooked white rice from lunch.

In return, my mom's virtuous sacrifices were met with the embarrassment and shame I caused at the grocery store a week later when she pulled out a wad of one-dollar bills to pay the clerk twenty dollars for the snacks and treats Johnny and I were habitually spoiled with.

"Mom, you're so stupid." I cringed with shame after noticing the impatient blonde clerk, whose hair was streaked with green from the pool, looking exasperated. "Don't you have a twenty-dollar bill?" I asked superciliously.

My mother looked up at the clerk to see whether she had heard what I said. She had. The clerk's smirky eyebrows lifted and the wrinkles on her forehead accordioned. I had single-handedly demoralized my mom in front of this asshat. My mother swiftly counted the compulsively organized dollar bills (all of George Washington's heads were uniformly facing up in the same direction), handed the clerk the money, and darted for the car. I grabbed the groceries and followed behind slowly, to the pace of my inner dirge, in complete terror of the scolding I was about to receive.

"How can you *umbarrass* Mommy and call me stupid in front of strangers?" My mom's eyes were the steady vessel of rising tears.

"I'm sorry, Mommy. We were taking so long, and I was getting nervous. That lady looked angry at us."

"You cannot talk to me like American child! How'd I do now? How can I go back there?"

My body heat rose whenever I anticipated danger. I had been worried about hearing an impending racial epithet hurled our way in the store for taking up imagined time and space. Thinking about these things engulfed me in a panicky inferno laced with sweaty chills that left an inky glaze on the black vinyl car seat. Because through societal reinforcement, Asians were expected to tread quietly, phantomly. I was ashamed of the clues —too many single dollar bills—that told everyone my parents worked in the service industry, that my mom got tips for good service. It was a reminder of the manual labor that my mom had fought so hard to avoid and that my dad had thought he was too good for. Yet, because of a twist of fate born out of his get-rich-quick entrepreneurial fantasies, they had landed in the world of restaurant manual labor like a lot of their immigrant friends.

Gate 4, like our apartment upstairs, was over sixty years

old. It seemed to be held together by black mold. It smelled like it, and it attracted drunks, like one of our part-time cooks, Jim, whose breath smelled like burnt rum and cigarettes. He didn't have any family, so he was always at the restaurant, either working or drinking and smoking near the jukebox after his shift. Jim was a longtime local, a carryover from the previous owners, who was endearing to the sailors, so my father saw him as an asset in controlling the crowds late at night. My mom didn't like the fact that Jim was friendly toward me. He would give me bags of Doritos to snack on near a fenced open field next to the restaurant that was overgrown with flowering white American Dogwood, Virginia's state flower. I picked the Dogwood flowers while I ate the chips.

"I'm going to report you to the police. It's a crime to pick the state flower," Jim teased with a smile that exposed his ecru teeth that became scarcer near the back of his mouth. I'd catch a glimpse of it whenever he tilted his head back to let out a chronic smoker's cough/cackle when he saw something inane, like beer bottles shattering when they hit the floor after drowsy, drunk patrons loosened their grip.

A week earlier my mom had overheard Jim telling Johnny and me that he wanted to take us on a field trip to visit his childhood neighborhood in Norfolk, about 30 minutes away. Johnny and I hated being cooped up at the restaurant or filthy apartment so we told him, "Yes!"

"You be good girl, stop talking to Jim. He's an old drunk man. I don't trust him, be careful," my mom warned as I walked outside to follow Jim to the fence to pick some more Dogwood flowers.

"Jim wants to give me a Mountain Dew!" I resisted.

"No, Mommy say no! You napun-gichibae, listen to me, he's dirty old man! He's going to do something bad to you!" my mom yelled at me from the kitchen as my dad walked by.

I ran out of the restaurant, made a hard right up the staircase toward our apartment, but not before turning back to yell at Jim, "I can't talk to you anymore!" while he leaned on the fence smoking a cigarette, nodding off to sleep.

I had crushes on some of the young Navy cadets who would arrive later at night to get drunk, around the time my mom would send us home to go to sleep. I was shy, so I secretly waited for one in particular named Steve: a tall, lanky, taciturn twenty-two-year-old who always swaggered to the jukebox after he picked me up and swung me around in circles. Even after he did all that and I laughed maniacally, I still pretended he wasn't there, turning my back to him so he'd have a chance to sneak up behind me to lift me up again and carry me under his arm like I was a clutch.

"What do you want today? Ice cream bar, french fries, a Coke?" Steve asked, offering to buy me things I got for free.

"Ice cream!" I screamed, exposing my newly erupting permanent teeth. I thought I was the only seven-year-old with a boyfriend until I saw him come in one day holding hands with a tall blonde woman. I was crushed. I stopped waiting for him, and when I did run into him, he smiled and winked at me as I ran away in embarrassment. I felt like the village idiot.

Aside from my parents' fighting and the disgusting living conditions, Newport News was oddly fun. It smelled like industry, trade, and nature: ship exhaust mixed with discreet river air. It was hardly a children's playground, but Johnny and I were doted on by the restaurant staff and customers. During our first winter there, school buses couldn't get through to our neighborhood for almost two weeks due to the four feet of accumulated snow, so Johnny and I used Gate 4's garbage pail lids to slide down the hills in the residential area beyond the fence where the Dogwood flowers once thrived.

As restaurant kids my mom couldn't spend time with us after school like the mothers of my classmates since she didn't get off at 5 p.m. She didn't get to go over our homework assignments or giggle with us as we helped her make dinner or bake cookies, no less help us make Halloween costumes. Instead she worked another full-time shift. She made Johnny stay at Gate 4 to do his homework and play arcade games and had me stay in the nearby apartment of their sweet twenty-four-year-old Korean hostess, Miss Kim, right before her evening shift. Miss Kim was married to a white U.S. Marine who was regularly deployed all over the continent. She liked me because I was shy and precocious, and she wanted children, too. Miss Kim spoiled me rotten with pizza and cookies and compliments like, "Yaepudda, ahgassi!" after she'd braid my long hair. I never thought of myself as pretty; cute maybe, but never pretty. Miss Kim was the first woman in my life to call me pretty, so I clung to her like a barnacle on an oyster shell that hid pearlescent secrets. I'd watch her put on her makeup for work and say how pretty she was—"Yaepudda, Miss Kim!"—and she'd pat enough blush on me that I looked like a Kewpie doll. I never wanted to go back home because I was smitten by Miss Kim's insouciance and the calmness of her apartment. My mom knew I hated returning home and was envious of my relationship with Miss Kim because she couldn't be the carefree, young mother enjoying time with her children; instead, she was overworked and encumbered by a difficult marriage. She just squeezed my hand and said, "Shodey-a, you have to come home now, you're going to give Miss Kim too much trouble."

My mom never wanted to be a burden on anyone. Always profusely thankful for the tiniest of kind gestures. If any of my mom's friends gave her a gift or did a random favor for her, she would pay them back threefold. After her coworkers took her out to lunch for Reuben sandwiches on her first day of work at Allstate, she showed up soon after with an elaborate homemade Korean meal including japchae, tteokbokki, and kimbap. My mom showed her appreciation by one-upping everyone with labor-intensive Korean street food.

Two years later when we returned to the West Coast when I was nine, my mom's side of the family had a picnic at a park near Redwood City where the redwoods took over the entire landscape. Koreans love a big family picnic with colorful banchan, barbecued meats, white rice, and cold beer. While the adults were cooking, my cousins Melissa and Renee (Aunt Min Jee's daughters), our youngest cousins Sophia and Shelley (Aunt Seo Yun's daughters), Johnny, and I got lost in the redwood jungle for about two hours. It was Renee's idea to play hide-and-seek and disappear farther into the mountains behind our camp. A few adults from another campsite sent their own teenage children to form a search party to find us. "Are you Melissa and Johnny?" one of the teenagers shouted behind us, signaling that they knew the oldest kids' names to ask for.

As we followed the teenagers back to our camp, I could see my mom off in the distance standing by herself at the entrance of the mountain path. She was fighting back tears of anger that we had made her worry. I was afraid of her bloodshot eyes and readiness to scream. She was the only person in the entire family who hadn't been able to eat until we returned. I sheepishly said, "Sorry, Mom," as I ran by her and sandwiched myself between Aunts Soo Jin and Yun See, the ones without children, and hid behind a plate of food while she tried to throw me dirty looks. I refused to look up.

I felt my mother's relief that we had returned in one piece, but instead of hugging and kissing Johnny and me upon our safe return, she yelled at us. This was how she showed affection. To chase that much anger and frustration in a stressful situation was her way of expressing love. My father sat quietly on the drive home, yawning from his beer buzz. His crimson nose and its blue-vein tributaries ratted him out. Instead of having the telltale signs of Asian flush on his cheeks, face, or neck, it concentrated right on his nose.

"You're one of the oldest, Johnny, think about what could have happened to Sophia and Shelley. They are not my children. Why you make so much trouble at lunchie today?!" my mom continued chiding Johnny through the door as he was using the bathroom when we got home.

"It was Renee's idea to go up the mountain, and Melissa is the oldest," Johnny defended himself, his whining echoing through the hallway.

"Doesn't matter, Johnny." My mom sucked in her teeth. "You are one of the oldest cousins, you are responsible for the younger ones! I said don't make trouble! If you make trouble like that one more time, no more family picnic!"

I understood "trouble" to mean *Don't bring me shame after all my sacrifices.* Those warnings only made us fearful and insecure that we were always doing something wrong. Even if my mom didn't know how it impacted us then, she understood, as an insecure immigrant, that it entailed not being a pain in the ass to anyone—to live as unassumingly as possible—as well as carrying a protracted indebtedness and gratitude in this new country by returning niceties with elaborate homemade Korean food—buffet style—at Allstate.

3

"I can't believe he did that, he's an animal." I overheard Aunt Min Jee talking to Uncle Terry when the family came to visit us during our first summer in Newport News. Aunt Min Jee glanced at me standing in the doorway to their hotel room, but she was too angry to care. A few days earlier my father had pushed my mom down the staircase that led from our apartment to Gate 4, injuring her hip and fracturing her right arm. Johnny and I woke up to news that my mom was in the hospital where my father told the staff that she "had slipped and fallen down a staircase." My mom returned home with a limp and a cast on her right arm. My father removed the stick of a broom he found in the restaurant kitchen for my mom to use as a cane. I wondered if the nurses and doctors at the hospital believed my father when they saw the swollen purple and blue of my mother's eyes.

I rarely saw my father strike her. A couple of times I caught my father's hostile, kinetic shadow pulling my mom's hair, but he always slammed the door before Johnny and I could see anything more. Or we'd scatter and hide first like feral cats dodging human interaction until the slamming, pounding, shouting stopped. Sometimes it lasted five minutes, sometimes fifteen. Young children adapt to disturbances faster than people think because of magical thinking. Like a conditioned dog I numbed myself to the sizzling I felt on my neck that quickly moved along my shoulders after hearing each blow, because I trusted my parents knew what they were doing and would soon stop. When we moved back to California a couple of years later in 1981, my cousin Julie and I babysat a one-year-old Korean boy who lived two apartments over from hers in Culver City. We noticed he had a dark-blue bruise over his butt crack so I assumed his father hit him too. It was completely normal for me to think that. I told my mom when she came to pick me up and she said, "No, that is the sign of the Mongolian, like a birthmark. Koreans are descendants of the Mongolians so many Korean babies have it. That's where our tail used to be." She laughed.

I thought only Korean men hit their wives and children because the white kids at my school looked happy and fearless, having never had to anticipate violence. As a child, I thought Korean men got a cultural pass to behave like animals because their raging tempers and inability to cope with any deviance of social mores were inextricable from their DNA. I was left to believe the tired trait, that my mom's corporal punishment at the hands of her husband was culturally condoned because ancestral trauma trickled down from one generation to the next. When I was twelve my mom told me my paternal grandfather had beaten my grandmother, so the violence was learned behavior. I'm not making generalizations about all Korean men; not all of them hit their wives and children (though, I cringe at the cliché). It took me many years to understand my father caused pain because he was born of trauma, which seemed to have fused with his core, fracturing his identity and making it difficult for him to heal.

My harsh judgment against the abhorrent abuses the men in my family committed was warranted because they authorized the next generation of men to follow suit. I thought my father would get over it after a few more years of living in this country; that he'd acclimate more and learn to respond to people in a reasonable tone of voice without raising an arm; that the optimistic American way would wash over him to cleanse him of his weaknesses.

"Please, Mom, stop fighting with Dad, stop talking back. He's hurting you too much. *Please*!" Johnny and I implored.

"He's a gaesaeki, ssang of a bitch!" my mom emphasized bilingually.

It took me years to realize how women are oftentimes blamed for domestic violence, that they're perceived as asking for it, or they're expected to refrain from defending themselves even when under duress. I was too young to see how the patriarchy surreptitiously manipulates our perceptions to blame the survivor or victim of violence. Even the magical perceptions of young children are bent—we thought my mom was the source of my father's violence. She was the one who talked back, made smart points, stood her ground. She poked the dumb giant. It was up to her to stop the bickering because she was also more reasonable, cooperative, soft, and, through the lens of the patriarchy, weaker than my father. So begging my mom to yield to her abuser was easier than actually stopping the abuser, it seemed to us, as though he was innocent during their battles.

"That son of a bitch, she needs to divorce him!" This time Aunt Min Jee whispered this to Uncle Terry. My aunt was livid.

"If we intervene, I'm worried Charles will take it out on Yong Cha and the kids. He might end up abusing her more," Uncle Terry whispered back, turning his back to me.

Uncle Terry made sense to me at the time because I was a scared seven-year-old. But it was this neutral, turn-a-blind-eye approach that well-meaning, informed adults took at the expense of others that made me wonder later on what families were for. My aunt and uncle were concerned, but not enough. I ran out the door and caught up with Johnny, Melissa, and Renee, who were playing hide-and-seek in the hotel lobby. "Why are you crying?" Renee asked me, out of breath.

"I want my parents to divorce!" I said, pulling up my shirt to wipe my tears and hide my face.

"Why?" Renee asked.

"Because my dad hits my mom." The words were muffled by my shirt.

"Mom asked me if it would be okay to divorce Dad when she got back from the hospital and I begged her not to," Johnny confessed. "I don't want them to get a divorce. We need him!"

Melissa, Renee, and I stood still for a minute with our mouths open until Melissa screamed, "Come on, catch me!" as she ran off to hide. She was always the vapid one.

My mom changed after my aunt, uncle, and cousins left Virginia, becoming more temperamental and falling into deeper depression. But she did what she knew best with that amount of polarizing energy: she cleaned our filthy, disgusting apartment with a vengeance. On the weekends my mother bleached and sanitized the floors of the kitchen and bathroom, removed the contents of every cabinet shelf, peeled back the aged lining paper, and scrubbed the shelves raw. She cleaned and organized the refrigerator and vacuumed everything in her path. I either got out of her way or pretended to clean just as vigorously so she wouldn't shout at me. Then she did load after load of laundry at the local laundromat. She cleaned to keep the facade pristine, orderly, and in control because it was all she could do from losing her shit.

My mom's temper grew louder: "Aish! Saekki ya, ssahng nyeon-a, stop leaving all your books and toys all over the house and help Mommy clean!" *Saekki*, meaning "baby animal" can be an endearing term, but when used in a vulgar sense, *saekki ya* means "bastard" or "asshole." She also called me "ssahng nyeon-a," which roughly translates to "low-born bitch" while sounding even more malicious in Korean, like all vulgarities. When she caught Johnny and me being lazy or sloppy on Saturday mornings watching cartoons she either shouted at us or gave us the silent treatment, but she never hit us. I felt her anxieties taking over her body. It gave her an intensity and rigidity that made my warm, cuddly mother the embodiment of fear, defiance, and rage. She projected this hostility onto Johnny and me because she felt helpless. When I didn't polish the coffee table well enough, she made me watch her scribble in the dust along the legs. "I don't know how you are my daughter, you are so dirty and lazy!" I was so scared once I locked myself in my bedroom for four hours and cleaned, organized, and dusted everything in sight until I got so hungry and thirsty that I crawled into the kitchen out of fear of my mom spotting me, even after I heard her eventually leave the house.

My home life spilled into school life. My elementary school teacher raised my right arm over my heart as we were pledging allegiance to the flag before class started. I was too tired and apathetic to remember the flag-worshipping ritual.

Johnny and I were in a joint second- and third-grade class at Epes Elementary School. "Chong!" our Black classmate blurted out after my teacher called my brother's name for roll call. The entire class erupted in laughter ridiculing Johnny's Korean name, which the teacher pronounced "John Chong In Pak."

"Here," my brother mumbled while raising his right arm and dropping his head down.

"It's not nice to make fun of *different* names, Michael," my teacher chided. "What if we made fun of your name?"

"My name ain't Chong!" Michael quipped to more laughter.

"Okay, stay after class, I'll call your parents to let them know how you're behaving today."

I looked over at Johnny whose face burned red with humiliation. He couldn't make eye contact with anyone, not even with me. The racism was more assertive in Virginia. We were two of five Asian kids at school. Johnny had punched a kid in the face for calling me "squinty eyes" on the school bus a week before. I saw how my father influenced Johnny to defend me and our heritage, like when he had brandished the monkey wrench in Tennessee. I was proud of Johnny for protecting me. But in that classroom full of laughing, mocking kids, all I did was sit quietly next to him, sharing his shame. I didn't defend his Korean name because I myself was embarrassed of our Korean names.

"You can ask your parents to change your name officially to Johnny Pak and Shirley Pak, just leave out your middle names," my teacher said cheerfully as we were leaving for the day.

"Our Korean names are our real names," Johnny said with his head still low. "Johnny is my American name."

"Well, it might be easier for everyone else to pronounce your American name, but it's up to you and your parents. It might be easier for you, too," my teacher responded with smiling eyes and a wink. Working three times my teacher's daily shift, six to seven days a week, my parents never had time for parent–teacher conferences to go over condescending recommendations.

Johnny always worked hard for my father's affection, acceptance, and respect, so he never told him about the incident at school; he didn't want my father to know that he had sat with his head down and done nothing. But my father was hardly a solid male role model with his volatile temper, violence toward my mom, habit of lying, and gambling problems. Johnny was smart, but his capabilities didn't translate well on his report cards.

"B-, C-, C+, D! What kind of a report card is this?!" My dad yelled at Johnny while holding on to a pool stick in the booth across from one of the pool tables.

"I'm sorry, sir, I'll try harder next time." Johnny's voice trembled and his body shook.

I saw everything from the bar directly behind the booth. I thought Johnny was going to pass out as my father struck his legs with the pool stick under the table while a couple of customers were finishing their meal at the other side of the restaurant. The irony of The Beatles' "Come Together" playing on the jukebox didn't escape me. The higher inflections of Lennon–McCartney muted Johnny's yowl as he grabbed his legs. My father struck him a second time, threw the pool stick on the floor, and stormed out of the restaurant.

I ran up to Johnny and whispered, "Are you okay?" as he cried.

His face flushed and sweaty, Johnny looked straight into my eyes and said, "You're right, I should have told Mom to divorce Dad."

My parents sold Gate 4 after a year and a half of ownership, at the height of its success. They made a lot of money from the sale, and we couldn't get out the door fast enough because everything in the apartment was falling apart: the plumbing was going out, there were more cracks and holes sending a mean, cold draft from the winter snowstorm while an army of rats erupted from all corners. Johnny went to the bathroom a few days before we moved, but the toilet wouldn't flush so the shit froze in the water, with micro cracks and fissures validating its existence. The landlord wouldn't send a plumber, so my parents were left to try everything they could to get rid of it. Nothing worked, so the shit stayed as we packed up our beige van and escaped to the suburbs of Chesterfield County where my mom and dad ran a pan-Asian restaurant called the Oriental Delicatessen. We were the butt of all of my Californian cousins' Chester-the-molester jokes.

They stir-fried vegetables and lo mein noodles and barbecued galbi and bulgogi for six months and to their surprise, managed to make a decent profit. It was heartening to feel the acceptance and demand for Asian food by white people, but pathological, too, that the same clientele were still racist toward us. They loved our food but hated us. Acceptance with a twist. So, my parents suffused our evenings with conversations about moving back west. They had had enough of the restaurant business and the lack of a Korean community in the American South. The only good thing about living in Chesterfield was the new, clean two-story town house we rented, which was the reprieve we needed after living in depraved conditions in Newport News.

The irony about that town house was my parents' fighting. It got worse and my mom had to go to the hospital again to stitch up cuts on her face and get X-rays for her beaten ribs. We thought he was going to kill her. I still don't understand how hospitals could turn a blind eye. My mom was so afraid of my father that she locked herself in her room at the top of the stairs for three days. When she'd use the bathroom in the hallway, Johnny or I would wait outside until she was done to check on her. But when she'd open the door she'd look at us with a stunned, hollow gaze, then cry or run back to her room. She was a series of shadows escaping to a soundless space until the fragile feeling of losing it broke.

After her third day of solitude she emerged from her room and declared that she wanted out of the restaurant business, that it or my father was going to kill her. The power of her confidence, after three days in isolation, didn't escape me as being New Testament biblical, like a rebirth or movement in her spirit. And this time this decision was on her terms. By the end of the evening, she had made my father agree to move. So, we packed up our creepy beige van and headed west, for good.

4

Growing up in the eighties was a different time. We didn't have to worry about predators stalking young kids at home or on the streets, or about drunk drivers and serial rapists in the suburbs my parents had selected for us. Home could be a living hell, but at least my parents always picked the safest residential neighborhoods with the best public schools.

Johnny was eleven and I was nine when we became latchkey kids in Palo Alto, back in the Bay Area. "Shallow Alto" to the people who didn't live there, as well as to the disaffected rich residents who did enjoy living there but were never going to show it. We lived in a gray area that wasn't in the shallow or "dangerous" East Palo Alto area either. The upscale Stanford Shopping Center was nearby, which my parents saw as status. Johnny and I dutifully came home from school to our apartment behind the Glass Slipper Inn, a Cinderella-themed motel on the famous El Camino Real.

My parents managed a liquor store near San Francisco and were gone all day and night, sometimes seven days a week, so Johnny and I were left alone a lot. As children of parents who ran service businesses, this alone time was both frightening and liberating. Frightening because I always worried something was going to happen to them; liberating because it set my brother and me free from the constant stress and bickering of overworked people. On Saturday mornings my mom gave Johnny ten dollars to buy us lunch at Taco Bell. Time revealed how lucky we were that nothing ever happened to him when he crossed busy El Camino Real. He wasn't abducted, assaulted, or left at the side of the road due to a deadly hit and run. Johnny was cagey like that, he could deftly disappear unnoticed into side streets and alleyways, blending in with the cars and shadows. I'd shout the same order to him as he walked out the door—two Taco Bell Grandes and Cinnamon Crispas—without thinking.

After school, Johnny and I made ourselves all kinds of plastic-wrapped, processed ramen manufactured by Nongshim before settling into a full dinner with my parents when they got home between 8 and 10 p.m. Neoguri was the front-runner, then later Shin Ramyun took the lead when our little Korean taste buds started to tolerate saltier and spicier prepackaged umami flavors. Late afternoons spent eating boiled dried noodles mixed with freeze-dried seasonings and dehydrated vegetables, with an occasional egg thrown in at the end, were an unlikely highlight to my elementary school days. I can attest to the fact that people ate their emotions back in 1981, too—Johnny and I devoured ours. We couldn't get enough, the hot ramen filled our craving for a normal family.

My mom had at least one day off on the weekends; instead of resting, she made copious amounts of kimchi in wide, multi-colored plastic buckets. It was always labor intensive. I'd alternate between catching Saturday morning cartoons and watching my mom chop, slice, and organize the green cabbage, green onions, chives, radishes, carrots, ginger, Asian pears, fermented shrimp, fish sauce, garlic cloves, and a whole lot of gochugaru. Then with some bewildering alchemy she'd combine and mix all these ingredients while assuming what we called the "kimchi squat" position—the position in which kimchi makers squat with their feet as close together as possible, heels on the floor, and thighs slightly wider than their torso—on the newspaper-covered kitchen floor, usually in her bra and underwear so her clothes wouldn't get stained by the menacing spices. Then hovering over a large, pink, plastic cabbage-filled bucket, Mom painstakingly spread the kimchi paste she had made on each leaf so that every wrinkle diligently soaked in the seasonings. After analyzing each bunch for color and texture and tasting for precision, she'd carefully fold the long strands of cabbage into a package that looked like a bojagi-wrapped holiday present before placing them into large mason jars. After about a week or so, when the kimchi was approaching peak fermentation, she would gift smaller glass jars of the coveted cabbage to her sisters. Her big family with a myriad of personalities agreed on one thing only: Mom's cooking and kimchi brought them to their knees.

The video rental world was hot in the eighties, becoming my father's new entrepreneurial focus after the liquor store. Uncle Terry's son from a previous marriage, Dennis, drove my father all around San Mateo County to find retail spaces for his latest vision. The video store did well even with the competition in neighboring cities, only because he stayed open the latest. Running this business lacked the drama of running a demanding restaurant, and we all appreciated that.

My mom wanted nothing to do with my father's latest business enterprise and, with steadfast determination and grit, got her old job back at Allstate. We only had the beige van, which my father drove to pick up supplies for the store, so my mom had to take the bus to go to work. One time she almost got mugged during one of her transfers and nobody tried to help her, which shocked her more than the attempted mugging.

Eventually she also helped out at the store in the evenings or on the weekends out of guilt because that was who she was—reliable, dependable, hardworking, born in the year of the Fire Ox. She was the only person I knew whose personal attributes precisely matched her Chinese zodiac animal sign. My mother's work ethic—her need to organize, to have a goal, to save money—made me love and respect her an inordinate amount while also feeling profoundly intimidated by her all at once. It also made me despise myself because she was doing all of this for Johnny and me.

In the summer of 1983, about a year after we moved back to the Bay Area, my paternal grandfather had a major stroke and was expected to die. My father, Johnny, and I flew to Seoul to pay our last respects. We didn't know how long my grandfather had left, so we scheduled our trip to stay for a month. My father hired a friend to tend to the video store while my mom stayed behind to work at Allstate. I had just turned 11. A day after we arrived, I saw my dying grandfather in bed with his head supported by a hard pillow filled with buckwheat. His high cheekbones that my father had inherited—and that, in turn, I had inherited—held up his hollowed, sagging face that looked like a thin layer of wrinkled tofu skin. His mouth was opened slightly to reveal the glimmer of his front crown and to release his fetid breath. My eldest aunt must have smelled the same odor and within minutes she brought his toothbrush, toothpaste, and a bowl of water to brush his teeth. She circled each tooth with minty toothpaste as tears filled her eyes. She then washed the utensils and returned with a razor, shaving cream, and another fresh bowl of water to shave his short, stubbly mustache and beard that had grown over the course of weeks. I could tell by the swelling of my aunt's eyes that she had been crying and had not slept for a while; it was the same kind of swelling that cursed my mom and me when we cried. We were both plagued with the most unusual tumid eyes when we sobbed. Our eyes didn't just get bloodshot like most people's; our eyelids actually blossomed like pygmy puffer fish for hours. We could never get away with just a casual cry.

I didn't know my aunt well, but from cultural osmosis I understood that she was performing her duty, filial piety: to show support, respect, and love to her parent; to display sorrow for her father's sickness and death; and to bury him and carry out sacrifices after his passing. As I stood there watching my aunt, I shook with panic when I visualized my mom dying and how I'd be there next to her bed to put lotion on her body, brush her teeth and hair, hold her hands, stroke her back, and say things only she and I would understand. I never wanted to imagine that day, but I knew what was expected of me. And what I expected of myself.

My grandfather passed away the next day, and my aunt's once somber house became clanky and loud with cooking and guests. It was a hot and humid July, but my aunts still made large batches of slowly simmered yukgaejang to serve with hot white rice and banchan; mul-naengmyeon that was always in high demand in the summer for its chilled, thin, chewy buckwheat noodles served in large bowls of cold, icy broth; and beautiful platters holding painstakingly sliced Korean summer fruits like small melons and oversized grapes, all to be passed around to mourners sitting on bamboo rugs. The Korean grapes were my favorite with their sweet, juicy, translucent green flesh and gelatinous texture. I'd pinch one side of a large, round slipskin grape to let the flesh ooze out, then stick it under my nose and walk around the house, slurping the sliding grape while saying *I like to eat my boogers* using the best Korean I had learned from my one year of studies. I was the hit of the funeral.

Aside from the funeral, the sweet Korean yogurt drinks with a tart finish (that everyone pronounced "yow-gu-rut"), unending adoration from family, public pools, and mogyoktangs (public bathhouses) made the summer of Seoul extra special. My cousins and I sang and danced to popular Korean children's songs: "Appa, umma jowah, umma appa jowah! La la, la la la la, la la, la la la la!" *Dad, I like Mom; Mom, I like Dad.* But I would only sing *Dad, I like Mom* over and over again until my cousins started to look at me strangely. The movie *E.T.* was a global cultural phenomenon, so we sang catchy songs about how the little alien made us laugh with its bread-loaf-shaped head, and that it was our best friend.

My grandfather's bedroom was quiet and calm for three days. On the first day, the bedroom was dimly lit with his corpse. My father and his sister put my grandfather in a traditional white Korean hanbok for men, which consisted of billowing pants and a vest worn over a jacket. His shrine was set on a long table covered in white linen two feet away from his head, brightly adorned with gilded, stacked platters of dates, rice cakes, nuts, grapes, and shiny apples. Both sides of the table were flanked by incense smoke, suffusing our prayers to aid my grandfather's spirit toward a peaceful afterlife so he would not become stuck as a gwisin, a ghost. My aunts assembled an Asian pear jenga pyramid with an inch perfectly peeled off the top of each pear, so his spirit could easily consume it. A fresh bowl of hot white rice with two chopsticks sticking straight up indicated this was the proper gesture reserved for the dead, though for the living it was bad luck. The ceremony left the air redolent, thick with cooking and prayer.

My aunts and female cousins wore black hanboks, some ajusshis wore traditional black mourning clothing for men, and my dad and uncles wore black suits. My father was the only man wearing a white armband with two black stripes on his left arm, signifying he was the oldest son of the deceased. Then for three days I witnessed grown adults entering the bedroom wailing in the traditional Korean way to mourn the dead. It wasn't just sobbing, it was a long, guttural, exaggerated moan accompanied by, "Ahboji, Ahboji, aigoo, aigoo!" Their tortured cries for their father were uncomfortable to watch and listen to, especially for immature kids like Johnny and me. When it was my dad's turn to wail, he bent down to whisper to me that I had to express my grief the same way. Up until that point I had never seen my father cry. Ever. So, when he proceeded with the dramatic gesture of showing respect for his father in that agonizing wail that sounded so affected and forced, I started to giggle with unease. My tiny eleven-year-old brain couldn't handle the hilarity of the ungainly situation. I was certainly not ready to mourn so publicly for a man I barely knew, a man I was told had loved and spoiled my brother and me before we moved to the U.S., but a man I felt no connection to. Then I looked at my devoted eldest aunt near the shrine next to my grandfather's body and remembered her sadness as she groomed her dying father and I let out the most believable caricature of wailing I could display. Johnny followed suit. We were successful.

Like many Koreans born in the Silent Generation my

dad witnessed the atrocities committed by Japanese officials and citizens during the Japanese occupation of Korea. He experienced the tragedy of famine, war, and human greed during World War II, and he also survived the Korean War, which upended our small country and further bifurcated it into two. My dad was born in what is now North Korea in 1935 to a father with a chronic gambling problem and an overbearing mother who kept the family together but lacked the nurturing skills my maternal grandmother and mother had. My paternal grandparents, father, and two aunts fled North Korea when my dad was seventeen, right before the end of the Korean War. My father's youngest sister had caught pneumonia right before they planned to flee so they had no choice but to escape persecution without her, fearing that her coughing would jeopardize their chances of making it farther south undetected. They had thought it would be temporary, that they'd be able to go back for her. My father never got over the guilt and grief of leaving his sister behind. This hardened him, but it also created an insatiable appetite for excess that was antithetical to the ascetic, spartan way in which he memorialized his sister—he never mourned for her in front of us. He took a minimalist approach to dealing with his remorse and a maximalist approach to living: he desired more money, more women, more cars, more glamour. His instincts and talents never matched his desires, which were too giant and out of reach, so he flew too close to the sun and got burned by a lot of trouble and debt. He spent his entire life as an entrepreneur with a gambling addiction bent on taking massive risks with no long-term plan.

A week after my grandfather died, my dad's family and friends came over to my grandparents' house to watch a wildly popular live program on KBS that followed families displaced by the Korean War. The program, titled *Finding Dispersed Families*, documented these families as they tried to reunite with their lost loved ones. Due to overwhelming demand, KBS extended their originally planned short documentary to air one lasting over 400 hours, spanning over five months.[1]

The Korean War ended in 1953 with an armistice that maintains the division between North and South Korea. The years of fighting had created a diaspora and Korean families were displaced beyond the borders. Over 100,000 applications, including my family's application, were submitted to *Finding Dispersed Families* in hopes for reunion. The reunions we saw on television showed a harrowing trauma and wound caused by those separations. There wasn't a dry eye in the room. My aunts, uncles, their friends, and older cousins wept openly. I was playing with my two-year-old cousin in the guest room when I heard people in the living room laughing and crying at the same time (an action my dad said would cause hair to grow out of one's butthole, such that to this day, I still fight the urge tooth and nail). As I turned to walk out the door to see what was going on, my father approached the guest room frantically, wiping away unruly, errant tears streaming down his face. He had wanted to cry secretly because it would be too embarrassing to weep in public as the eldest and only son, and as a formidable father; he wanted to be seen as stoic and impregnable. But I had caught my dad in the act of expressing the turbulence inside him, all the accumulated years of furtively hardened emotions.

Aside from the seemingly contrived wail fest during my grandfather's funeral, this was the first time I witnessed my dad truly cry from a place so primal and true in his heart that he couldn't deny the overwhelming grief he had felt his entire adult life. The sadness and shame of leaving his younger sister behind in North Korea had festered inside him for thirty years and made him implode, turning him into a difficult-to-love, unhappy man. In some ways he was a sort of superhuman hero, bravely seeking freedom for his family and himself, a freedom that was so easily handed to Johnny and me.

But I was too scared to try and support him through his tears. We weren't like that. We returned to California the following week, never speaking of it again.

5

A few years later Allstate relocated my mom's department from Menlo Park to Brea in Southern California, in the bastion of conservative Orange County. My parents were excited to rent a medium-sized house with a sprawling, unkempt brown lawn full of overgrown weeds and parched trees from years of drought in a sleepy suburb called Yorba Linda. The birthplace and home of Richard M. Nixon and the Brea Mall put this suburban city on the map. My parents had learned that Yorba Linda held "high-class status" from the emerging Korean American community in OC for its good public schools, trickle-down economy, private golf courses, and brand-new identical-looking homes. My parents finally found a home behind the orange curtain. Johnny and I were entering our junior high school years, hormonally chaotic in another predominantly white community, which solidified our sense of being complete misfits.

A month after our move to Yorba Linda, my paternal grandmother moved in with us. It was Korean custom for the eldest son to take care of his parents when they got older, which meant having them move in with you or the other way around. My grandfather had died four years earlier, and my father brought his mother to live with us in the summer of 1986. My grandmother smoked until she was seventy-four and made spicy, greasy kimchi jjigae that gave everyone Montezuma's Revenge at some point. She also burped out loud, had a fierce limp, and loved hamburgers. I wasn't used to my grandmother's affection, which came across abrasive and forced: she'd pound Johnny and me on the back and say how spoiled we were as children, then give each of us twenty dollars.

My mom didn't get along with her mother-in-law as she was, in my mother's Korean words, "uneducated and loud, from the country," while her own mother was "classy, demure, from the city." Even without these descriptors, I had always favored my maternal grandmother over my paternal one, and it showed: I'd avoid my paternal grandmother and grimace when she said in Korean every night over dinner how precocious I was when I was the length of her arm. I wasn't sure whether my mom was right or whether I unfairly disapproved of my grandmother simply because she was guilty of being my dad's mother. When my mom came home from work exhausted, she still had to make dinner and clean up after my grandmother, who was robust but made a mess. "I don't like how she wash-y dishes. She wash-y dirty dishes with soap, then rinses. Supposed to rinse dirty dishes first, then use soap, then rinse again." My mom's obsession with cleanliness and her lack of patience for my grandmother's habits caused my parents to lock horns. My grandmother adored Johnny and me, but we knew she was homesick for South Korea. Yorba Linda lacked the Korean bodegas that she could walk to during the day to gossip with other halmeonis. She stayed with us for one year before my father found her a studio apartment in sprawling Koreatown in LA surrounded by other halmeonis she could socialize and cook with. It was the first time my father broke tradition in favor of his mother's (and wife's) happiness.

Mom was an eager student. She used to line up her stuffed animals on stools when she was seven to teach them things. She respected her teachers so this was her dream job, which entailed being listened to and telling people what to do. Working at Allstate was never the job she romanticized; it was a practical, life-preserver ring that pulled her out of the drowning demands of American manual labor, which gave her another kind of purpose—her appearance. She loved putting on business suits or high-waisted flared pants and silk tops propped up by platform sandals or heels every morning. She spent time curling her permed hair and putting on eye shadow, blush, and lipstick. My mom never wore jewelry at home, so work was a time to let her fingers shine on with her wedding ring and diamond and sapphire cocktail rings she called "gojussu," which was how she pronounced one of her favorite descriptors. She had gotten her ears pierced at the Brea Mall after I did and wore the small diamond studs she had bought years before in Seoul, which she promptly took out whenever she got home, lest they fall out doing chores. My mom's tight domestic routine reflected the order of her repetitive job at Allstate, which gave her a reliable discipline that she needed for stability in her life. Meanwhile, fashion gave her an outlet to loosen the line.

When my parents lived in Seoul in the late sixties, Mom was thrilled when she was eventually promoted to be supervisor of her department for the U.S. Army. Her job allowed her to devote herself to one program, brainstorm ideas from inception, focus on minutiae, and execute a successful project. Her brain moved in a linear direction that didn't suffer anomalies well. She admired the fact that Americans usually promoted employees based on merit and not by the nepotism that was common in Korea. I imagined her being a fair and understanding boss, but taking no bullshit. Professionally sucker free.

"I was a fox back then, I had a big goong daengie and my hair was more ba-ronde-y." My mom laughed out loud as she reminisced about her big butt and blonde hair, which she meant was light brown from sun exposure. "The GIs always pulling on my ponytail!"

"Did you want to marry a white man?" I asked, curious if she fantasized being like Aunt Min Jee.

"They like me, but my father doesn't like Yankees, so I married your daddy. Aunt Min Jee married your Uncle Terry after my father died. If I marry a Yankee, you cannot be here." She laughed while patting my thigh.

During the humid summer months in South Korea my mom jumped on and off trains to and from the U.S. Army offices in Yongsan-gu, one of the twenty-five districts of Seoul. My mom would be crisp and clean in her white summer dresses or blouses, then became sardined between hot and sweaty commuters just to get off drenched in other people's sweat. I pictured her swollen agitation and cringed knowing she always kept her clothes in impeccable condition, permeated with the scent of mothballs trapped in long, plastic garment bags.

"Mom, why didn't you wear something you didn't care about on the train and change at work?" I asked, revealing my American preference for comfort over style.

"Ladies don't do that one in that time, we always looking fancy. We not tomboys like you girls in this country," Mom said in a tinkly tone. "When I was thirteen, we never had maxi pad, we used cotton cloth. During summertime, when I have menses, it was so hot and uncomfortable. You never know that kind of sticky hot like Korea."

"Did you have to wash the cloth pads by hand? Ew!"

My lackwit question made me want to gag as I thought about having to hand-wash my own non-cloth, bleached, plastic-wrapped pads that I could easily toss into the trash.

Mom laughed. "Of course! You could never do that kind of thing!"

Allstate was founded by Sears so we always got discounts on our back-to-school clothing there. My mom really wanted me to be a "girly girl," whatever that meant, but I was born a tomboy, and in preschool and elementary school, I threw a fit if I couldn't wear my dusty-pink OshKosh B'Gosh corduroy overalls and torn T-shirts. Mom bought me frilly dresses that only went to use during holidays and birthday parties. When she tried to dress me up in sundresses in the summer, I'd whine hysterically, to which she'd suck in her teeth and say, "Aicham gijibae-ya, I buy you all these pu-dey dresses, and you want to look like a boy!"

By the time I reached junior high she was too exhausted to try to make me wear dresses. But I also hated wearing the generic, trendy button-up shirts with shoulder pads and stirrup pants from Sears in the mid-eighties, the same outfit my mom would ask, "Did other girls say anything about your clothes? Did they say it was pu-dey?" Maybe she was living through me, the young pubescent teenager without any responsibilities, or maybe she wanted to remember what it felt like to be admired for one's fashion sense, as she had been in Incheon and Seoul. To her, shoulder pads and stirrup pants were the current blueprint of style and acceptance. I didn't tell her that an obnoxious popular girl had pressed on my left shoulder pad and sarcastically cackled, "Nice shoulder pads," as we were heading down the steps to lunch.

6

Aunt Min Jee died of liver cancer in the fall of 1986 at the age of forty-five, taken away too soon from her husband and young daughters. Her doctor told her that mothers can unknowingly transmit blood infected with the hepatitis B virus to their children. He also mentioned he saw many cases among East Asians, specifying that the same modern standards of sanitation didn't exist in war-ravaged Korea. So my grandmother could have been a carrier of the hepatitis B virus from something as innocuous as a cut from an HBV-contaminated object, passing the infection quietly.

My mom and Aunt Min Jee shared a love of fashion, movies, glamorous actresses, and Elvis. When Mom returned from the Bay Area after visiting her sister at the hospital before she died, she broke down in my arms crying, "Aunt Min Jee asked if I got my ears pierced." I wondered how my aunt could have remarked on something so banal when she was facing the ultimate truth. Wasn't she afraid of death? My mom's weeping was pure and she felt limp in my arms, eerily like floating deadweight, both heavy and light. She was unassailable when it came to defending Johnny and me so I felt energized knowing I was consoling someone impregnable, and her grief was empowering to her because it was affirmation of a beloved sisterhood.

I didn't want to imagine the day I'd lose my mom. The anticipatory grieving was paralyzing, knowing that one fateful, mysterious day controlled the circumstances that would take away my mother.

Aunt Min Jee's death kick-started my lifelong fear of cancer killing my mom. I was worried she was going to succumb to some sort of incurable organ cancer because she had been exposed to the same environmental hazards as her sister: industrial chemical exposure during the wars and DDT used to control insect-borne diseases among U.S. troops. My mom said children were even exposed to the toxicity, and she heard that DDT was even used in children's hair to kill lice.

A few months after Aunt Min Jee died my mom started to complain of sharp pain in her right hand and wrist. At first it was manageable with aspirin, but then it got worse when she could no longer make a fist with her right hand. The condition made her right middle finger contract toward her palm due to chronic nerve and tendon damage so she went through two botched surgeries to try to correct the tendinopathy and neuropathy. Even with six months of physical therapy she was never able to completely straighten her right middle finger and her range of motion was compromised. The hand surgeon told my parents that the antiquated IBM keypunch machines my mom had used for over twenty-five years required her to make hard strokes to depress the buttons. Although her OCD tendencies proved to be helpful for her to perform her tedious job that required accuracy, efficiency, and speed, it created such a severe case of tendinopathy that she had to go on permanent disability at the age of forty-eight. The job she loved ended up ruining her.

"Mom, you're so lucky to get to stay home now!" I said with excitement, thinking she'd look forward to the time off.

"Why you say that?! I don't want to retire, I want to

work!" my mom screamed at me in tears. I had made a careless statement with the frivolity of a fourteen-year-old who wanted to stay home and do nothing. I didn't realize I would strike a new nerve so raw that she hyperventilated while her mind raced to make sense of the nonsense. This was the same work ethic that intimidated me, that made me copy the chores my mom did in our filthy apartment in Newport News.

"I didn't mean it like that, Mom. I'm not saying be lazy. I'm just saying you can take some time off to relax after working so hard. Maybe this is just temporary." My heart hammered as I urgently tried to defend myself.

"Shut up! How'd I do now?!" My mom slumped over the kitchen table with her hands embracing her face.

Instead of resting her arm, Mom took on a punishing workload cleaning the spotless house. The busy work kept her focused and sane in the midst of her worsening depression. She became the overzealous homemaker who did everyone's laundry, to the point that Johnny and I didn't fully learn how to wash our own clothes until we moved out of the house. She tried to revive our brown garden, but the statewide drought-induced water restrictions made it impossible. I'd come home from school to see my mom on all fours scrubbing the kitchen and bathroom floors or dusting the furniture, paintings, and baseboards I'd already cleaned. She was also usually preparing stocks for stews, which took time and planning. We had a spacious patio with an ever-growing container garden of begonias, tropical plants, small shrubs, and lemon trees that mingled with clay ceramic pots of doenjang (fermented soybean paste), used as a base for soups. The older doenjang made a home in their traditional earthenware containers for years to seal in their piquant flavor, but on one unusually warm spring day, my mom decided to thoroughly scrape out and clean one of the nearly empty doenjang containers. I smelled the sharp, pungent scent on my way up the hill toward the house. I was embarrassed because we were the only Asian family for miles, so we were a dead giveaway as the source of this provocative smell.

"My hand give me hard time when I squoosh the wet towel . . . squish?" Sweat beads slid down my mom's face as she crinkled her lips and nose. The dankness was getting to her, too. "I cannot cleaning the doenjang pot. Aigoo, too much-ey!" She walked toward the house to get more hand towels while doing her OCD tap walk: her left foot always leading and her right foot tapping back and forth three times.

"I can do that for you, but why are you cleaning something nobody else would clean? It stinks so bad, it's embarrassing. The whole neighborhood can smell it!"

Mom was enthralled in her project wearing a muumuu and SAS sandals. Immersed in a job so labor intensive, distracting, and unnecessary, it was respectable enough for her to be satisfied with her work. Disheartened, I realized my mom's work ethic was rooted in the notion that females were brought up to withstand absurd amounts of labor, which may contribute to a sense of self value. Watching my mom bend over to clean out a clay container that had no business being cleaned made me see her tolerance for adversity and hardship, which may have been the way she showed her devotion and love. I saw this in her relationship with her overbearing older sister, Young Soon.

The dynamic between my mom and Aunt Young Soon was always competitive and volatile. My youngest aunt, Chan Mi, told me a buried family story about the time Aunt Young Soon came home drunk one night from a party when she was twenty and my mom was seventeen. Aunt Young Soon had smashed her hand through a window and smeared blood all over the walls and furniture after my mom dared to tell her not to make a mess in the house since she had spent all day cleaning it. My grandparents were furious at Young Soon but still more intimidated by her to kick her out of the house. They always favored my mother because she was the "good, responsible girl" while Young Soon was fearless, loud, and borderline feral. Envious of the adulation my mom received from their parents and teachers at school, Aunt Young Soon condescended to my mom for being obedient, while my mom publicly humiliated her older sister by calling her trashy, classless, and manipulative. They both had to have the last word when they fought, and neither side could abide without it, so their feuding nearly always ended with Young Soon slamming a door in my mom's face and screaming incoherently in Korean, while Mom shouted back before hard-charging away just so she felt like she had the last word.

My mom may have received praise from her parents for being the reliable, selfless daughter compared to impetuous Aunt Young Soon, whom my grandparents dismissed as wild and desirous. But I wanted a bit of that for Mom. I wanted her to desire.

My father's violence went on hiatus somewhere along the way, and by the time Johnny and I noticed it, he was fifteen and I was fourteen. The screaming matches were still around, but the beating ended unceremoniously. I was furious that it had taken an inescapable, permanent injury for him to stop beating her. I remember it vividly: Johnny and I came home from school on an overcast day in May, and as we entered the kitchen, we heard from our parents' bedroom the distant and familiar high-pitched screeching and indecipherable barking that was reaching that unsettling point where my father would usually resort to violence.

"Johnny, tell Dad not to hit Mom!" I yelled. "He's going to fuck up her wrist!"

Johnny slowly approached their closed door like a panther, a sly animal gracefully inching toward its prey so as not to alert it of its fate. He opened the door to my father hovering over my mom who was sitting on the La-Z-Boy with her arms and legs crossed like a mob boss. Her expression was decisive, calm. It looked like my father was about to jerk my mom from her seat when Johnny grabbed him by the shoulders and said, "Stop beating Mom up, she can't take it anymore! You're too old for this!"

At this point Johnny outsized my father and could have probably pinned him to the ground if he wanted to. My father angrily shook himself out of Johnny's grip, headed to the bathroom to clean up, and left the house for six hours just to return straight to his bedroom in time to catch the Korean dramas at 9 p.m. My mom slept on my bed while I took the floor.

I was disgusted by our cowardice, that it had taken Johnny and me that long to intervene. We had been terrified of my father's temper as young children, fearful of him raising an arm at us. In some ways, it was also maddening that speaking up was all it took. I fizzed with bitterness that Johnny and I had to shoulder the guilt. It wasn't right that the responsibility of stopping the abuser fell on us because we also received my father's abuse. The generational cycle of suffering and sacrifice made Johnny and me feel a specific flavor of inferiority of never being able to live up to my parents and repay their sacrifices. Right then and there, I was ready to recognize this life marker as just how things played out. But it was time to try to terminate this cyclical narrative.

"Dude, we finally grew some balls. Fucking tired of Dad's bullshit." Johnny said confidently, as we high-fived over dinner that night.

7

My parents bought our first home six months after my mom officially went on disability. It was a medium-sized three-bedroom, two-bathroom house situated in a cul-de-sac adjacent to Weir Canyon, about four miles away from our old house. It didn't occur to me that our house was in a tract home development, which meant that it looked identical to all the others, just blue. We were the only blue house for three tract blocks so we were already different on top of being only one of two Asian families in the sprawling neighborhood. I felt sorry for the quiet Filipino family who lived next door because we were a noisy, quarreling family. If my parents weren't fighting, I'd be shouting from my bedroom on one side of the house to my parents' room about thirty feet away to tell them to turn down the tinny volume of their daily Korean shows, which featured Korean news, song and dance segments, and K-dramas from 7 p.m. to midnight. I knew my parents were homesick for Korea when I saw how mesmerized they were by the entertainment and food that reminded them of their youth; albeit a newer, shinier culture that seemed to have had become modern overnight. I barely saw our next-door neighbors, but when I did, I'd quickly run away out of embarrassment for being the loud ones. Our neighbors smiled at me warmly, knowingly, like there was an unspoken agreement that Koreans were the hot-tempered Asians.

There was a Costco a mile away that was the paragon of abundance for my mom—an enormous warehouse that embodied excess and privilege. Plus, she loved buying Johnny food court favorites like whole pizzas and Chicken Bakes for under fifteen dollars. A Honda dealership and El Torito rounded out the canyon. Across from our tract community, an Albertsons shopping center was situated in the middle of a strip mall with a Ruby's Diner on one side, where my mom and I ate breakfast nearly every Saturday morning, and another set of bigger, "realer" homes on the other.

"Oh, you live in one of the tract homes," my friend Ashley said, giggling, when she came over to see our house. Ashley lived in one of the "real" homes. She was naturally pretty so I didn't understand why she wore vibrant turquoise eye shadow, thick layers of mascara, and frosted pink lipstick every day. Her overly processed hazel-colored hair with frosted tips stole attention away from her beautiful blue-gray eyes and soft features.

"What do you mean?"

"Your house looks like all the other homes here, they're just cheaper. And can you understand your mom?" Ashley's giggle turned into a well-rounded laugh.

"Yes. Why? Can't you?" I snapped.

I never had problems understanding my mom, even when she spoke in Korean interspersed with English. She added extra sounds, like *e* and *u*, after certain words: *go-juss-u* for *gorgeous* and *lunchie* for *lunch* because the phonology of the Korean language isn't accustomed to ending a word with certain consonants.

"It's hard for me to understand her because of her thick accent. It's, like, broken or something," Ashley admitted with hesitation after she sensed my defensive body language and glare.

Up until that point I didn't have a solid idea of what broken English was. Ashley made my mom's English sound damaged, and in turn, it made me feel damaged. My mom's Korean accent identified her to me. I was ersatz trilingual because of it—a third unique mode of communication in which my mom and I interacted. My mother's English unequivocally symbolized perseverance to me. She dared to speak *broken* English to non-Koreans out of necessity, to survive, even when she was embarrassed and insecure about how she'd be ridiculed for it.

"You need to get out and travel more, Ashley! You're very Orange County." I mocked, knowing full well that I was sheltered, too.

My mother mourned the end of her career and needed to restore her independence, so cooking, besides cleaning, became her discipline. Even when it was difficult for her to carry heavy pots and pans of hot bubbling broths, stews, noodles, and meat from one side of the kitchen to the stove, she rarely asked us for help. She continued to cook the food she was celebrated for in her family. Mom made jjigae with beef stock, meat, bean sprouts, old ripe kimchi, gochujang, doenjang, soy sauce, and fermented shrimp. As a loose vegetarian since age fourteen I was fine with whatever she made as long as I didn't have to chew any meat. Before serving, my mom always ladled my portion, without the meat, in a small bowl.

During hot summer days, my mom made mul naengmyeon. My father always requested this ice-cold noodle dish because it, and he, hailed from Pyongyang, North Korea.

My mom would start the mul naengmyeon with a broth made with dongchimi (brine of radish water kimchi) that she had frozen in advance. She added a halved boiled egg, sliced cucumbers, and julienned Asian pear to round out the savory broth. After my mom boiled the buckwheat noodles, she added them to a large bowl of ice water to cool and then transferred them to the broth that had been chilled with floating ice cubes. When it was scorching outside, I channeled my inner harabeoji when I slurped and gulped the ice-cold broth and noodles.

Mom made a pact with Aunt Min Jee before she passed away to be there for Melissa and Renee, both emotionally and financially. Koreans are good at handing out cash to family so Melissa and Renee knew this offering would be a given whenever they visited. My cousins were complete opposites. Melissa was a beautiful teenager who loved that her Asian features were subdued compared to Uncle Terry's more dominant French features: prominent, pointy nose, orblike light-brown eyes, fair skin, cheeks stippled by charming little freckles. Melissa garnered a lot of acceptance and adoration from her friends and my aunts who swooned at her every whim or cheered at her deafening, hackles-raising laughter. She looked like Nia Peeples from *Fame* circa 1985, but I'm not sure Nia Peeples was unconditionally caught up in her looks the way Melissa was, preening in front of every surface that offered a reflection, or fulfilling materialistic urges by compulsively shopping at Brass Plum in Nordstrom's young adult department. Melissa later landed a job there because the staff loved her enthusiasm for their inventory.

Renee was much more introverted, cerebral, and

sensitive. Her lifelong point of contention with Melissa was her insatiable quest for external validation. Renee yearned for the love of a mother. She could never turn to Melissa for help with her grieving since, in Renee's words, "Melissa is too shallow and selfish to help anyone but herself. I've never seen her mourn my mom's death. She even told me once that she never liked my mom." Renee was fifteen, a year younger than me, when she asked to live with us for a semester during my junior year.

Renee had boy trouble and was distracted by Uncle Terry's rushed marriage to another Korean woman who had finagled a way to make him sign over their house to her when he died, leaving Melissa and Renee nothing. Renee slept on the floor next to my bed snuggling a brass picture frame with filigreed corners holding a photo of her codependent, sketchy, pathological boyfriend who manipulated her to stay with him one day then ghosted her the next. "I know Robert loves me because he used to hold my milk carton during lunch," Renee said as I rolled my eyes and cringed with embarrassment.

My mom thrived in her new role of caring for another teen because it protracted her desire to be relevant, but with far less pressure of being a mother. But I knew my mom was exhausted, and she quietly complained to me about having to spend more money than she wanted to on the Korean snacks that Renee "enjoyed like a chipmunk." Mom drove to Arirang Supermarket in Garden Grove a couple of times a week to buy various unnaturally-white Korean rice cakes like kohng dduk, with a mix of beans and dried fruit, or songpyeon—chewy, nutty half-moon-shaped rice cakes filled with mung bean paste or red bean paste. She greeted Renee and me with these chewy treats every day after school while we wondered how some of the parallelogram-shaped rice cakes could be insanely sweet and nutty with the slightest aftertaste of sesame. In that order.

Renee was busy some weekends, which gave Mom and me time to hit Arirang Supermarket and our favorite soondubu (Korean tofu stew) restaurants together. Sometimes we'd get our brown late-seventies Toyota Corolla hatchback tuned up at Golden Auto Body Shop because my dad always made mom drive the crappier car while he got to drive the newer Oldsmobile, until one day she bought herself a brand-new Nissan Sentra whose keys she hid from him. I was relieved whenever Renee wasn't around because that meant I could have my mom to myself.

As a teenager I was particularly fond of my mother. Aside from her nagging pleas to help with chores, I never felt any need to assert my own burgeoning independence because I knew our mother–daughter dynamic was built on a foundation of innate trust. She was *home* to me because of our shared history of domestic violence. I also wondered whether my teenage affection for my mom was a result of the trauma I had experienced as a latchkey kid who had always worried whether her mom was ever going to return home.

Mom was someone I wanted to hang out with. She was a confidante with a nimble mind who didn't judge me for my idiosyncrasies. I smoked the occasional weed, but she knew I wasn't out partying past midnight, because I probably would have told her anyway. When I was gone all weekend, I was usually with other introverted girlfriends at Disneyland, Balboa Island, or the massive South Coast Plaza in Costa Mesa where we ate junk food and coyly flirted with skater boys. She let me be me, for the most part. However, when I lied to her about anything, like promising to meet my teenage curfew of midnight, but cavalierly returning home an hour later, I suffered a wrath no human should experience. It felt like a harrowing descent into hell where I was relegated to a burning, thorny corner to reflect on my trespasses, and when I was allowed back to earth, I endured a weeklong silent treatment that drove me to the cusp of near lunacy. *Just hit me instead!* I'd shout in my head, begging for corporal punishment instead of the guilt my mom used whenever she thought I had betrayed her.

On our weekends without Renee when we shopped for food, entering and leaving the strip malls of Garden Grove in one piece was a modern-day running-the-gauntlet. Garden Grove Boulevard invited drivers with little to no regard for human life, speed limits, or oncoming traffic, even with controlled lights at intersections. My mom often became overwhelmed with agitation trying to get over to the farthest lane by suddenly switching lanes, cutting off drivers, and receiving the bird in every direction. I was usually white-knuckling but was more worried about my mom's sanity navigating the aggressive streets with vehicular diarrhea. We heard a lot of, "Go back to your own country, chinks!" and "Fuck you, gooks!" But my mom was a focused driver, coolly shaking off the racist missiles. Though, I couldn't. It burned me to the core as a teen. I'd glance over at my mom after some overweight, pugnacious white man finished screaming at us while mirroring our car, but without fail, my mom looked straight ahead with a slight smirk, arms on the steering wheel at ten and two, like Sully Sullenberger landing his Airbus A320, while I slowly raised my left hand to flip off the fat fuck, disgraced. She was boss and drove on poker-faced while a bloated, balding white man foamed at the mouth losing his shit. It was a boon that my mom didn't have the luxury of being humiliated like I had. She blithely ignored the epithets like she snubbed my father's shouting.

At Arirang Supermarket we'd fill rice-paper-thin plastic bags to the brim with oversized Fuji apples that Mom insisted I select because I was "good at that one" and stocked up on boxes of large Asian pears, each wrapped in their own Styrofoam fishnet mesh. She memorized each aisle of the market and picked packages of Pulmuone soft tofu, shrimp crackers, udon kits, boxed kimbap, egg-battered fried fish, mung bean pancakes, melons, chestnuts, and Korean grapes. On the way to the register we hauled boxes of Shin Ramyun for tawdry late-night snacking.

We were always starving by the time we finished navigating the narrow aisles of the grocery store and dodging the sharp jabbing elbows and carts of other Korean shoppers, who I'd learned early in life had a different concept of personal space. We were creatures of habit and always ended up at our favorite soondubu restaurant with a neon sign that read "Soondubu" in Hangul hanging over their door. The restaurant's shiny epoxy flooring was covered in stacked boxes of aloe juice and tiny yogurt drinks with red foil tops, the same sweet and tart yogurt drinks I had fallen in love with during my childhood summer in Seoul. The alienating fluorescent lighting didn't match the coziness of the food.

Mom and I usually ordered our food to share so we'd get meals that complemented each other. I'd usually order vegetarian bibimbap, which sometimes came in a stainless steel bowl, but after my mom opened my eyes to the world of dolsot,

I never turned back and carefully devoured the soul-scorching bibimbap right out of the sizzling vessel. Dolsot pots were a game changer. The Korean granite stone bowls retained inferno-level heat, which cooked the rice to a golden, chewy, crispy layer (akin to socarrat in paella) at the bottom of the bowl, adding a nutty flavor to each bite. My mom regularly ordered the piping-hot seafood soondubu, also served in dolsot pots, which came out looking like percolating spicy lava. The raw egg that accompanied the stew on its own banchan plate would cook in mere seconds after it was cracked open and hastily stirred. I never liked the flavor and texture of meat, but I made exceptions for some seafood and always helped Mom finish her soondubu.

I could never finish my food, so Mom always requested a to-go box whenever we ordered, neatly packaging the estimated leftovers before we ate to ensure that my food stayed fresh for later, uncontaminated by my own saliva.

8

I loved my brother growing up. I looked up to him as my leader. We only had each other after elementary school, or when we cowered in a corner liked caged baby animals listening to my parents fight. I used to mimic the way he'd wiggle out of trouble by being cute as a child. He was good. It started with a sweet smile and a tilt of the head, then, if my mom didn't start yelling at him, he'd put his arms around her waist and say, "I'm sorry, Mommy, I'll never do it again," which always disarmed her. But Johnny couldn't try this ruse with my dad.

Johnny always let me win when we played catch. When he turned nine, he pulled that shit older siblings do and started running away from me when I wanted to play with him and his friends, who would tear off screaming, "Run away from the crybaby, don't let Shirley play with us, crybaby, crybaby!" leaving me alone to bawl my eyes out. When he came home after playing with his friends, he made up for his inattentiveness by letting me torment him again. I was a spoiled, bratty, younger sister who pounded him on the head, but he took it like a champ. When I was barely a year old, I hit Johnny on the soft spot of his two-year-old head with my steel spoon, nearly arresting my mom's heart. Johnny cried for five minutes but came back to my crib an hour later to smile at the non-ambulatory creature in the house. Indeed, I was what you call a true crybaby. I cried for attention, food, sleep, for the hell of it, and Johnny was always there for it.

"Johnny always feeling bad when you cry and asking me

what's wrong," my mom said. "He watched you and touched your leg softly to calm you down. He look at me sadly like he wanted you to stop crying." It turned me upside down knowing that my sensitive, loyal brother was rattled by a demanding father and loved by a nurturing, vigilant mother because she felt like she had to compensate for her husband's deficits.

I was about sixteen when I started to despise Johnny for the burden he was becoming to my mom. He became moodier and more withdrawn; his transformation insidious and stealth that I almost missed it at first, which later turned spectacularly loud. Johnny would shut himself in his room next to mine and crank Black Sabbath or Guns N' Roses to the point I considered drinking Liquid Drano. Or when I walked by I heard my mom's quieted whispers become more clamorous through the cracked door, "Aishhh, saekki ya! Why you wasting all the money I giving you? You just like your daddy! Eotteohge hal su issni?" *How could you?*

At eighteen, Johnny had never dated or had a girlfriend, even though I know he wanted one. He was seen as the chubby, goofy, nice guy that helped people out of a jam but didn't seem to need to be in a romantic relationship because, to his friends, he resided in a safe, vague area where he was everyone's easy-going, fun, asexual friend. Johnny had a handful of good friends, but they were always up to mischief and got him into a lot of trouble by making him skip classes with them to get drunk or stoned, or to gamble. So Johnny went along with them mostly because he knew he was smart and could catch up on school work with panache and good acting. This was his practice for future years of deception.

The summer before Johnny started his senior year he

asked my parents if he could apply to the College of Architecture at the University of Colorado. My father shut him down. I linked my father's refusal to Johnny's nascent hobby of gambling, which was evolving into a problematic source of peer pressure and acceptance. My mom also told me that my dad didn't have a lot of confidence in Johnny's talents, though I think he was just too cheap to pay for out-of-state tuition. Johnny sank into a bigger funk, skipping more classes, disappearing mysteriously. As Johnny's senior year came to an end, I overheard my mom broach the topic again to my dad in Korean: "Johnny feels bad, you don't believe in him. Let him apply to the college he wants to go to. He's very smart and hard working!"

"It's too expensive when he can get the same education at Cal State Fullerton. He might not even graduate from high school!" my father exclaimed.

It was a self-fulfilling prophecy: our high school principal called my mom a month before Johnny was supposed to graduate to inform her that he was probably going to be held back a year because he was failing all of his classes. Mom sobbed in front of the principal, who turned to Johnny and said, "Look how sad your mother is. You're a good student, but this last year, you showed no effort and skipped most of your classes. If you promise to attend summer school and pass your subjects, I'll let you graduate."

Johnny just sat there like a lump, breathing out of his mouth, while my mom lit up with prospects and hope. "Oh, thank you so much for this chance, my boy is such a good boy!" she cried.

Johnny went to summer school, aced all of his classes,

and finally graduated high school. He never applied to Cal State Fullerton like my dad wanted and went straight to Fullerton College, a community college, where he felt he didn't need to take his classes seriously and could continue working and getting high with his friends at a nearby miniature golf course.

When I asked Johnny if he skipped classes he said no so I believed him because he seemed to always be around to drive me home or drop me off at friends' houses after school. This was way before I learned you can never trust a junkie. My mom's anxiety over Johnny's burgeoning gambling problems festered and needed releasing, so it was during this time that she unleashed on me stories from the vault about my paternal grandfather's gambling addiction when my parents lived with them in Seoul for a few years after they got married. To pay back his debts my grandfather had enlisted his daughters' husbands as well as my dad and mom to help him reimburse his creditors and pay his bills.

"It was a hard time for Mom. So stressful living with your grandparents, always bothering me to born baby when your daddy had a problem making me pregnant for long time. That's why I born Johnny when I was thirty-two and you when I was thirty-four! Korean custom of women living with the husband's family is so hard for women only. The husband's family always push the daughter-in-law." My mom had had two miscarriages before us, after which she wasn't able to conceive for a couple of years. The preexisting stress she received from her in-laws and husband didn't help. The patriarchal family my mom had married into blamed the woman for not being able to carry out her wifely duties of producing a son, though after many clinical tests, it turned out my father was the reason; he was shooting blanks. "His gochu not working," Mom said laughing in an effort to lighten the mood. After nearly ten years of trying, she finally became pregnant with Johnny, who became holy to her, a real-life baby saint delivered from heaven to provide succor to her grieving. My mom was ecstatic like a religious zealot and spoiled him like a little emperor.

"Then your daddy asked me for money to gamble when he spend all his paycheck, and your grandfather wanted money, too. I working so hard for U.S. Army and wanted to save money, but sometimes my entire paycheck go to your dad and grandfather. Gambling runs in the Pak family blood, not my family. Now Johnny has the same problem! It's not his fault, he learned from your daddy!"

My mom usually had the patience of Job when it came to unearthing family secrets; she would have rather internalized her anguish than snitch to protect her offenders out of a sense of duty. But in this case, my father and paternal grandfather were getting the full brunt of her anxiety. As I was getting older she probably thought I could handle these concepts of inherited and intergenerational legacies of gambling addiction, the vices that continued their damage through my father's bloodline to her son.

I'm hard-pressed to say Johnny didn't culturally "inherit" his gambling addiction, learning it from our father, because my mom and I witnessed it firsthand. Scientists have explored this question of whether chronic gambling is hereditary and an impulse control disorder, suggesting that, certain people may be genetically inclined to an addiction to gambling. And that people who have these genetic markers could pass them down from generation to generation. Conversely, reading books by some contemporary therapists who have argued against the popular notion of addiction being a genetic disease offered a more forward-moving view of addiction and the impact childhood trauma has on its development. If I had known then what I align with now, I would agree with the idea that addiction isn't an individual moral failure, but rather a case of human development gone awry, which, in turn, restores dignity and agency to the addict. It gives them the hope for growth and healing, as opposed to the pessimism and prison of genetic determinism.

But back when I was sixteen I was just a self-absorbed teen, dissociating like I was an audience member of our real-life, unpolished K-drama. I didn't know whether my paternal grandfather could have passed down any gambling genes to my father, who, in turn, could have passed them to Johnny; I also shared my brother's upbringing and emotional baggage with no gambling addiction to show for it, which muddied my own vision. What gave me the most pain was to see my mom smothering Johnny with treacly sympathy even when she knew he was taking advantage of her. He took and took, while she gave and gave.

My mom could read the room, but to say Korean mothers spoil and dote on their oldest sons is a colossal understatement; my mom wanted Johnny back in her womb. Her seismic concern for Johnny blinded her. I wasn't as tolerant as my mother was when it came to my father's and Johnny's pathological lying; to balance the way they took advantage of her generosity and naivety, I felt an intense need to do the complete opposite. She was mostly skeptical but often caved in to their fantasies and lies out of pure exhaustion. Then when she learned the truth about their lost wages, she had nervous breakdowns that immobilized her for days. By the time Johnny turned forty, my mom had probably spent close to fifteen thousand dollars bailing him out of his debts, paying off his bookies, and providing him with an income to gamble more. She didn't see her role in the enabler cycle. If Johnny were a part of any other family, including other Korean families, his ass would have been on the street before he turned twenty. It was textbook self-destruction. Ultimately as the years went by, I grew frustrated with my brother for losing his will, gaining a lot of weight, and being a major source of anxiety for my mom.

While my mother enabled Johnny, my father was always hard on him. My mom knew full well that my father was unnecessarily unfair, and her heart bled oceans for her first nearly-impossible-to-beget son. My father wanted Johnny to be tough and aggressive in business like he was, take no prisoners, be an intimidating leader. But Johnny was too decent of a guy and was never going to live up to my father's expectations. The truth was Johnny was loyal to his friends and family to a fault, and I got hints that his friends took advantage of his generosity when they blew through their own money to gamble, which trickled back to us.

"I think Dad's disappointed in me," I overheard Johnny tell Mom when he was nineteen. I could sense his self-loathing, too, but instead of starving himself like I eventually did, he couldn't get enough to eat. My brother had been chubby since he was twelve, then he became fat, then he straight-up morphed into an obese adult. When anorexia dominated my life at nineteen, I'd watch Johnny shovel food down his throat without taking breaths in between mouthfuls, so I lived vicariously through him. His eating filled me up with the food I craved but didn't feel worthy of.

Along with carrying on my dad's gambling addiction, Johnny picked up my father's filthy habit of smoking a pack of Marlboro Reds every day. My dad was a poor influence on Johnny in other ways, too, like disrespecting women and lying about playing golf to be a chump at the poker table. Then, it was no surprise when Johnny started beating me.

I clearly remember the first time Johnny beat me up; he was twelve and I was eleven. It happened on the heels of my father slapping me so hard in the face that I fell to the floor, nearly hitting my head on the sharp edge of the coffee table. He did this in response to my refusal to share my Halloween candy with my cousin Julie, it was the trick-or-treat loot I had collected in a large pillowcase with Renee in their affluent Belmont Shores neighborhood where her neighbors handed out full, not fun-sized, candy like Snickers, Hershey's, Twix, Starbursts, Smarties, and Jolly Rancher Stix. Instead of addressing my behavior like my friends' parents did by pulling them aside to persuade them to see the error in their ways in a reasonable tone of voice, he raised his right hand and slapped me thunderously on my left cheek, and with stony eyes said, "I hate you," which was only audible to me. He hardly hit Johnny or me only because we were too chickenshit to confront him the way my mom did. But something came over me that evening.

I fell to the floor from the force, stunned by the red, hot humiliation that he had slapped me with such hatred in front of Julie and Johnny who were watching from the kitchen. I got up and walked to the bathroom where Julie chased me, apologizing profusely. Why was my little cousin apologizing for a grown man's fucked-up behavior? I didn't let my dad see me cry, earning the pride my mom had taught me. I grated with hatred for him, not out of revenge for my father's own declaration of hatred for me, but because I felt it swim through my blood. He had just said it out loud first.

A month later Julie crashed at our house for a week. My parents were working so we ordered Kentucky Fried Chicken. Johnny laughed in between bites of his gravy-drenched mashed potatoes and biscuit, "Look at the massive zit on your nose! Gross!" At first it was funny and I laughed with Julie and Johnny, until his ridiculing lasted too long.

"At least I don't have your moon-sized pizza face, Johnny!" I laughed as I threw a piece of fried chicken at his face. "You pizza-faced sumo wrestler!" I taunted, running away.

Thinking we were playing, I ran around the house yelling, "Pizza-faced sumo wrestler, pizza-faced sumo wrestler, you're nothing but a pizza-faced sumo wrestler!"

Johnny caught up to me, looked me in the eyes, and with a shit-eating grin said, "You're a minority and a female. You're never going to make it in this world." Which, at the time, I'd quietly considered, but the fact that he had announced this platitude out loud, most likely learned from some racist at school, engulfed me in a blinding rage. With both fists, he beat my head back and forth like a punching bag for about five seconds until my yowling scared him enough to stop. I called and left a dozen frantic, rapid-fire messages with the receptionist at Allstate until my mom called me back twenty minutes later and told me with an unsettling calm that belied her beating anger, "I'm so embarrassed at work because you call too much crying. How do I go back to work now? I'm coming home soon, and you better have a good reason."

"Mom, I have bruises on both sides of my forehead!" I screamed into the cordless phone.

"Why did you call me so many times at work, they think we're crazy. What can I do from here?" I could tell my mom was more concerned about her reputation because, in the same way I assumed all Korean men beat their wives and children, she probably knew her son would imitate his father, and there was nothing she could do to make him unsee or unlearn my dad's abusive propensities. She reprimanded Johnny, but the truth was he needed to be held accountable by my father because he actually cared about what my dad thought. He mindlessly told Johnny to stop hitting me, but also told me to never call my mom at work unless it was a *true emergency*.

Thirty years later at a Gam-Anon for Families meeting I told the group that Johnny had beat me because it was learned behavior from my father, and I had forgiven him for that. But I couldn't forgive him for taking advantage of my mom when she went out-of-body desperate to enable him. He didn't seek help when his friends and I gave him the resources. He knew better but was out of his mind. I realized that the addict was not evil, just broken, and that my brother was suffering more than anyone could have ever understood. But I didn't have the mental and physical capacity at the time to care for Johnny, my capable older brother who was supposed to look out for me.

As the group was leaving our last session, one of the Gam-Anon moderators stopped me before I reached the door and said, "I wish someone had told me to prioritize myself and my loved ones while I was breaking down dealing with my son's addiction. I'm encouraging you to take care of your mom's and your health first. Even if your mom can't stop enabling your brother, let him know your priority is her and your health, and that you don't have time for his bullshit. It's like animal whispering: don't allow the difficult animal to penetrate your harmonious circle; instead, you instill discipline and respect through calm training methods. In this case, set boundaries that will limit his interaction with your mom to make it very clear to him that you won't tolerate anything that compromises her health and peace. This helps her and you regain some control while basically making your brother understand that you don't care if he gets into trouble for his gambling. He'll think harder before he blows his next paycheck because he'll figure out his safety net isn't there anymore."

This advice was revolutionary to me. I had never thought it was an option to think about my mom's health only, let alone my own, because her health was contingent on Johnny's. So with nothing to lose I started setting firm boundaries with Johnny, and it worked. My mom's health became my sole focus, taking the power away from him. My brother knew I'd never be like mom, the martyr; I wouldn't be his safety net. I still held on to the memory of my protective older brother who defended me on the school bus from the ignorant kid who called me "squinty eyes," but I wasn't going to bail him out when he blew his cash.

9

Toward the end of my senior year, I applied to UC Berkeley, UC Irvine, UC Santa Barbara, and UC Riverside. I was accepted to all of the colleges except high-ranking UC Berkeley. I chose to enroll at UC Riverside.

"You will be a UC graduate. Whaaaa! I'm so proud of you. Jalhaess-eo!" *Good job*, my mom said to me, but I felt unworthy of her adoration. She didn't know UC Riverside didn't rank in the top ten colleges of California and that it was inferior to the others, a lesser school, at least in my eyes. When I told her that she just smirked and said that Aunt Young Soon was jealous because her only spoiled child, Steven, had gone to Pomona, which was "not a UC school." Steven had graduated ten years earlier with an engineering degree; at least he knew what the fuck he wanted to do with his life because I had no clue. Meanwhile my dad lied to his friends and told them I had been accepted to Berkeley; he even wore a Cal baseball cap when he golfed with his rich friends. It was so sad.

Within the first week of classes, my perception flipped. I was impressed with the curriculum UC Riverside had for their literature and creative writing programs. There was no law or medical school during my attendance, and the intimacy of the campus made UC Riverside unique compared to UCLA and other colleges. I discovered that the professors there were world-renowned in their specialties, and teacher's assistants from around the country clambered to help teach ambitious courses. I felt like I was cheating compared to other students at more prestigious colleges because I had access to a similar program of studies and teachers with niche specialties that didn't force my parents to refinance their house. We were the cool underdogs of the Inland Empire.

A college advisor told me UC Riverside had a solid reputation for their economics, plant sciences, and agriculture programs and that nearby asparagus fields, citrus groves, and avocado trees surrounded the area. The aromatic scent of jasmine and freesia when the summer breeze hit just right was glorious. I was thrilled and challenged reading the works of Toni Morrison, or studying Chicano and African American literary movements, eliminating any sediments of embarrassment I once unfairly felt about the school. Back home, my parents and I didn't discuss cultural icons and art over dinner, but whose family did anyway? I only wished my parents and I had more meaningful conversations about Life instead of having to listen to their scattered squabbling.

I was overwhelmed by many simultaneous urgent interests, all of which I abandoned just as easily. I wanted to be a paragon of utter excellence at each thing I cared about before panic set in and I froze in my steps. Having no idea of what I wanted to do with my life, I finally chose English Literature as a discipline, which I felt was a transferrable degree in many trajectories: law, education, or teaching. I was a useless Korean, meaning I was terrible at math and statistics, and on top of that, I didn't eat meat, smoke cigarettes, or drink a lot of alcohol as though our bodies were built for it.

I lived at home and commuted the thirty miles to campus. I wanted to save my parents the money that would be wasted on dorm living, and I knew my mom would be lonely without me. I also knew I'd be lonely without her. In some ways, we had a codependent relationship.

Codependency has always gotten a bad rap because neediness—a dysfunctional, stifling trait of codependent relationships—must exist for such bonds to flourish: one person, the "giver," sacrifices their needs for the sake of the other, the "taker." I didn't know what codependency was until it was first brought to my attention by Renee when we were bickering about something I've since forgotten, and she told me I lived a sheltered life in Orange County, in a codependent relationship with my mom. But in the early days of my mom's and my functional mutual codependency, she and I were both insecure immigrants living with a hostile man in a new country so our so-called *unhealthy* relationship became essential, a source of comfort and *health.* Codependency became generous, selfless, as we looked after each other.

I wasn't ready to live without my mom in my first year of college because she was a sense of consistency to me when I had no idea what I wanted out of school and life. I *needed* her community. I felt an urgent necessity to protect her from the dangers of my dad and Johnny. I also sensed my mother wasn't ready to give up our sisterhood that had helped support her during her most difficult times with the men in my family.

In my early twenties I confided in a college friend about my father's abuse of my mother and she tried to connect my mom to a state of victimhood: "Your mother stayed with your father even when he hit her because she didn't have the strength to break the ties to your dad. She probably wanted to keep all her stresses deep down inside, but she had you to vent to. It was your mom's choice to stay with your father and be a kind of a recluse." To which I responded, "Nah, we're not *Grey Gardens*, Oprah," referring to the 1975 documentary about the lives of two hermits, a mother and daughter, who lived together in a derelict mansion in East Hampton, New York.

Abused women have left their abusers before. But this superficial assessment was familiar to me: a shallow, tired regurgitation of ersatz feminists and self-empowerment gurus I heard on late-afternoon talk shows who lacked the comprehension of real life's complexities and conflicts. How could my white friend who came from a wealthy family understand my mom's gnashing fear of raising two small children by herself in a new country on one income, and her dread of not being able to communicate well with her limited English? I didn't have it in me to explain to her the cultural disapproval of divorce in the Korean community in the seventies and eighties because her comments were mind-bogglingly asinine like insults blasting through the air.

In a country that values self-sufficiency and independence, the idea of codependency can be quite embarrassing. I don't wear it as a badge of honor either, but the truth was Mom and I pulled each other out of casualty.

By 1991 my parents were estranged yet still living together. The vibe was eggshells. I didn't know why they stayed together but for the comforts of habit and financial security. I avoided coming home for as long as I could by hanging out at Ashley's dorm room until it got dark, the same Ashley who had laughed at our tract home and my mom's "broken English." On a Wednesday before winter finals I came home early to see my mom sitting on the couch with an impassive expression on her face.

"Where did you go?" she asked.

"What are you talking about, Mom? I was at school."

"Where do you go to school?" my mom asked mechanically.

"Mom, what happened?" I immediately thought she had hit her head and lost consciousness. "Where does Dad work? What is your oldest sister's name?"

"I don't know where he work. My oldest sister name is Young Soon." I looked around; nobody else was home. I called 911.

Two ambulances arrived ten minutes later. The EMTs checked my mom's head and limbs, and I glanced inside her muumuu for any signs of assault. Two of the EMTs drove my mom to the hospital while one stayed behind to recon the entire house. After fifteen minutes, the EMT called me over to show me some skid marks at the entrance of the crawl space under our house where the screen door was busted open. There was a single SAS sandal left behind on the ground. "I think she fell here. The footprints match, and there's a pile of weeds. She might have been gardening and slipped and fell into the entrance of the crawl space."

In the waiting room of the ER a Vietnamese doctor came out to tell me my mom had minor ischemic strokes and that it could have been worse. "She lost her short-term memory for a bit, but it should come back within twenty-four hours," he said like this was a cautionary tale. "She's very lucky and will need medication for her hypertension."

My maternal grandfather had died of a massive stroke and thoughts of her going the same way were rappelling into my mind. I was already fearful that cancer was going to take my mom, like Aunt Min Jee, now I dreaded a stealth stroke was more menacing—it was quieter and swifter. I looked up from sobbing over the gray tile floors of the waiting room when my father appeared out of nowhere to snidely tell me, "Your mom is making this up for attention."

"She is not! Are you crazy?! How can you say that, and why would she go through all of this trouble to fake it? Why do you think such terrible things about her all the time?" As I ran away from my dad down the hallway and into my mom's room, I remembered a year earlier when my mom had catered an elaborate Christmas meal she bought from Costco. Instead of just heating up the premade food, she made extra vegetables and Korean food to accompany the turkey, gravy, mashed potatoes, and pie. She was overworked and stressed from having to cook for us and extended family that she got shingles on the inside corner of her right eyebrow. I had never seen her stunned in pain like that. I took my mom to her stern, laconic Korean doctor after the holiday and told him she seemed fine but stressed. He responded, "People like you have no idea the feelings of those who are suffering," as though he knew I was oblivious. Her stoicism under pressure was undetectable. And I knew my father and Johnny were also conditioned to seeing my mom as a dependable workhorse who rarely complained.

The one significant thing that differentiated my dad's cynical remark and my nineteen-year-old selfishness was that his comment was based in spite, whereas my inattentiveness to my mother's stress levels had been based in pure ignorance. He was the parent and husband; I was the child. I sat on a chair next to my mom's bed and rested my head on her stomach and cried.

"Mom, where do I go to school?"

"UC Riverside," my mom answered.

"Where does Johnny go to school?"

"Fullerton College," she answered correctly again.

"Mom, what happened? Do you remember anything?"

"I don't know. I'm scared," she said.

"I'm scared, too. Please promise me one thing, Mom, stop doing so much housework and gardening. We have a gardener so you don't need to clean up after him."

"Okay. I try. Too many happening," she said, exhausted and confused.

I shuddered to think what could have happened if I hadn't arrived on time to call 911. My mom could have incurred serious paralysis, speech impairment, or death. I couldn't imagine life without my mom at the age of nineteen. I had to be on high alert when it came to my mom's health. In that moment I realized my mom was a series of comebacks from heartbreak, health scares, and injuries. She was hardwired to survive the most arbitrary, tragic situations, but I couldn't take that for granted anymore. She was getting older. The audacity of my father to assume my mom had ulterior motives repelled me. It confirmed that he didn't trust or love my mom, and even more disheartening, he didn't even like her, which required a level of respect. It also created a fantasy world where he was dead to me because I didn't like him either.

Just as the doctor said at the hospital, my mom regained her short-term memory the next day. We had dodged a bullet, and I was determined to keep it that way. I accompanied my mom to her follow-up doctors' appointments, and even though she was already on medication for hypertension, I made sure she was prescribed every appropriate medication for her preexisting conditions; pills that were most offensive against potential blood clots that blocked vessels from making vital associations.

It was around this time that I stopped eating. At family barbecues I was the weird vegetarian my aunts thought belonged to a cult. I had always been some sort of vegetarian since I was fourteen, mainly lacto-ovo vegetarian, and then pescatarian when I was twenty. I considered fish an honorary vegetable as it was a staple in the Asian diet and didn't have the dense, fleshy texture of bulgogi or galbi. I also lost my period that year for a couple months from drastic dieting and got it back after taking progesterone for ten days. The Korean gynecologist my mom found through a church friend said I was still an average weight for my height, ninety-two pounds, but since I was "medium-boned," I could afford to put on more weight. I was so offended by her generous judgment call on my body frame (*why wasn't I small-boned?*) that I decided I hated her and never returned to her office.

During my senior year in high school, I weighed 135 pounds after gaining 20 pounds on my five-foot-four frame by liberally eating Taco Bell burritos and tacos every day for lunch. In college, seeing all the smart, skinny white girls with dark, sunken bags for eyes made me reevaluate what I thought it was to be unique. To stand out was to be austere, aloof, and thin, while I was chubby, average, and disappeared unnoticed into the mass of all the other Asians girls. In the early nineties, MTV and Gen X movies flooded images of waiflike Winona Ryder and Kate Moss into the mainstream imagination. I wanted to be skinny like they were. Becoming thin looked like something rarefied and meaningful to do. I especially wanted control over my chaotic life. My parents never separated or divorced years before they should have, so witnessing the consistency of their fighting left me depressed and combative, with emotional needs that were never satisfied. Specifically the emotional needs that a solid male role model provided, whatever that meant, the kind that cultivated trust in men without fearing corporal punishment if you dared to talk back. I was choked by my dad's censure of what I wanted to tell him and that was to be a better husband, father, human.

My family didn't go to psychiatrists or psychologists, and we were certainly never medicated for our depression. So I isolated and starved these new twisted feelings. I saw how lonely my mom became when my dad disappeared for days, presumably to be with his longtime lover. When my father did return home, she'd sleep in my bedroom with me. I was escaping into my own pain and thought I deserved physical suffering, which meant I never wanted to feel the fullness and goodness of food. I wanted to disappear. And in a bizarre way this deprivation was a sign of self-love because I poured all of my attention into myself and only myself.

Anorexia was right up my alley because my wheelhouse was control. Bulimia never appealed to me because it was messy, and I couldn't voluntarily vomit for the life of me. Once, as a child, I vomited so much after being dehydrated that I started to barf bile, which gave me a mild case of PTSD. I never became the anorexic who lost an egregious amount of weight that forced my ribs to distend over my concaving guts. The least I'd ever weighed was ninety-one pounds, but in the thick of my disorder, I was so fucked up and wanted to drop down to eighty-eight pounds because it was more respectable—symbolic of monastic self-sacrifice and discipline. I finally had a purpose.

Anorexia made me pull desperate, global-war-level shenanigans like hiding boxes of fat-free snacks from Costco under my bed. I was the resident squirrel that never forgot where I stored my nuts, hiding snacks for safekeeping so I could go back and eat them on my terms, without feeling rushed or fearful that the bigger, hungrier squirrel (Johnny) would get to them first. The snacks were a benevolent security blanket, dependable things that would always be there for me and never let me down. I ate the snacks conservatively, sometimes in place of full meals, in hopes of losing weight. It wasn't unusual to find commercial-sized boxes of Nature Valley Crunchy Oats 'n Honey and Peanut Butter Crunchy Granola Bars tucked under my bed next to old yearbooks. Or the ridiculously capacious 10-pound bag of round whirligig peppermints that restaurants served with the receipt on plastic trays, gifted to me by a friend when I told her I preferred mints to any other dessert because they had no fat content. I got through half the goddamn bag neurotically sucking on the hard candies with a running mantra in my head: *I've got to fit into the size 23 waist vintage Levi's I just bought.*

A college friend took speed regularly to help her keep up with her studies so she offered some to me after she noticed my interest in its appetite-curbing capabilities. I took it twice within a week and it worked; I didn't crave any food for days, but the intense migraines I got from not sleeping were insufferable so I stopped as quickly as I started. I was too controlling to release myself into the uneasy, clichéd white light of drug addiction; and plus my body was a hyper-sensitive wuss that could only parry this college experimental phase for a week. I was completely clueless to the effects of illicit stimulants when I was 19, but the euphoria I experienced made me rattle off to my mother in extravagant detail about how I was going to pursue journalism after I graduated—for at least 30 minutes straight standing over the kitchen sink—which she genuinely and enthusiastically supported. She had no idea I was flying so high, basking in the freedom from my usual anorexia-induced moodiness. I couldn't stand myself the next day for bullshitting this inauthentic ambition to her, but its deceptive delivery via methamphetamines that Mom thought was earnest wrecked me the most.

"I'm fat." It was the only thing I could listlessly come up with, hungry for my mom to see how fucked up I was. A week earlier my mom and I had run into one of her Korean church friends at the store and I overheard her tell my mom that she thought I still had baby fat on my face, which sent me over. That same week I ate a two-pound bag of peanut M&M's, then went to Family Fitness and rode the stationary bike for two hours after finishing three consecutive aerobics classes. I took aerobics classes so determinedly that my arches started to collapse, causing smarting, throbbing plantar fasciitis that my podiatrist mollified with custom orthotics.

My poor mom tried to assuage my rage. "Mrs. Kim hasn't seen you in a long time. You look like you're sick, like Aunt Min Jee!" I could tell she was confused about my beauty standards: had she just told me that I looked as emaciated as her beloved sister who had died of cancer? That my baby fat was a compliment, a sign of health and youth?

"She didn't mean it like that. She meant you look

healthy. That's what Korean old ladies say, they always talking about what you look like to make conversation." Living in South Korea or watching Korean television with its aggressive advertisements for beauty products that promised flawless, porcelain skin and cosmetic procedures that guaranteed lifted eyes and faces would have further disturbed my cognitive dissonance. No wonder the casual passing judgments on appearances by well-meaning church folk. My mom was tired of my disordered eating she hoped I'd drop as though it was another one of my transient caprices. But I was profoundly immersed in the cult of *me*.

"Sure, she didn't," I said with a snarky roll of the eyes. The thing was, I got off on the notion that I looked sick.

The inflection of sarcasm from a spoiled teenager was often lost on my mom, making her take some expressions literally.

"See, I knew you'd understand," my mom smiled.

My mom had to put up with my unpredictable mood swings and compulsive eating habits for at least four years during college when I was still living at home, and five years after I moved out. She was a pragmatic woman who didn't understand self-imposed starvation in this "first-world country." A product of strict food rationing and famine during World War II and the Korean War, she had never had the luxury of deciding not to eat. Aunt Seo Yun's husband, Uncle David, used to call my mom "the onion" because of her slight midsection girth; her riposte was that his distended paunch looked like the aftermath of eating ten Thanksgiving dinners. My mom could never fathom renouncing food just because she didn't feel worthy, loved, or pretty. Who wouldn't want to eat when you were hungry? "Waegurae?" *What's the matter with you?* she asked, because, unlike me, she never had the time to indulge in her own self-pity. I was frustrated that my mom lacked the Western perspective to understand my eating disorder in a hemisphere of the world where food was plentiful enough to be considered optional; though at the same time I stored quiet desires for her to get help for me. She even cleaned and saved aluminum foil and saran wrap to reuse because she wanted to save money. My mom's unintended, prescient environmental activism came before the fads and trends. She had a survivalist mentality that helped her get through the next series of natural disasters and personal wars, and her vigilance during events like the Southern California drought of the late eighties and early nineties impelled her to urinate in buckets to save and pour down the bathtub drain to save gallons of water per flush.

"Never waste one grain of rice, you don't know real hunger. People in this country make so much food, then waste it all. I want to punch them hana." Mom said that during the Korean War, U.S. troops would drive their vehicles through some residential areas to give boxes of provisions to people who lined up on the side of the road. These boxes contained candy, chocolate, crackers, canned foods. My mom was thirteen when she saved her sickly, emaciated three-year-old sister's life. She hoisted Aunt Yun Hee on her shoulders so the troops would hurl extra supplies at them. When Mom returned home with more boxes than she could carry, her father shouted at her for accepting gifts from the "imperialists," even though his family was hungry.

"My father said we were Yangban, educated upper-class people, and we had a little money because he doing business for

Japanese when they occupy Korea, like helping their army."

"Mom, I saw a picture of harabeoji, and he had a Hitler mustache," I said, remembering a weathered black-and-white photo of my grandfather I had found in my mother's address book when I was eleven, trying not to shriek at the odd reveal. "Do you think he was an ally of the wrong team?"

"No! That was the fashion back then. Lots of men had that kind of mustache-y in 1940s, not only Hitler!" We both laughed. "My father was smart, he had to be sneaky and pretend to respect the Japanese. They stole from our land and used people like slaves and wouldn't let us speak our own language, but my daddy used the Japanese to make money for his family and keep us safe. He heard about raping and kidnapping, so he walked my older sister and me to school and waited for us after school so nothing happening to us. I was only five years old. He also gave my Japanese school teachers money and food so they would be nice to my sister and me. The Japanese teachers gave me Japanese name, Ako Masuyama." My mom lit up talking about her family. "He was such a good, responsible father. He was very proud of our ancestors because we come from ruling class. But during Korean War, everyone was poor and hungry, we lost everything."

I was satisfied with my grandfather's subversion, events that seemed a million miles away, because if it hadn't been for his indignant propensity for action, it would be hard to know whether my mother, her family, Johnny, or I would have ever existed. Hearing my mom recount details of the wars made me realize we were still not that far removed from the Korean War, the atrocities of which were still palpable to survivors like my mom who was alive during the diaspora. Sharing her intimate accounts with the next generation was my mom's way of collectively revisiting her traumas, to seek meaning and justice, so her world resisted becoming invisible.

10

Coffee culture in the early nineties pales in comparison to how hot it is now, but the scene was still simmering. I worked at a successful coffee shop in Anaheim Hills during my first year of college, owned by two veterans in the coffee industry. Independent coffee shops were cropping up on every other corner, even in sleepy, lackluster Yorba Linda whose streets rolled up at 9:00 p.m.

My father was intrigued by the long lines for hazelnut-flavored coffees, espressos, double mochas, cappuccinos, and lattes when he came to visit me at work. We used an industry grinder and scale and a precise measurement of six to eight grams of finely ground Italian roast for a single shot of espresso to create the perfect demitasse with crema. My boss, Matthew, taught me to pour very cold low-fat milk into a stainless steel pitcher and dip the wand of the frother at the surface level of the milk to start the foam. Once the foam got frothy, I dunked the wand into the milk to heat the body of the milk. When the milk became warm, I moved the pitcher up and down so the wand reached the surface level of the milk again to sustain the foam and heat the milk to the desired temperature. My dad saw I was good at my job. Out of nowhere he proposed opening a coffee shop and wanted me to work it, which entailed quitting my job at Matthews's shop. I didn't want to be sucked into the vortex of another one of my dad's cockamamie plans; I had planned to work at Matthew's festive coffee shop through college. I begged my mom to talk my dad out of forcing me to work there after classes at UC Riverside, but my father responded defensively, "I want you to inherit this business, we're going to make a lot of money and you'll be set for life!"

"What's the point of getting an English degree if I'm going to end up making coffee for the rest of my life? I don't want to do it, I like working for Matthew."

"You'd rather work for a stranger than your father?" he asked, cornering me with guilt. *Yeah*, I thought, but could only roll my eyes. My dad and I fought until eventually I felt I had no choice, which only made me more self-destructive. I turned in my notice three weeks later.

My father found a strip mall in Rowland Heights in the suburbs of the San Gabriel Valley to open Gourmet Coffee Unlimited (GCU), the name I christened the shop as a joke but that he loved for its length and even number of syllables.

"It sounds intelligent, European," he said as he wrote the name on his business plan for this new entrepreneurial venture, which he'd helm while some lackeys, namely my mom and me, would do most of the grunt work. When my parents worked in the service industry they endured grueling schedules and performed tasks that compromised their health and sanity. But they had also operated successful and busy restaurants, convenience stores, and video rental shops. To my father, GCU would be a more civilized enterprise that lacked the greasy hamburgers and fries to serve to drunk patrons.

In the early nineties the San Gabriel Valley was composed of a large Chinese and Southeast Asian population, which couldn't be more night and day compared to the majority white population of Yorba Linda. I walked into 99 Ranch Market in Rowland Heights with alacrity, knowing I was now a member of the majority as opposed to being one of the few Asians at the Costco down the hill from our house. Being both ignored and scrutinized for being Asian in a white town like Yorba Linda tripped up my perception of reality. On the one hand, I could live in the careless haze of anonymity, but on the other, I could be heckled by a racist as I walked down the street. It felt fresh yet intimidating being part of the larger crowd in Rowland Heights in that everything important could be taken away in a split second. I became paranoid that a bitter white supremacist would walk into our shop with an AK-47 and take us out.

My father didn't have the vision to create GCU into the cool destination for wannabe coffee snobs. He had the walls painted eggshell and populated the tea cabinets he had bought at an estate sale with antique-inspired coffee cups and tea sets that his good friend's wife made by hand. He didn't have the foresight to see that the college students from neighboring Mt. San Antonio Community College and Cal Poly Pomona didn't resonate with faux antique porcelain. They wanted brown XCF Made-in-Italy ceramic latte cups with matching saucers in which to sip their coffee outside on the patio, or at least paper cups with stamped logos of edgy, abstract imagery that they could carry off to class. Coffee shops were still competitive with each other in the early nineties, and my dad didn't look around the room; he was out of touch with café culture, aesthetics, attitude, and history. My father was of a previous generation whose demographic probably couldn't afford a two-dollar cup of brewed coffee. Ironically, he didn't know how to appeal to people with disposable incomes, the folks he wanted to hang out with. He just saw the lines outside of Matthew's coffee shop waiting for drinks that looked fairly easy to make and wanted in on the fast money.

I drove thirty miles from Riverside to Rowland Heights after classes on Monday, Wednesday, and Friday to fill the evening slot from 3:30 p.m. to 9 p.m. On weekends, I worked from 4 p.m. to 9 p.m. I was made manager via nepotism, not experience, even though I did all the grunt work like sweeping, cleaning, mopping, sanitizing, and refreshing the coffee inventory. I made coffee drinks, too, but I lost the bright-eyed vigor I once had working for Matthew who inspired me to be good at my job, to be proud of it. Matthew taught by encouragement and suggestion, not by dictating orders. After years of doing what my dad told me to do I realized he never inspired me to do anything I *wanted* to do. He always judged me for being me, like my decision to pursue an English Literature degree and not take the law or medical school route that the children of his golf friends took. He never encouraged me to follow my interests the way my mom did. She never judged me for my choices; the crazier the better because my mom was fun though she lacked the opportunities to grow her interests. But I usually played it safe due to my own diffidence about the things I fantasized doing, like going to fashion school, an art-oriented profession that didn't require a traditional college degree. But this inherently introduced greater risk to my bus route of a life going from one stop to another, clutching onto a recognizable bachelor's degree.

My father also conscripted my mom to make copious amounts of chicken, tuna, potato, and macaroni salads for the sandwiches we started to offer, when he could have just ordered prepackaged salads from a deli or bought them from Costco.

But my father was too cheap. My mom's salads were delicious, not heavy on the oil or mayonnaise, just the right amount of dill, herbs, mustard, salt, and pepper. The sandwiches and salads were a runaway hit and our customer base grew quickly, but the intensity of the work caused my mom's right wrist to flare up again. She'd groan while trying to wring out the water from the tuna that came in large commercial aluminum cans, which I helped open with a can opener since our automatic one couldn't handle the size. I helped Mom make the food when I could, but it didn't help curb the pain.

Making salads for GCU was not what my mom wanted to do during her premature retirement. She enjoyed constantly creating busy work for herself at home. Our meandering garden with zigzagging pathways lined with pretty weeds, jubilant bushes, and tall trees that constantly shed their leaves drove my mom bonkers. She needed to control the unpredictability of nature and stop it in its tracks—before a single wayward leaf fell on the grass—so she didn't have to worry about cleaning it up after the gardeners had left. Instead of spending hours making food for patrons she never met, she wanted to go to the Korean market and acupuncturist to stock up on bottles of aloe vera drink and herbs to mollify her menopause symptoms; she wanted to walk down the fancy jewelry and accessories aisles at a boutique near Arirang Supermarket to obsess over the Omega watch she finally bought herself after watching an alluring commercial on Korean TV; she wanted to get her eyebrows and lips tattooed with aunt Young Soon; she wanted to attend her Presbyterian church during the week to sing for the choir; she wanted to live her life without being affected by my father's latest caprice. His ambitions became her obstacles.

"Your daddy always using people to do his work. One day I dropped off food and I saw him sitting really close to an American woman. Butt almost touching butt. I walked in and he moved away a little. I couldn't believe it."

I felt the heat of my mom's humiliation. The American woman was a jovial, affable teacher who had no interest in my father. She was just nice to everyone and he fell for her charm since he wasn't getting any affection from my mother. I've always tried not to imagine my parents having sex. It was an act that had happened in an alternate universe that produced Johnny and me, and that was it. I knew my father was a lothario but wondered when my parents had last done it, and whether my mom had ever experienced a time with my father when she didn't feel like she was merely surviving. My mother wasn't turned on by my father. It was obvious. But I knew my father had his needs. I just wished he was classier about it.

My father may have been anemic in the male role model department, but he had a knack for identifying trustworthy, hard workers to fill in when he played golf. One of his hires was a girl named Lucy. I developed a close friendship with Lucy, who was artistic, efficient, scrappy, and honest. And she was exactly my age, nineteen going on twenty. Lucy had a great sense of humor and a vetted taste for literature and music. She was sensitive with a side of gloom, and she shared my skepticism of people as well as the nascent feminism one develops during their first year in college. Lucy was raised in the San Gabriel Valley and was one of the few white girls in school where Asians made up the majority. "I have a lot of Asian friends, but I noticed that Koreans are the most temperamental," Lucy said in passing as she was cleaning the countertop holding the display of biscotti and multi-flavored Pirouline rolled wafers.

"I think the body language, gestures, and pursed lips throw you off. Along with the inflections and consonants of the Korean language that make everything sound a lot worse than they really are. It always sounds like we're stressed or pissed when we're just talking, man," I said stolidly.

Unbeknownst to my father or me, he also hired a well-respected Latina singer named Lysa Flores who was friends with some members of the band X. Lysa was charming and energetic; her effervescence was the yang to Lucy's and my yin. She introduced us to D.J. Bonebrake, the drummer for X, and his artist wife Diana (who went by Dinky), an effortlessly cool, casually intellectual, down-to-earth couple who surprised me with their goofiness. Lysa invited them to visit our sterile, unadorned shop a month after we officially opened in November 1991 to consider hanging and consigning a couple pieces of Dinky's art. I felt like a fraud that Lysa thought so highly of our little shop, enough to persuade Dinky into trusting us with her pieces. To me, Dinky and D.J. were giants in the art and music world and our humble, uninspiring coffee shop was insufficient.

"I don't eat junk food," D.J. said after I offered him a cheese muffin that we ordered wholesale from a Korean-owned bakery in Fullerton. I copied my mom's hospitality of offering guests food and drink as soon as they stepped into our home. I looked at the unusually large, unappealing yellow muffin with jiggly lava puddles of sweet cream cheese poking through random corners of the cake. It was the sort of pastry only Koreans could concoct. What other culture could devise such a witty, hilarious dessert but Koreans who love decadence wrapped in the common-sense shape of an archetypal muffin? When I starved myself for a full week and felt worthy enough for a treat, I reached for a day-old cheese muffin at the end of my shift. I'd cut it into quarters, then dunk one of the pieces into a small cup of nonfat chocolate and vanilla swirl frozen yogurt from Golden Spoon, a frozen yogurt chain store on the other side of the strip mall. When I was in high school, I overheard a skeletal student tell a friend she poured salt on her leftovers before throwing them away so she wouldn't be tempted to pillage the trash to eat more later. I didn't want to submit to the same temptation so I'd crumble and smash the remaining bits into fine pieces of flour and cheese. Instead of wasting my mom's salt, I churned the remains with dirt from our garden and the rot of our garbage. I'd be damned if that wreckage seduced me.

D.J. Bonebrake was one of the original members of X who helped put the LA punk scene on the map. When I was sixteen, I listened to cassette versions of 1980's *Los Angeles* and 1982's excellent *Under the Big Black Sun.* And I always thought 1987's *See How We Are* was superb and underrated. I imitated Exene Cervenka's moves for hours: I stood tall, arms straight down my sides, and, hinged at the hip, moved my torso in all directions like a twitchy Tin Man with my long hair whipping my face. X was the first LA punk band I took seriously. And I was embarrassed I had offered a lumpy cheese muffin to its cool drummer.

Lysa was the cool kid of the shop and Lucy and I were chill by association. Sometimes Lysa invited her musician friends over when my dad wasn't around and performed impromptu sets, which serendipitously created interest as passersby popped in to see what the crowd was for. Her friends weren't assholes and never destroyed anything. My father was too cheap to spend money on advertising so these gatherings actually helped us out. But after Lysa's parties ended the only buzz we heard was from the mini refrigerator that contained my friends' clattering beer bottles.

Business was slow out of the gate without the usual bustle of Matthew's coffee shop, where the wealthy Anaheim Hills clientele had too much time. GCU was nestled in a corner of a cursed, low-foot-traffic area of a Rowland Heights strip mall where the clientele had less money and even less time. Besides the Golden Spoon frozen yogurt shop, where I got my usual nonfat yogurt dinners after a long, boring day, there was Happy Noodle where they made my weekly meal of vegetarian lo mein noodles that I'd slurp up while driving home. I salivated when I saw Lysa slowly eating the noodles while talking about her latest show and I needed to have them in my life. I needed the whole visual package, the gesture of twirling the noodles around my fork, analyzing each strand, resting the fork on my chin to think of something clever to say between languorous bites. I wanted her levity, the image of what I thought happiness was. After my voyeurism of Lysa's lo mein appreciation, I made a Friday night ritual of taking home an order of greasy noodles that came in a giant Styrofoam container for my ride home. After a full week of studying, working, commuting, and depriving, I felt that the tawdriness was warranted; I was finally worthy of eating. On a few occasions after my mom helped me close the shop she'd catch me precariously balancing the Happy Noodles Styrofoam container on my right leg while I drove. She shouted, "Why don't you eat at a table like normal people or when we get home? We're going to get in a car accident!" She sucked in her teeth.

"Nah Mom, we're good," I said, cocky and high after my first bite, my body singing from the sugars and nutrients overloading my senses. Anorexia took me out of my body and dictated its own absurd rules that made flawless, logical sense at the time. Five was my lucky number so after eating five medium-sized forkfuls of lo mein, I'd close the Styrofoam container, which was handy for its hinged lid-lock system, and stop eating. I gave the greasy leftovers to Johnny when I got home.

Routine and control are essential to anorexics. I had to eat the same thing and amount at the same time every day, and if I didn't, I suffered agita that couldn't be shaken for at least two days. For 9 a.m. breakfast I ate half a burnt cinnamon raisin bagel (my dysmorphic wishful thinking led me to believe that more fat and calories were charred off when I set the toaster on high) with the scantest spread of nonfat cream cheese, half a large Fuji apple to ease my constipation, and coffee with nondairy hazelnut creamer. Then I'd fast (without hydrating, because liquids made me full and anxious) until 4 or 4:30 p.m. and eat ten Wheat Thins, or two Fig Newtons, or one SnackWell's Devil's Food Cookie Cake (snacks I carried with me in case I wasn't at work or home at exactly 4 or 4:30 p.m.), and a nonfat cappuccino stirred with half a packet of Equal. I lived for my next snack. For dinner, I had a small bowl of white rice and kimchi jjigae or other stew, or, if I was at work, I'd slice a piece of wheat bread in half and scoop barely a tablespoon of Mom's tuna salad on it to eat along with two tablespoons of mustardy potato salad. If we went out to eat I ordered salads (vinaigrette on the side) or veggie burgers with mustard atop one bun. I was that person who ate only half the veggie patty and poked at the shards. I'm sure I lost some brain cells. I was also a secretive eater. I didn't want people, even my family, to know I ate so that they could make a correlation between my eating and any resultant weight gain.

Feeling full made me antisocial, shut down. Being full of nutrients and energy supports people to do meaningful things with their lives; being hungry, gaunt, and malnourished kept me small, passive, and weak that I felt no pressure to do anything at all. Fullness was my nemesis; even a spontaneous midday snack of juicy grapes would have sent me spiraling into a fragile, frenzied state of self-hatred; instead, I loved the hunger pangs that satiated me and were proof of my resistance. I craved so much control over my life, but felt stuck and afraid of doing anything I'd possibly fail at.

Knowing that my Friday night feasts of lo mein would throw off my metabolism, I'd leave work at 9 p.m. and eat by 9:15 p.m. to finish by 9:30 p.m., so I could get home twenty-five minutes later to walk laps around my room for about half an hour in order to feel completely digested, empty again. I once saw Aunt Chan Mi do that when she lived with us in Palo Alto and it stuck. She'd walk circles in our living room for twenty to thirty minutes after dinner, like a blind cat creating a map of its surroundings. Aunt Chan Mi, my mom's youngest sister, was known as the grumpy feckless one who couldn't hold down a job for her life. She bounced from one sister's house to another every three months or so, leaving whenever they tired of her bullshit.

We weren't prepared for the 1992 Los Angeles riots. On the first day, I drove to work from school hearing about it on the radio, not thinking about any significance it would have on relations in Los Angeles communities until I watched footage of Korean store owners in Koreatown standing on rooftops with rifles and guns.

That same week, my history professor said race relations between African Americans and Korean Americans in LA had already been poor in the seventies and eighties, but after the shooting of Latasha Harlins on March 16, 1991[2] by a Korean liquor store owner named Soon Ja Du (who was found guilty of voluntary manslaughter, but was sentenced to only five years of probation without jail time)[3], [4], they drastically worsened. The riots started after four officers of the Los Angeles Police Department were acquitted in 1992 after using excessive force in the beating of Rodney King the previous year.[5] The tragedy of Latasha Harlins' death further divided communities and the acquittal deepened the outrage and anger in LA. Hostile confrontations followed, leading to the violent unrest and widespread destruction.

Many Korean American business owners in Koreatown (as well as those in parts of South LA and other affected neighborhoods) felt neglected while police protection was concentrated in wealthier areas farther west like Beverly Hills.[6] Months later my dad told me he knew some store owners who felt like they had no choice but to defend themselves to protect their families and livelihoods as the violence continued.

Up until that time we had lived in tone-deaf, ultra-conservative Orange County for nearly a decade, sheltered, not from racism and bigotry, but from most of the violence. I'd never heard of Latasha Harlins until the LA riots and didn't have any context for the existing conflict between Korean shop owners and Black communities across the country since the seventies. One of our Black customers told Lucy and me that Black people felt that Korean shop owners overcharged them for goods and that they were sick of the racist stereotypes and structures that predominantly privileged whiteness, which portrayed Black people as economically dependent, while Koreans were perceived as self-sufficient. Years of abuse and racism pit Black against Korean, Korean against Black, and buttressing those tensions, white against both Black and Korean. The devastation of the city playing out on the news was surreal. Even with the volume turned down the helplessness rang and rang.

It was hard for me not to take the attacks on Korean-owned businesses personally even though ours was protected from the fires and looting, being nearly an hour away from the riot's epicenter. My parents had run restaurants and convenience stores on both sides of the continent, so I felt violated on behalf of the Korean shop owners who had to defend their businesses against ineluctable violence and arson. My parents worked their asses off to clear paths so we could reach for more. Most Korean immigrants in the seventies didn't speak or understand English well enough to easily apply for mid-level corporate jobs, the comfortable roles my parents dreamed of; all they had was their intrepid entrepreneurship, which was in the genetic makeup of the immigrant. At the same time, I felt that people who had moved to a country built by racist, egregiously exploitative labor systems should know their history in order to become a viable part of society. But the real-life politics were more complicated than the idealism of my freshly scrubbed twenty-year-old brain that understood we were all fucked.

The riots and not eating were making me delirious. One of our regular customers asked Lucy if I was sick or recovering from cancer because my "hip bones were jutting out." The delirium led me to watch more footage of the armed Korean vigilantes on their rooftops, which filled me with both empathy and shame. I wanted to be jettisoned from the coffee shop, a symbol of immigrant entrepreneurship, an Asian process. "It's what we do, we open restaurants and shops to make a lot of money so we can create a better life for our family," my dad explained to me when I was eleven. At the same time I also heard in my head, *we open shops due to our limited English and racism because who would hire us?* I was witness to a series of entrepreneurial setbacks, successes, and sacrifices my parents had experienced and endured, which ultimately made me feel that being an immigrant family that opens businesses was a tired trope. *It's what we do.*

"If you need anything let me know," my father said, seemingly oblivious to the events of the world, while heading out the door to go home so I could work the evening shift during the throes of a maniacal riot. "I installed a security system yesterday."

Yeah, that was going to stop them from throwing shit through the windows, I thought.

"Are you sure we should stay open? It looks like a lot of stores are closing," I said futilely.

"No, why? That craziness is over an hour away. You think all those thieves are going to drive together in one car to loot this shop? You're being crazy like your mom. She's worried, too, so she told me she's coming later to stay with you."

Lucy piped in, "It's just to be cautious, Charles. People are desperate and angry now. Maybe you should close for a couple of days. You shouldn't think about money right now." I was impressed by her soft judgment of my dad.

"You lazy girls! You just want time off! You don't know true scary history, this is nothing! I'm proud of those Koreans. We fight back when nobody will help us. I'd do the same thing if I owned a store in Koreatown. They're defending everything they have to try to make it in this goddamn country. I'm less worried about them than about you two spoiled girls who want everything given to you for free. You haven't lived through real wars and starvation!" My dad knew national war stories one-upped regional ones.

"We want to keep it that way!" Lucy half-laughed, half-scoffed.

This wasn't going anywhere, and my dad was pissed and tired. All he wanted to do was go home, eat dinner, and watch Korean TV in his pajamas. I understood my father's primary focus was to protect his business and livelihood, but his denial and shock limited his awareness of the larger political, economic, and historical realities that affected the people in his own community. My father was a fiercely proud Korean who defended our culture to the marrow. He was glued to the Korean news during the riots and for months afterward, nervously watching the destruction and its aftermath unfold, stunned like he was running through hardening concrete.

The shop did very well during the two winter holiday seasons we were open. We couldn't keep the bags of ground and whole bean coffee from flying out the door. During our first

Christmas, the entire crew, including my dad, worked ten hours straight without eating. We were all amped up on caffeine and biscotti and needed nothing else. My anorexia thrived. My hair and clothes shed coffee detritus every night. When the rush of the holiday season ended, we were back to long, quiet mornings and afternoons of selling about thirty cups of coffee, ten sandwiches, and maybe four bags of coffee. I knew we weren't making what we needed to break even.

My father started talking about filing for bankruptcy around spring 1994, which to his surprise elated my mom and me. I couldn't believe how unbothered he was of our resentment for the work my mom and I had put into the shop. He also had no idea about my anorexia, how it made me feel like a cotton-head zombie. The only thing he ever said in recognition of my disordered eating was, "Eat a hamburger, you're getting too skinny." Then he patted me on the back on his way to golf. My mom was relieved she didn't have to make salads anymore, and I was reeling over the fact that I no longer had to watch the figurative coffee house catch on fire. There were days Lucy and I didn't move from our bar stools to greet anyone, because there was no one. The overhead costs eclipsed the revenue, and soon our customers started going to the new Starbucks five blocks away.

11

I turned to music in between the vague, crazy days of my imminent college graduation and liberation from GCU. The alternative music scene in the early nineties was lit up by grunge whose essence became less inspiring with bands sounding more derivative and monotonous. Like MTV, the music on LA's KROQ in the early nineties was repetitive and mundane, except when the DJs played eighties flashbacks, particularly the ones that Mom loved like Depeche Mode's "Just Can't Get Enough," to which she tapped her thighs to the plucky percussion, and The Cure's "Boys Don't Cry," to which she'd exclaim, "Johnny cry!" then release an infectious chortle.

I loved English rock of the early and late eighties, like Love and Rockets, The Smiths, Pulp, Joy Division, and Bauhaus. Up until then most of my musical heroes were men, but then came Polly Jean Harvey, known as PJ Harvey, with her 1992 debut album *Dry*, which obliterated the vanilla from my ears. She hit the alternative music world with a welcome tornado and confronted grunge music with her own intrepid art school sound of bluesy hard rock and punk. Defying categorization with influences by Willie Dixon, Howlin' Wolf, Captain Beefheart, and Bob Dylan, Harvey's songs were confrontational and mighty, as well as tender and clever. The unusual sounds, phantom whispers, and occasional discomfort of her unconventional musical landscape disassembled me and left hope for something new. The female characters in her songs are longing, smart, flawed. I liked to think she was singing about herself rather than any feminist ideal.

I wasn't prepared for my first PJ Harvey concert in the summer of 1993 at the Hollywood Palladium. I watched in awe as she stood undaunted and motionless on stage with her girthy, oversized electric guitar wearing no makeup, a vintage sequin dress, and sparkly sunglasses, showing off her unshaved armpits and unkempt eyebrows. I felt victorious. I swooned over her athletic vocal range and endurance that could go from high-pitched warbling to bass operatic lows in seconds. Harvey's live shows told the truth of her artistic gifts, it was just her and her music.

I bought *Dry* on cassette, which was on nonstop rotation in my car and bedroom in Yorba Linda. I imagined how tickled she would be to learn that far-flung fans like me listened to her in the most random, plain towns across the globe. I twitched and danced neurotically to "Sheela-Na-Gig," "Dress," and "Victory" when I got back home from school or work. I competed with other fans about who loved her more: who had the OG first-edition cassette tapes of her first two albums; who had all the B-sides and rare live recordings burned on CD; who had stayed up until 1 a.m. in 1993 to record on VHS her live performance of Willie Dixon's "Wang Dang Doodle" on MTV's *120 Minutes*, where she wore a vintage red minidress, gold metallic platform sandals, and a crooked smile. She was the type of artist who attracted the envy and territorialism in her fans.

I noticed similarities between my mother and PJ Harvey: they were both extremely private, courageous, imperfect, thoughtful. My mom taught me to *never make trouble* when I was a young guest at other people's homes, which instilled in me an insecurity to do anything outlandish and a reason to always overthink my actions and take the safe, practical approach; all while maintaining my integrity the way she did with my father. Meanwhile, Harvey gave me a strong sense of agency and confidence to be outrageous and creative, even when I knew she was hiding behind an alter ego, costumes, and thick layers of stage makeup during her later live performances. My mom taught me to be considerate and gracious at the expense of suffocating my impulses, but as I got older, Harvey's influences helped me to be more innovative and autonomous and less apologetic for my urges. These binary effects, with their own limitations, made my identity porous, flexible, and ready for change.

After a friend flaked on me, I took my mom to a PJ Harvey concert at the Mayan Theater in downtown LA in 1995 in support of her album *To Bring You My Love*. I told my mom to stay near the back so she wouldn't be bothered by the noise and crowd while I spent the entire evening standing up against the stage—I was that fan who sang along with every word. When the show was over I found my mom sitting near the entrance of the theater, laughing with a group of people my age. A couple of kids giggled, "Is this your mom? That's so cute she came with you!"

"All the young people want to know how come I'm here. The fashion here is so crazy," my mom said, riding on a high of adoration and excitement.

For as long as I could remember, my mom always sang and danced to old Elvis songs. She learned to sing "Can't Help Falling in Love," Neil Sedaka's "Oh! Carol," and Patti Page's version of the Jessie Mae Robinson song "I Went to Your Wedding" phonetically, the way I learned to sing Korean children's songs the summer I went to Korea for my grandfather's funeral. There was even a Korean version of "I Went to Your Wedding" that she knew by heart. The song, a memory of a wedding attended by an ex-lover who was still in love with one of the parties getting married, captured a popular theme of unrequited love in the early 1950s. Koreans love sad songs, especially songs about longing and the one who got away.

My mom explained the contrasting emotion of regret and hope as Han, a specifically Korean characteristic whose central tenet is described as a form of grief and resentment that pertains to oppression without payback. The origins of this niche concept stem from the Japanese occupation of Korea and is also connected to the division of families during the Korean War; a protracted melancholia, much like the loss my father experienced after escaping North Korea without his youngest sister.

The phenomenon of Han can also make Koreans hear everything, including happiness, as crying. I often remember my mom crying whenever she was happy or comforted because there's a sliver of hope in Han. This explained her tears when she was relieved to see Johnny, my cousins, and me emerge from the redwood forest near our picnic site after being lost for hours. She felt hope in this good fortune. Bubbly tears burned my eyes when my mom, cousins, aunts, and Johnny sang "Happy Birthday" to me on my fifth birthday over Jack in the Box and Lucky Supermarket cake. I was moved by their attention, but instead of squirming in my seat anxious to blow out the candles, I cried through my inchoate joy.

I knew some of PJ Harvey's songs about desire and unrequited love would resonate with Mom—at least the acoustic versions. Or her desperation songs for their inherent drama like "Rid of Me" in which the protagonist begs their lover to never leave them lest they suffer a vengeful punishment. During some early live performances of this song, PJ Harvey sang with a wink and sly impudence. I wish there was an app back then in which songs could be translated to emote feelings and context into the Korean language so my mom could have experienced the same survival sounds I heard as I sang along to lyrics that wandered the world in search of a deeper resonance with life.

At fifty-seven, my mother was thrilled by the fever pitch and energy of the PJ Harvey concert, to finally see the musician I talked about all the time—the artist I was obsessed with, admired, and wanted to be. She got a kick out of her lurid magenta cat suit and deranged makeup and called her "michin gijibae," *crazy girl* or *bitch*, which could be construed in a playful or not-so-playful way. In this context, *gijibae* held an endearing quality, like the informal familiarity of family. She was just thrilled to be my wingman when I was in my early twenties, and for one evening, entirely alive.

12

"You get sankapul surgery in Korea, I pay for it for your college graduation present," my mom said to me. "Korea does best job for sankapul surgery in Asia."

My mom wanted me to have an upper blepharoplasty, double eyelid surgery, one of the most common cosmetic surgeries often seen as a rite of passage for young adults, mostly females, in South Korea. Young women faced an inordinate amount of pressure to alter their appearances with fillers, botox, facial contouring via jaw surgery, and facelifts especially with the rise of Korean pop culture in American metropolitan areas, which created a surging demand for sankapul surgery. Arguably this new aesthetic standard of beauty linked more "open" eyes with increased opportunity and prosperity. My aunts once sang, "Ay, yaeppuda," *pretty*, in the most patronizing way to my half Korean, half white cousins who all had natural double eyelids.

Koreans are vain. I'd catch my mom strut in front of her full-length mirror in her bedroom to check out her silhouette while swaying in her pleated skirts and dresses to judge the movement. She'd catwalk in wedge platform sandals to see if her butt looked big. When she applied her lipstick it was like watching a surgeon slice open skin with laser-like precision. She also often pulled on the bridge of her nose with her right thumb and index finger to sharpen and contour her nose, as though the repetition was going to miraculously lift and reshape it. She did it to me sometimes, too.

Mom said the "present" of sankapul surgery would be

in my best interest. The conversation naturally occurred at Korean restaurants where she had a good undistracted view of my face. "Your eyebrow is so perfect, not too thin like Mom, just right. Don't cut too much. I cut too much, and it never grows back. Sankapul make your eyes look much bigger. We go to Korea and you get that one, okay?"

Sankapul surgery is sought after in Asia because many Asians are born with monolids, like me: my eyelids are smooth and don't have the crease that some people think offers a more alert appearance. Mom and Johnny had natural sankapuls, but my father and I didn't. It felt like a curse to have inherited my father's physical attributes. My mom was softer and had pretty, round features and unusually supple skin, while my father and I had sharp features, underbites, and bowed legs. For my slight underbite, he took me to see a dentist when I was eleven to get fitted for a retainer I had to wear for a year. "I didn't have this opportunity growing up and I don't want you to have to suffer the headaches I got," he said after we left the dentist's office. I was surprised by his empathy and that in the fog of his flaws, there was a thoughtful provider somewhere in there. My mom also judged me for my bowed legs, mostly as an incidental observation when she caught me in my underwear or when I wore shorts in the summer. "You have Daddy's legs. I wish you had mine, see how my knees are straight? Johnny has my legs." She shook her head sucking in her teeth.

"I don't know, Mom. I think society places way too much pressure for non-white women to live up to Western standards of beauty. Plus I'm scared the surgeon will mess up. You can always see the scar from the surgery. I can tell when other people have had sankapul surgery. It seems so desperate to be white." I was on the heels of finishing *The Beauty Myth* by Naomi Wolf. I had been turned on to the book by a friend in college who thought my anorexia stemmed from misguided vanity. She thought this book would be a quick salve.

"No, it's so beautiful. Everybody doing this one!" My mom was determined.

"It's a waste of money and people won't recognize me. It changes your entire look and who you are," I snapped back.

"You are so stubborn-o, sankapul surgery looks natural," my mom cringed, aggressively sucking in her teeth. "How did I get such a tomboy daughter?"

The truth was I was curious about double eyelid surgery and furtively researched the multiple types of surgery options. I tended toward the tapered shape and lateral flare that would suit my heart-shaped face. If we had lived in South Korea, insecurity and pressure would have probably made me lean into a decision to have that undesirable layer of fat cut from my eyelids. But I couldn't get myself to fly twelve hours to Korea to get it done. It reeked of desperation and planned regret. I was sure if there were to be a cosmetic surgery disaster, it would happen to me.

I also lacked the ample bosom of my mother who had had two natural childbirths, two babies she breastfed for nearly a year. "When you have baby, *boos* will get bigger." My mom offered unsolicited information about my boobs when I got up to go to the bathroom to pee. I never held any fierce objection to having kids; I loved babies and children. But I didn't want them for myself, especially at the age of twenty-one. My thoughts caromed while I stood in front of the mirror, trying to picture myself with double eyelids and a distended pregnant belly. What I really thought was my parents had fought too much and I didn't want to have any offspring that might carry on that lineage. But I couldn't tell my mom that just yet. Her obvious dissatisfaction in my not wanting sankapul surgery was enough disappointment for one day.

I graduated from UC Riverside in 1994, completely blindsided by my appreciation for it. I excelled at all the liberal arts courses, even with my distracting, steadfast anorexia. My mom was proud I was a UC graduate and told everyone at church that I had gotten straight As, selectively forgetting my B- in statistics. I didn't have the mental dexterity to navigate scatterplots.

That same summer when the bankruptcy filing for GCU was complete, I spent a month at Aunt Soo Jin's house in Hayward, about twenty miles southeast of San Francisco, thinking I wanted to live and work in the city. I wasn't going the cliché post-college New York route because I wanted to stay close due to Mom's health problems. Unfortunately, living with my aunt entailed living with her overbearing husband, a retired Scottish American engineer twenty years her senior. My mom didn't want me to "bother Aunt Soo Jin and Uncle James too much," but this time she was on to something. Uncle James was impatient with a quick temper. He snickered at Aunt Soo Jin for the way she pronounced her words. He'd purse his razor-thin lips, which made his Scottish Terrier mustache quiver like a worm that was being sprinkled with salt, and mock the way Aunt Soo Jin said "Mochart" instead of *Mozart*, "all light" instead of *all right*, "Sholey" instead of *Shirley*. When Uncle James ridiculed Aunt Soo Jin for her mispronunciations and malapropisms, he was also mocking the way my mom and all of her siblings spoke. It was demoralizing and racist and I wasn't going to sit and watch. "Aunt Soo Jin's English is better than your Korean," I snapped at Uncle James over dinner, cracking myself up inside for talking like my mom.

"She's been in this country for over twenty years. She should know better," Uncle James mumbled, crumbs clustered at the corners of his mouth.

"Her accent isn't going to change. You try taking on a new language as an adult. You don't understand how Hangul converts to English." I felt like a fool for arguing with a clown.

"Okay, let's finish dinner. I have to sleep soon to wake up at 5 a.m.," Aunt Soo Jin said, trying to defuse the situation. She had a one-hour commute over the San Mateo bridge every day, after Uncle James had unreasonably made them move to a bigger house situated near an industrial wasteland in a neighborhood undergoing slow gentrification. They didn't have shouting matches like my parents did, as far as I knew, but the toxicity was there. It seeped out of my aunt's pores and made her cringe with a smile at each of her husband's efforts to humiliate her.

I wondered why Uncle James had married my aunt if he had such disdain for her. Was it because he thought she'd be a gormless Asian wife who'd submit to his demands after being married to a bossy white woman for many years? Did he have yellow fever? Gross. And did my Anglophile aunt marry him because his Scottish heritage was the closest thing to being English? Did she think he'd give her more credibility and status in this country? Uncle James's pettiness was rubbing off on my classy aunt who was our family historian that played the piano brilliantly. I wanted to bitch-slap him and grab Aunt Soo Jin by the shoulders to shake some sense into her, to tell her she was too lovely for him. Uncle James, and the three low-paying, unpromising job offers to be a media assistant, public relations coordinator, and marketing associate in the city were making my anorexia flare up. I didn't feel like faking it to make it in industries I didn't care about and that were notorious for underpaying women.

I wasn't like my father who could work his wile in any entrepreneurial situation, and I certainly wasn't like my mom who had a saintly amount of patience and devotion to stick with a middle-class job. I unequivocally knew my mom's work ethic was superior to mine. So I packed up my mom's red Nissan Sentra a month later and drove back south to familiarity. I woke up early on the morning of my departure to throw some clean clothes from the overnight laundry into my car when I noticed the passenger door handle had been jimmied and the graduation jewelry gifted to me by good friends was stolen. Some clothes and toiletries were missing, too. The sharp pang of feeling violated evaporated when I saw that my shoes had remained. I took that as an auspicious sign that I had made the right decision to get the hell out of Dodge.

A month after I returned home from Aunt Soo Jin's house I applied for an administrative assistant position in the botanical department of The Huntington Library, Art Museum, and Botanical Gardens. I got the job and moved to Pasadena two months later. The one-way commute from Yorba Linda to San Marino, near Pasadena, was over an hour long most days so I found a small three-hundred-square-foot studio in Pasadena that I called "the Hovel" to rent on my $7.25 hourly salary. I was basically camping indoors every day. The kitchen boasted an RV sink, hot plate, and one cabinet to store dishes. The bathroom was so small I couldn't open the door to full expression, so I constantly slammed my face into it. I missed having a bathtub, and the corner where the toilet was situated was so narrow that I hit my head on the side of the sink when I got up to stand. I was living on top of myself.

Being away from home was chaotic and oddly peaceful at the same time. Aside from the fact that my parents weren't fighting as much during the last couple of years I lived at home, the actual promise of peace in the Hovel was delicious. I started drinking red wine every evening with dinner to curb my hunger, which upset my stomach. It also gave me heinous ulcers that I combatted with Pepcid AC until that stopped working and I had to curb the red wine for good. I was doing uncouth things like dunking my vegan chocolate chip muffin into low-fat ranch dressing because I was desperate for mad flavor in my bland anorexic diet. The free time by myself enabled me to eat more because I was a closet eater. Still haunted by the cancer that ran in my family, I started cooking and eating macrobiotic food after I scoured information on diets that were lauded to prevent, even cure, cancer.

The other reason I launched head-on into macrobiotic eating was because, a week before, I had collapsed on my ass at Boardner's in Hollywood when I stood up from a barstool to use the restroom. When I regained consciousness ten seconds later, my friends picked me up and as soon as I was able to balance myself, I fell flat on my ass again. I was rushed to the ER only to be told I was moderately dehydrated. I took that and my mom's subsequent relentless worries as signs to make drastic changes. Anorexia was constant, distracting chatter in my head that exhausted me, and I could tell it was also exhausting to those around me. I was getting bored with it, too. At twenty-two, I was five-foot-four and ninety-one pounds of gaunt that hid well under baggy clothes. The thrill of resisting food and eating like an ascetic monk was still there, but the circumstances started to get dangerous and old.

A common characteristic of anorexia is that anorexics enjoy cooking or like surrounding themselves with food without actually partaking in a meal. This was true for me. Like we were strong enough to deny food to feel some dominance over our emotionally chaotic world. In my experience I loved celebrating other people enjoying my creations and being nourished by it—the frisson of living vicariously through others to experience the sensation of being satisfied without ever having to feel full. Through starvation and self-denial, I became even more obsessed with food, driven by thoughts of my next snack and scant meal.

Cooking macrobiotic meals by and for myself was artful and time-consuming. It became the gesture of creating and consuming just enough to get by. The beauty of the macrobiotic diet to an anorexic is that you can eat carbs in bulk and not gain any weight. The food goes right through you. So did large amounts of protein, iron, and vitamins B12 and D. I may have been deficient in core vitamins and minerals, but I was high on cooking in my bite-sized Barbie Dream Kitchen. I indulged in caring for precise measurements and the deliberate, meticulous handling of each ingredient. I channeled my mom's talent for chopping and mincing vegetables. I tried to mimic her dexterity and ability to slice vegetables into symmetrical pieces without wasting too much of the "butt pieces." Mom usually gave me a ribbing when I explained macrobiotics to her at my apartment.

"Remember when you told me to never waste a grain of rice?" I asked, looking for space to set down my mini rice cooker.

"I'm teaching you to save food and not waste money. Wash the rice good, at least ten times, until water is clear. Why are you eating brown rice when white rice is more sweet and de-lish-uss-u? White rice gives you shiny, healthy skin and hair." I visualized the fifteen-pound bags of Kokuho Rose sticky rice my mom used to pour into our large, round, yellow plastic storage bin that was so old and overused, the white lid stopped fitting over the top at some point because the rim had become jagged like Jack-o'-lantern teeth and lost its grip. She'd scoop out the rice in a retro, pea-green plastic teacup from the eighties that had a modern aesthetic with its round simple shape and square handle.

I loved preparing and steaming the chickpeas, kidney beans, kale, broccoli, pumpkin, and brown rice, but only up until the diet was clearly giving me some off-putting, protracted gas. I was imbalanced, my yin was overwhelming my yang: according to one of the tenets of macrobiotic cooking, yin foods have high water content while yang foods have dense energy. Maybe this explained why I was anemic and flatulent. I was also poor. I was sub-broke, in the red, and couldn't afford the vetted expensive tools and cooking utensils to make macrobiotic food, like the cast-iron Dutch oven, stainless steel and cast-iron cooking pots, and large stone mortar and pestle used to grind ingredients. Macrobiotic cooking and eating was exhilarating and exhausting—it was the same way my mom made all of our meals fresh from scratch and laid them on the table for my family to devour. It was a ritual and an act of love and gratitude I had come to appreciate even more especially when I now knew that food wasn't going to magically appear on my table by default. Gradually, the effort of creating my own meals eradicated my concerns of taking inventory of the fat and calories in each meal.

So I slowly started eating more than two items on a plate, then whole meals to experiment with what it would feel like to feel full again, which made me feel like a foreigner in my own body. Over time the anxiety that had once baffled me about feeling full diminished. If there was any epiphany as a result of my brief stint with macrobiotic foods, it was that my anorexia was inextricably connected to universal things that confound people, like feelings of self-worth. And it was especially connected to my father and his inability to provide emotional security for us. I can't completely blame my father for the disease, much of my distorted sense of self was beyond him. But when I wasn't in my dad's presence I ate more because my emotions felt more grounded to the earth. It was my body that got lighter *with* food.

A grateful refugee at The Huntington I was granted asylum from the dysfunction of my family in an institution devoted to classic European and American arts. The art gallery and library honored dead white people, but the landscape offered peace to the misfits and broken-hearted. I spent nearly four years in the botanical department performing administrative tasks, helping with special events, fetching mail, serving pastries and catered lunches, and making coffee for botanists, researchers, and rich docents. I also carried heavy items from one large meeting room to another, hardly the glamorous life my friends thought I had. I loved it, though. I was a peon in a low-level job that delivered the ass-kicking I needed in front of a backdrop of beautifully manicured lawns scattered with seventeenth- and eighteenth-century sculptures, obscure purebred and hybrid roses, naughty-looking orchids, and supernatural cacti and succulents. I ran into Dinky and her new baby daughter roaming the gardens during my last year there and because she was an artist, I gave her a pass to paint on the grounds. Dinky was still Dinky, goofy and cool, even four years later under a completely different set of circumstances. I just felt a million years older.

A milky fug of anxiety startled me when I was barely able to pay rent with my measly salary. I subconsciously turned to stimulants again—something over the counter this time—to find reprieve from the lack I was feeling close to my last month at The Huntington. Two or three times a week I'd take a single dose of Sudafed in the morning to help me blithely and twitchily get through my menial tasks, with an occasional cigarette surreptitiously lit in between the bamboos of the Jungle Garden. Then I'd crash by late afternoon and try to cure my migraines with two cups of sludgy coffee. The migraines won, so I stopped. In my defense I did have allergies, but my self-dosing had less to do with quieting sneezing attacks from the airborne pollen of the garden's grasses and shrubs and a lot to do with jolting myself out of a malaise of being dirt poor.

I quit after I turned twenty-five and needed to borrow six hundred dollars from my mom to pay for food and rent. The eight-dollar-an-hour final salary at the nonprofit wasn't cutting it and I didn't want to be a burden on my mom the way Johnny was by continuing to live at home. I paid my mom back from the last paycheck I received and moved to West LA where I answered an ad looking for a word processor at a telecommunications software company. The position was more editorial, such as proofreading and editing technical documents. I was thrilled that it paid three times more.

My parents helped me to throw a going-away party at the Hovel, which had a large courtyard for my neighbors and me to share wine and cigarettes. I was a social smoker for six months and had one or two cigarettes a day, maximum. The cigarettes went well with the buzz, but they sometimes made me nauseous and blow sooty snot from my nose; I stopped after I once excavated a substantial chunk with a Q-tip and feared my lungs looked worse. It was easy to quit nicotine when you were a poser. My parents came with trays of banchan, namul, kimchi, lettuce, and white rice and laid out the spread on two long tables that I had borrowed from one of the conference rooms at The Huntington. My dad barbecued galbi and bulgogi, which disappeared almost immediately.

Watching my parents arrange plates of food together like they had at Gate 4 made me surrender to the mystery of how life transitions and works—how these two random humans had created me and laughed and fought together. Their experiences defined the best and worst of family, and now they were operating as a cohesive unit showing off their talents and charms in front of my coworkers, in solidarity for me. They actually looked like a pair of retiring Korean DJs fussing with their decks, reaching over each other, swaying to the momentum, and focusing on their distinct roles. I was stupefied and disarmed enough to release the dependable, ubiquitous grudge I held against my dad, at least for that day. My parents were getting older and the soberness of that reality slammed me with heartbreak that bordered on mourning, so I went to my closet of a bathroom and cried for a few minutes. I was going to lose my parents one day. I was going to be an adult orphan one day. I always turned to my parents with questions about Korean food, culture, current affairs, and history, and I was going to lose the tenuous Koreanness that bound me to them one day.

13

Aunt Soo Jin passed away in 1999 from colon cancer. My mom was bereft, Aunt Soo Jin was one of her favorite sisters. It was a gift to be with her at her home before she died. I watched Renee put one of Aunt Soo Jin's music boxes up to her ear as it played "Für Elise," to which Aunt Soo Jin played the air piano. I was moved and emotional, not wanting to imagine the day I'd perform end-of-life rituals for my mom. Two days before Aunt Soo Jin died, I told her I was sorry for being hard on Uncle James and for squabbling with her over politics when I lived with them. She waved her hands and nodded her head like she was saying, *oh please, I get it.*

My father eventually left the house later that year, and I wasn't surprised. I had a fleeting clairvoyant moment after I graduated college that my father was scheming his departure; I just didn't think it would take him five years to execute his mission. "I sleep in your bedroom now, not with your dad," was one of the first things my mom admitted to me after I moved to Pasadena. I had wanted my parents to divorce since I was six years old during the peak of their hostilities. I wondered what the point was now that they were both in their early sixties. Still, I was ecstatic for my mom. His exit was anticlimactic and didn't happen overnight. My father dragged on the charade by slowly removing his clothes from the closet and chest of drawers. It started with a handful of shirts, then some pants a few days later, then finally boxes of shoes and golf club bags, until my mom demanded he leave without humiliating her anymore. She was destroyed, calling me every night trying to fight back tears, her voice quaking and words incoherent. She was too proud to tell me my father had left her to move in with his mistress in Seal Beach. At first I didn't understand what was happening, so I'd snap at her and ask why she was calling me multiple times a day.

I was a late bloomer, acting out my frustration and late-onset need for autonomy at the age of twenty-seven. I unfisted ideas of attending graduate school in New York or traveling the world so that I could offer emotional support to my mom. I felt beholden to her, guilty for wanting to leave after all the generosity she had shown me, and as a result I locked in a vault a resentment of her that lasted many months. I squirmed with a gnawing ache in the pit of my stomach, thinking I was acting like my father, the perpetrator who manipulated the person he subjugated into believing she was just being whiny or dramatic. I carried the dread that I had learned to permanently view my mother as a martyr. Or worse, a doormat.

I was also coming out of a recent breakup around this time. I had met Jamie through a friend in college and exchanged numbers, though we didn't stay in touch until a few years later when Jamie called me out of the blue, a week before I left The Huntington Library, to see if I wanted to go to a party with him in LA. We started dating almost immediately. Jamie was half Indonesian, half Dutch, and hardworking, so I thought he'd be a passable surrogate for the Korean son-in-law my mom wanted. Absurdly, what I didn't notice at first was that he also had a gambling addiction. In hindsight, Jamie was Johnny's doppelgänger with their shared ability to function through an addiction. I was in denial right up until he told me he couldn't help pay rent and lied that he wasn't gambling, which raised the final red flag despite previous warnings from friends and family —even my mom, with her radar. I still felt the wound my dad and Johnny left after taking advantage of my mom, and I'd be damned if I was going to enable Jamie. So I packed up my things and moved out the following week.

I was left frustrated by my mom's neediness and loneliness on top of my needing my own space to process my failed two-year-old relationship. The belligerence of my lingering anorexia still made me intolerant of anyone else's pain. I was ruthlessly selfish to the woman who was always there for me because I couldn't see straight. Living with my mom had inured me to any criticism of our happy, functional mutual codependency; living away from home, wrapped up in the dense haze of my chipped heart, now made me question some aspects of what seemed to be a smothering relationship.

"Ay, why you so mean to Mom? You change-y so much after you moving out. That stupid boy was using you! You are smarter than him. I'm hanging up, my heart is bumping, and I need peace by myself." My mom sounded so defeated I felt my heart crumble.

"I'm just tired, Mom. I'm sad about Jamie. I'm sorry." I didn't question, this time, how she could not see that Johnny was doing the same thing to her.

I thought my mom was infringing on my independence, but over time I eventually released this resentment, knowing it was an unfair grudge and that she wasn't the true reason for my stagnation. Anorexia, a directionless career, and the sadness of the breakup had jumbled up my identity, making me want to chase a life that departed from anything I resolutely embodied.

After my father left I visited my mom every weekend. I told her how much I had prayed for her to divorce my father since I was a child and that she had always been too good for him. All the things best friends said to each other after a breakup: "You're a queen, Mom! Dad never took you traveling like you wanted. He hit you! He was a terrible husband and father. I'm glad he moved out, now you can start your life over. I'm just angry he moved out after I did. Why didn't he move out sooner? Why did he make us all suffer with him for so long?!"

My mom sat on the couch crying and laughing so I warned her that hair was going to grow from her butt. She laughed that I had inserted my self-involved wishes into her open grieving and felt regret and shame for not leaving the relationship first instead of being abandoned by her husband for another woman. Mom was lonely and needed a constant stream of distractions so I accompanied her to buy groceries at Arirang Supermarket, eat pancakes at Ruby's, stock up on mass quantities of anything at Costco, and get lunch at soondubu restaurants.

She also started attending church again after a brief hiatus. "In Korea, long times ago, my family was Buddha-ist, but American missionary come and convert us to Christianity when I was teenager."

"Did you like being Buddhist, Mom?" I asked.

"It's okay, it teaches respect for everyone, my family was longtime Buddha-ist. But Buddha-ists did terrible things, too, and created corrupt government. And I don't like that smoky smell, it's that Buddha smell."

"Incense?" I asked.

"Yes, incense-u. Too strong, giving me headache."

My mom was a private person and reluctant to confide in her church friends because she didn't want to be the source of gossip in the Orange County Korean Christian community. Some of her church friends judged too harshly when stories got scandalous; the hypocrisy was real. Though my mother's faith was tenuous at times, it helped pull her out of madness on many occasions. And she counted on being reunited with her parents and deceased sisters in the afterlife—*jibae*, meaning "home," as she called it. Who would dare take that away from her? She was a quiet believer, never a Bible banger or bombastic about her faith. Thank god.

"Let's celebrate freedom, umma!" It was a tender, heartfelt moment—a culmination of decades of pain and worry—and I felt compelled to call my mom umma, the Korean term somehow bringing me closer to her.

I craved something bold and spicy on this brisk fall day to pair with Mom's new sense of opportunity. Kimchi kalguksu (handmade, knife-cut wheat flour noodles) sounded appropriate. My mom made seafood kalguksu from scratch, creating the dough, rolling it, then cutting it into chunky, wabi-sabi slices. I'd always loved that kalguksu noodle slices looked undulating, meandering, novice-rendered. The broth was thick and consisted of anchovies, clams, water, seaweed, zucchini, onion, green onion, carrots, garlic, and salt, which supported the dense, chewy noodles. I wasn't a vegetarian on the days my mom made clam kalguksu—I slurped the noodles and when there was no more, I methodically picked up the large bowl of broth and gulped it all down as a chaser.

This time we drove to a clamoring kalguksu house in

Garden Grove, where I made sure they served soju for toasting. While we negotiated the unimpeachably hot, slippery noodles, I encouraged my mom to take small sips of her soju. She hated the way alcohol heated her up and never smoked cigarettes, so the two tiny sips made her loquacious, turned her face a muted poppy, and gave her endless chortles.

My mom started to crack me up. "When I was fourteen we had an American teacher who taught English at Incheon Girls School, where I graduate high school. A big *moss* flew by and all my classmates and I screamed, 'Bul-Ba! Bul-Ba!' That means, *look at the bug! Look at the bug!* But my teacher thought we say, 'Vulva! Vulva!'"

I was undone by the comedy of errors. "That's crazy, Mom! How did anyone explain the miscommunication?"

"The teacher didn't understand Korean so we all got in trouble by the principal!" My mom laughed out loud. "But finally we all told the principal the true story and we got to go home. The teacher was so *umbarrassed*."

My mom drowned her noodles in broth with her chopsticks as she continued sharing stories from her past. "After you born, I get *botion*."

"Wait, back up, you what?" I asked wide-eyed, trying to recover from the heat of the soup as my nose and forehead beaded with sweat, after hearing Mom say she had an abortion that she didn't tell me about until I was sitting in front of her at a busy kalguksu house at the age of twenty-seven. I sat stupefied gaining access to a new side of my mother I'd never known before, both of us adults. I felt the layers of warmth and security of our ever-growing bond, which dilated into a more overpowering, staggering love that was built on an indefatigable trust. My mom kept her secrets in a tightly sealed safe, never to see the light of day, the same way she kept another secret from me, until I was thirty-two, about a woman my father had impregnated when she was nine months pregnant with Johnny. I wondered who the secrets benefited. Did she want to altruistically shield my father from our contempt? Or herself from unendurable pain? Regardless, I was relieved she had told me. We both benefited from the release of secrets that tethered her to an unpitying time and place. I stared straight into her eyes, searching for tears, but she sat tall and undaunted.

"They go under the baekkob and cut." My mom said brightly because the Korean word for belly button always made her giggle.

"Ohhhhh, you mean you had your tubes tied! Ha!" Relieved she didn't have to undergo an abortion, I still wondered why my dad couldn't have just as easily gotten a vasectomy.

"Your Daddy say another baby is too expensive and we not happily married. Finish your lunchie," my mom responded nonchalantly, like she was telling me to get the check.

But I couldn't finish my lunch. "I'm glad you made the decision that was right for you, umma. I know it must have been a difficult one. You're so strong," I assured my mom, impressed by her self-restraint.

"It's not big deal, another baby would have hard life." My mother smiled while she picked out a piece of spice between her teeth with the toothpicks every Korean restaurant seemed to supply, like they knew you were going to need it.

We bickered about who was going to pay. In Korean culture, the eldest always foots the bill. Like, *beware, I love the most.* But the occasion was bittersweet and I wanted to celebrate in honor of my mother, to treat her for this milestone. My mom prioritized Johnny and me in every situation that it caused quakes in my heart when I felt like we didn't live up to her ideals. I needed to pay because I unequivocally loved the most that day.

"Aigoo! I'm the mom, I pay!" my mom said perturbed, her face twisted in a knot, now a glinting coral color from the soju. I could tell this was going to end up in the wrestling match I'd seen play out many times before in public spaces with my mother and her younger sisters. It was a shameless display in packed restaurants each time the check arrived: my mom sucking in her teeth, her arms weaving into one of her sister's arms, like a game of Twister, rabidly grabbing for the bill, shoving each other around as one sister made a breakthrough and rushed toward the cashier with the bill and cash in hand. It always ended with my mother grabbing the arm of her younger sister and pulling it—knees bent, hips at an anterior tilt, haunches back—the way I tugged at her when she dropped me off at kindergarten and I wanted her to stay. My mother always won.

The waitress started to move toward my mom to hand her the check, obviously knowing the custom, but before she got close enough I leapt up to grab it midair, nearly body slamming her onto the epoxy-coated floor.

"Nope, I'm paying!" I was victorious. Buzzing and laughing with my mouth wide open, spices sandwiched between each tooth, I skipped to the cashier and threw down cash, the transaction type Koreans love most.

At age twenty-nine, I officially reverted back to my Korean name, Sun Yong, because Shirley always made me self-conscious, like a stranger hiding in my throat. So I went by Sunny, a typical nickname for Korean female names whose first character starts with *Sun*. Most people caught on, though some of my family and oldest friends still called me Shirley, which I thought was an asshole move for not respecting what was already a soul-shaking decision to publicly and officially change the name I had long lived with; now I see that they were just too lazy, or old, to rewire their consciousness. When people continued to call me Shirley, I broke the ice and flashed the deadpan "and don't call me Shirley" line that Leslie Nielsen's Dr. Rumack character immortalized in *Airplane!*

Around this time the grip of anorexia loosened unceremoniously. It wasn't an overnight, mysterious release. It felt *just like that*, as anticlimactic as my father leaving the house. I had always been afraid that this eating disorder would plague me for life after reading blogs and firsthand accounts by anorexics who emphatically declared that the illness never completely went away. I could see how that happened because anorexia was a lifestyle, a subculture with its own rules of discipline and devotion. But the triggers and demands of my father weren't around on a daily basis anymore to throw my mind into complete chaos, and I grew out of my need for him to love me for who I was. The food hoarding stopped because I didn't have to hide snacks anymore from Johnny so I could have a chance to eat them on my terms. I learned that hiding food was a way to control my environment. I had adopted my parents' need to ration food to suit my needs, not for basic survival, but for authority and suppression.

When I moved out of my parents' house, I slowly ceased being the weird, difficult friend who'd ask about the ingredients in every item on restaurant menus, before ordering only steamed vegetables with lemon for dinner anyway. It was my newfound allowance of feeling satisfied after eating a full meal that made me realize I was overcoming something giant, when I had resisted that sensation for too long. It had taken nearly ten years to get to that point, with some body dysmorphia setbacks, but I slowly realized that a handful of fries or two slices of pizza wasn't going to blow me up.

Anorexia had also been a response to my constant concern for my mom's health and happiness. As a child I tied my self-worth to my attempts at defending her from my dad's beatings, and as an adult, I tied it to my efforts at protecting my mom from what I thought were Johnny's gambling predations. The good fortune of getting home from college just in time to call the paramedics to rush my mom to the ER after her strokes impelled me further to control her health and protect it from bad fortune. My ambition for control was one fulcrum that catapulted my eating disorder.

I had entered anorexia stealthily and quietly and I was exiting the same way. I outgrew a mindfuck of a disease that had brought me to my knees and kept me there for too long. I never saw a psychiatrist or popped antidepressants for it, and I'm hardly stoic or a better person because of it, either. In retrospect I wish I'd sought help for starving myself; the pathology was honest. But my family didn't see doctors for dysphoria. Whenever I brought the idea of my mom seeing a psychologist for herself, she was never into it.

"Mom, I found a Korean-speaking psychologist in Fullerton. I don't think it's that expensive. I can take you."

"Aigoo, I don't like wasting money! I don't want to talk

to stranger about my family problem, it's so *umbarrassing.* I think the doctors are more crazy. Why they not pay me to listen?"

She never wanted to admit that something was wrong with her family or herself. It was an invasion of her privacy to tell a stranger her problems and batshit crazy to have to pay for it. Mom felt like she would have been judged in a psychologist's office. But I had distorted things, too—I considered anorexia a rite of passage.

If I knew then what I know now about plant medicine and how it has been proven to help people with OCD, PTSD, or depression, I would have signed my mom up for a clinical trial where there was less direct talking and more internalizing and experiencing. My mother was interested in the unusual so she would have probably been into something like this. Mostly because it would have been free.

14

I was thirty when my mom sold our house in Yorba Linda in the summer of 2002. I found out my father hadn't contributed much toward the down payment so my mom scored on the sale. The fact that he didn't have the savings was more hurtful information that my mom withheld from me to shield me from his indignities. She didn't want me to *look down* on him when she was always bad-mouthing him anyway.

"Your daddy asked for joint bank account with me after he moved out. I laughed and told him, 'You really think I'm stupid?'"

"Dad thinks everyone is stupid compared to him," I said spiritlessly.

My mom loved the suburbs; the newer the homes and wider the streets, the better. She became interested in Rancho Cucamonga after Uncle Young Soo and his wife, Aunt Helen, moved there. We celebrated birthdays, Thanksgivings, Christmases, and the Fourth of July at Aunt Helen's and Uncle Young Soo's house. Mom would dress up in bright red or green dresses for Christmas, which matched the vibrant banter of their squabbling family made leaner over time with the deaths of Aunts Min Jee and Soo Jin, even if it was just for the sake of nostalgia.

Aunt Helen had also paid most of the down payment on her home so my mom shared a kinship with her hardworking sister-in-law. Their son, Paul, kept their marriage afloat. Aunt Helen was a surgery nurse at Kaiser Permanente, an overachiever in a subdued way. She liked Cheap Trick and had *Zen and the Art of Motorcycle Maintenance* on her bookshelf. Every New Year's Eve she'd either prepare for me or let me make my own mandoo (Korean dumplings) to add to the tteok guk (rice cake soup) we'd eat on New Year's Day. She'd set aside a mixture of tofu, glass noodles, cabbage, onion, and seasonings, without the beef or pork, to stuff into the wrappers. I loved having loud reunions with my cousins in Rancho Cucamonga; I just didn't want my mom to live there.

I had first heard about Rancho Cucamonga during my freshman year in college when I read that Frank Zappa had built Studio Z recording studio in what was then called Cucamonga (he even created an eponymous compilation album), where he lived for a couple of years in the sixties. Zappa was straight outta Cucamonga. The how-cool-is-that feeling was short-lived after I heard a massive mall development was on deck around the corner from Aunt Helen's house. I couldn't stand Rancho Cucamonga (often referred to as Rancho) and felt guilty for that when Mom loved it. Maybe my mom and Frank Zappa were ahead of their time and I was clueless.

"God, Mom, Rancho is so boring, it's worse than Yorba Linda! Move near me in LA and if you don't like it you can move to Rancho. Give LA a chance."

"I don't like all the cars in LA Downtown. It's too crowd-y and loud." My mom thought the metropolitan area of Los Angeles was all downtown-ish.

Rancho's cookie-cutter homes set in sprawling tract communities was like Yorba Linda on steroids, except not as developed. Rancho was in the heart of the Inland Empire (a term coined for what I think referred to its rambling sparseness at the time), an hour east of LA in San Bernardino County. It got too hot there in the summer, so deliriously hot you could see the mirage of the heat two feet in front of you. Rancho in the early aughts was attractive to Koreans because the homes were affordable and you could drive down the streets without being assaulted by an endless stream of manic, aggressive drivers. Somnolent strip malls jammed with fast-food restaurants and big chain grocery stores arbitrarily clustered around the main tributaries of Foothill Boulevard, Baseline Road, and Haven Avenue. At the time Rancho was a spacious food desert, a dearth of decent Korean, Vietnamese, or Thai restaurants for long stretches. It was where a Starbucks had finally moved in and offered a strange hope to the sleepy neighborhood. The one Korean restaurant that opened a year after my mom moved to Rancho gave me such caustic diarrhea that a Jewish friend, who had accompanied Mom and me, joked that returning there "would be like the Jews and the Holocaust—never again."

For soon-to-be seniors like my mom who loved driving crosstown to Costco on easy, wide-open streets, Rancho was perfect. Rancho was my sensory deprivation chamber, but serenity for Mom, who said the snowcapped foothills were beautiful in the winter, *like Korea.*

She found a two-story condo in Rancho through a Korean real estate agent who told her the area was "ripe with growth and potential" that I assumed the agent got from an industry marketing campaign. The condo eerily reminded me of our town house in Virginia, in that my mom's room was the first room on the left at the top of the staircase. When I visited, I still saw my mom's shadow run back into her room.

Johnny was still living with my mom so he was part of

her move. The deal was that she and Johnny would split the mortgage, which was ridiculously cheap. Johnny was responsible for about seven hundred dollars, including utilities, but he couldn't even pull that off, and within six months he blew all his money gambling. So, my mom was forced to sell the condo and incurred a capital gains tax.

"After Johnny told me he gambling all his money, I drove fast like a crazy person on the freeway. I didn't care if I died," my mom said bawling, realizing she'd have to make another mentally and physically exhausting move. Mom's home was a sanctuary to her and this displacement was a cruel joke, a subversion by her only son. I heard the panic in her voice from being uprooted from the one thing that gave her comfort and peace. I never loathed Johnny more for making my mom homeless. It was a direct assault on her identity and humanity. His addiction blinded him and my mom, his forever enabler. I had a job an hour away in LA that I was tempted to leave, and even if I could, the thought of living in Rancho made me nauseous. I hoped this was the final wake-up call for her to stop enabling Johnny, and that this series of events would force her to move out of Rancho.

"Promise me, Mom, when you find a new house, please don't let Johnny move in. He's never going to help you pay the bills. You have to let him hit rock bottom on his own," I implored.

"I'm so disappointed in him. Your dad make him like this. But how'd I do? He's my son," she responded feebly.

My mom stayed with Uncle Young Soo and Aunt Helen for a month until old wounds reemerged. Ten years earlier, when my dad had run a part-time janitorial service at an engineering company in Santa Ana, He had hired Uncle Young Soo as his assistant in the evenings. Instead of helping out the crew when it got busy, my father showed up in business suits, flaunting his elevated status, while forcing Uncle Young Soo to perform most of the janitorial duties. Uncle Young Soo's misdirected misogyny and blame drove my mom to rent a bedroom in the house of a Korean family in Torrance for three months, because she had never wanted to *make trouble* with her brother. This humiliation crushed her. I begged my mom to stay with me in my tiny studio apartment in West Hollywood, but she repeated, "I don't like LA Downtown," and that was the end of that.

In Torrance, she serendipitously remembered seeing signs for a new senior apartment community in Rancho situated a couple miles north of her old condo. It was directly across the street from Dr. Strange Records, a record label and store that started in 1988 and featured many well-known punk bands. I loved that it was so close to my mom's reach even though she was completely oblivious to the history of this punk rock landmark. My mom drove to the apartment community from Torrance, which was an hour and a half away in treacherous traffic, and put herself on the wait list. She called the manager every day to check her status. Within three months her name was up and she hauled ass back to Rancho.

I came back from a trip to Thailand in May 2004 just before my thirty-second birthday, a week before my mom moved into her apartment. I was delirious from jet lag, but couldn't confuse my mom's elation as I entered her box-filled apartment. Even with the mess of moving in, her place already looked clean and organized.

"Hi, Shodey!" my mom exclaimed behind a tall box containing part of her wardrobe. My mom was one of the few people I didn't mind calling me Shirley; she adored the name and our history had earned it for her.

Her 550-square-foot second-story apartment was cozy, tidy, and new—exactly what my mom wanted, the perfectly manageable size after she had gotten rid of all of our old patio furniture. She was a proud home owner for many years, but now she was back to renting. I wanted to absorb any humiliation she may have felt with this curve ball, but she seemed oddly at peace with her bright, bite-sized apartment. Because it was finally all hers.

"I don't like big house and garden to clean and pick up leaves. I don't miss that about Yorba Linda house," she said. Her apartment wasn't one of those trapped inside a dank building; it was an open community with apartments that faced inward into a large common courtyard lined with two old sycamore trees and benches. You could smell the star jasmine from her small, private patio and pick oranges and lemons off the trees in the back near a communal garden. The community was quiet except for when the elementary school let out next door, but that was kismet because my mom loved children and found their distant shouting to be a salve. I was proud of my mom for her fortitude and tenacity. I had felt, seen, and heard her anguish of being homeless for three long months, but her scrappiness and determination to find a new home against all odds made me realize she was unwavering and indomitable. She had moved a mountain.

"Mom, how are you doing all of this by yourself? I know Johnny's going to eventually follow you here so why don't you wait until he gets here to help you move the big things?" I asked bitterly.

"Too many happening right now. I don't like him helping me, he make more mess. I want to buy the apartment manager, Patricia, a Korean jewelry box. She say she like mine so I'm going to buy an old-time-style one for her. She save this brand-new apartment for me." My mom owned at least ten vintage medium and large Korean lacquer jewelry cases decorated with mother of pearl or abalone-embedded peonies, cranes, and waves. Every Korean household has at least two.

"You don't need to spend so much money on a gift, Mom. The manager was just doing her job," I said, trying to rein her in. It was just like her to give much more than she received. She always had to pay back the kindness manifold. But she felt she owed her life to Patricia for her kind gesture, and in a way she was right.

Mom peeked around her tea cabinet that was blocking the entrance and smiled impishly. I sensed something was on her mind.

"When I was living in Torrance and having hard time finding new house, I thinking about your future. When you going to born baby? I need a grandchild!" she said excitedly.

The pressure bogged me down. I cynically interpreted her statement as: *I was thinking about your future, and mine living alone. I need a purpose as I age so hurry up and have some children so I can move in and take care of them.*

"Mom, I don't even have a boyfriend!" I laughed. In Thailand, I had had a three-week fling with an Englishman who was breaking up with his girlfriend, at least that's what he told me. I was too shy to flirt with guys I liked so they thought I wasn't interested, and the ones who liked me were white men with yellow fever. I had issues with men. I feared I was searching for the cliché father figure because I lacked one. It usually started off great with some of the guys I was interested in, but the attraction would flatline when I saw a pattern of bad male behavior: hints of misogyny ("Are you on your period? Why so cranky?"), disturbing tempers, or expecting me to be passive and docile. I dated this one German guy who walked me home, but when we reached a portion of the sidewalk where an old magnolia tree split the path in two, he told me to walk on the street so he could take the sidewalk. A bad omen, according to any Korean mother who believes men should always walk on the outside, closest to the street, while women walk on the inside. I pushed him toward the street. When we got to my apartment and he wanted to hook up I told him to fuck off. He called me a bitch then stormed out the door.

In this ass-backwards patriarchy I was dumbfounded by the deficit of gentle, smart, emotionally stable men. I was also going through the great anorexia unlearning process where my ideals still didn't match the reality in front of me. I was picky about the type of guys I wanted to date and desperately tried to make them fit a mold that was unattainable, which only created a dead-end relationship pattern. I fell into a state of dating inertia that made me numb to any kind of intimacy like the insensitivity to an injury before the aching starts.

"I'm getting old, Shodey-a, please have a baby," my mom said under the kitchen sink where she was lining the bottom with layers of plastic to catch any future leaks and prevent the wood from getting moist or dirty.

I felt pressure and pure sadness for not having the right

partner and circumstances that would have made my mom happy. But there were so many other things I wanted to do, like travel untethered. And I still had no career path. I was working comfortably as a freelance writer, editor, and project manager for Yahoo! Music, small startups, and big software companies, but I also wanted to do something more tactile like arrange flowers for a quarter of my salary. My career path was disjointed, scattered all over the place, and out of the lingering fear of failing at every interest I had, I did nothing about it and continued working decent-paying but uninspiring jobs.

Another Korean woman who was about my mom's age lived on the side of the building facing the main street. Grace happened to be a devout Christian who relentlessly bugged my mom to attend her Korean Presbyterian church in Rancho.

"I told her I don't want to go with her. I have my church in Fullerton," Mom said.

"But Mom, Fullerton is so far. It's an hour away near the old house. You can make new friends at her church. You can't just do the same thing every day and drive to Stater Bros. and Costco just to buy chicken bakes for Johnny." I was starting to worry about my mom spending so much time alone.

"Can't you go to the senior community center down the road? I took you there once. They teach tai chi and yoga."

"No, I don't want to go there, they don't understand my English. What's wrong with going to *Statee* Brothers and Costco?" My mom was antisocial. She just wanted to be with Johnny, me, and her future grandchildren.

After Mom moved into her apartment, we discussed buying a house together in LA but hit an impasse after she realized my stance on Johnny tagging along was never going to change. There was no way in hell I was going to let Johnny move in with us just so we could support him. Johnny worked in LA as a freelance IT guy for a sports network and did a nasty one-and-a-half-hour commute to and from my mom's apartment every day. He traveled a lot for work, but when he wasn't on the road, Johnny had the gall to say that he was helping Mom feel less lonely by crashing at her house. This was his way of justifying being thirty-five and living with his mother in a senior apartment community.

Johnny and I couldn't have been more different as adults. I always paid my bills on time and had excellent credit scores; he continued to live at home with my mom from his twenties into his forties. I don't think the arrow on the credit rating scale could have tilted more to the left or gotten redder for him. The one thing Johnny had over me was his work ethic that he'd inherited from my mom. I didn't have it in me to work grueling sixteen-to-twenty-hour days like he did. He worked his ass off to feed his gambling addiction.

"I work hard to play hard," was Johnny's hackneyed motto.

"That's a disgusting racket, Johnny. You're the casino's mascot, a clown. You know the books are all cooked and the slot machines and poker tables are designed to make you lose. Do you really think you'll strike millions?" I taunted.

"The most I've ever won was fifty thousand dollars," Johnny said, jaded.

"Why didn't you stop? That's a lot of money! Why can't you walk away?"

"I don't know, I make all that money and it gives me a

huge rush so I want more. I get greedier, and greed doesn't turn off for me when I'm winning or losing. It only stings when I have no money left to pay people back."

Soon Johnny stopped taking my calls and blocked my emails. I shook with rage leaving unhinged messages on Johnny's voice mail. "Johnny, you're the reason Mom gets sick and stressed. You're killing her with your gambling. You know she'll give you the money you ask for, then you blow it all! Mom doesn't think she enables you, she thinks she's helping you. If you take her money again or make her lose this apartment, I'll call the cops and APS. This is senior abuse! You need to get help but you won't. You'll always be a junkie. I'll never bail you out or give you money!"

My mom begged me, "Don't be jealous of Johnny. I love you both."

"I'm not jealous of Johnny!" I snapped back, offended by something so absurd. I worried whether she actually believed me. "But you keep giving him money and a place to live. What's going to happen when you're not here, how's he going to take care of himself? I'm not going to help him."

"Aigoo, Sun Yong-a, please understand me, I'm his mother, and he's your brother. Johnny had a hard life, your daddy didn't help him. He need us to help him."

We didn't talk for five days after this standstill, the longest we'd ever gone without speaking. Mom and I talked every day even when I traveled out of the country, so this silence was loud.

A week later on the morning of Thanksgiving, 2005, I was getting ready to pick up my mom to take her to Aunt Helen's for dinner. Johnny was out of town on a work trip. Thanksgiving was an unspoken agreement—we always went to Aunt Helen's, brawl or no brawl. My mom called me as I was heading out the door: "Sun Yong-a, you can't come here anymore because they don't allow visitors."

"What are you talking about? What's wrong with your voice?"

"Patricia said people cannot stay here."

"That's for people who stay longer than two weeks, like Johnny. Are you okay?"

She hung up.

When I got to my mom's, she was lying in bed moaning about lower back pain, with all of her medication next to her on her nightstand. She looked pale and pasty, but there was no sign of a fever. I went to the bathroom to find vomit on the toilet seat and a trail of soiled hand towels. I helped her get changed and drove her to the hospital, which was ten minutes away.

The ER nurse said my mom had a compression fracture on L5-S1 and that she was moderately dehydrated from taking her blood pressure medication without eating or drinking much for what she thought had been a few days. Her potassium levels were low so my mom was admitted to the hospital for a few nights so that they could catch up. I told Aunt Helen we weren't going to make it for Thanksgiving.

I stayed in the hospital with my mom on the first evening, and as I watched the potassium, electrolytes, and saline slowly dripping into her tiny veins, I realized the dehydration had caused her remarkable confusion. It explained why she had called to say I couldn't come to visit her because she would have never said that to me with a sound mind. As my mom became more alert she recounted what had happened: a few days before Thanksgiving, she was in the shower when she heard pounding on the front door. She threw on her clothes and ran to answer it when she tripped and fell onto her stomach, causing the low back compression fracture. My mom crawled to the door and hoisted herself up to see Grace standing outside with a box of Asian pears. My mom screamed at Grace and told her to take the pears away.

I was mortified for being so petty. I swore to myself that no matter how hard my mom and I fought in the future, I'd call her every day. Had I called her a few days before Thanksgiving, I may have been able to prevent this needless suffering. My mom had dodged another bullet, again. But this time she was sixty-seven, not fifty-three.

I could tell my mother was becoming incrementally lonelier with little left to clean and organize and fewer errands to run to fill her refrigerator and cabinets with things she never used. And when she was bored, she got tenacious. One day she answered the door with a knuckle Band-Aid on her left temple.

"What happened to your face, Mom?"

"Oh, I cutting a dark mole," my mom giggled, waving for me to come inside.

I removed the bandage and blood oozed from a small seborrheic keratosis mole my mom had attempted to slice off with a razor blade. Her dermatologist had frozen it a year before, but it returned a few months later.

"Mom! Why did you use a razor blade? Was it clean? Does it hurt?"

"It's not big deal! It's so ugly, it was easy to cut off," my mom laughed.

I cleaned the wound with alcohol and hydrogen peroxide, applied a lump of Neosporin on it, then sealed the haphazard mole-execution job with gauze and another knuckle Band-Aid since those were the only ones in the house. Within a week the wound had completely healed, but the mole was still there to drive Mom bonkers. I made an appointment with another dermatologist two weeks later to freeze the mole again, but it returned two months later, again. I immediately threw away all the razor blades in the house.

A month after she fell my mom applied for a position at a new Korean grocery store a mile from her house. She had more resolve and strength to get out of the house because waiting for me to have children was taking forever. The manager told her she was "too old" to carry heavy items or to help make kimchi in the back. Then she called my mom "halmeoni," *grandmother*, which my mom wasn't in the mood to hear. Social hierarchy pervades the Korean language so I understood that terms of seniority were used out of respect, but through my Korean American ears, these honorifics inadvertently felt like they did the opposite—they flat out made someone feel old. Another such term, ajumma, connoted something more senior and frumpy to me than ma'am and needed to be used with prudence unless you wanted a screaming match on your hands; it burned like *old lady*. Ajumma was an attitude, a state embodied. The archetypal ajumma almost always wore a perm, bucket hat or visor, the occasional arm-length gloves while walking or driving, and puffy down coats any time of year, which somehow worked. The trademark fortitude of ajummas made them undeniably *boss*. But being called halmeoni by a stranger, even when it was customary, was unsolicited and far too condescending. I went with my mom to the grocery store to talk to the manager the following week.

"Ajumma, why did you call my mom halmeoni when she's only a few years older than you? My mom can run circles around your kimchi. She practically invented kimchi." I was a complete dick.

"No your mom told me she has arm problem and I don't want her to hurt herself. She's very thin. Koreans call older ladies halmeoni out of respect," the store manager snapped at me, shooting me the dirty side eye.

Full of spite, I continued hurling ajumma missiles at the poor store manager, hoping it burned under her skin.

"My mom is stronger than you think, ajumma, and you should give her a chance. I guarantee you she has worked harder than you or any of your employees have ever worked. Please don't call my mom halmeoni, she's not into it." I was talking trash. I didn't want my mom working there anyway.

"I'll call her if I need someone to handle light things. I don't want any of my employees to hurt themselves." At that point the manager was spooked and was saying anything to get me out of the store.

"Thanks, ajumma. We'll wait for your call." I winked at my mom and turned to leave. I knew she wasn't going to call.

15

My father and I stayed in touch after his mother fell and broke her hip in her studio apartment in Koreatown. My dad was getting older, too, so he moved my grandmother into a nursing home in Anaheim. He must have loved his girlfriend since he didn't ask her to take care of his mother. My mom and I didn't look forward to our monthly visits with my grandmother to see old people in wheelchairs parked in the hallways like abandoned cars on the side of the road. Each time we left her room we'd hear her heart-wrenching yowl for us to go to her. "Yah! Yah! Yo-gi-ro oh-sae-yo!" It was a mournful cry that made us want to hide for the rest of the day.

"I'm so sad for your grandmother. I never want to be in a nursing home," my mom said.

"You're never going to a nursing home, Mom. I feel horrible knowing she's desperate to come home with us." I was thirty-three whining like I was thirteen. The lingering stench of urine in the hallways, or seeing seniors eat and drool puréed foods or being infantilized by the staff who gave them creepy dolls to coddle was unsettling. My grandmother was an ox who was once unstoppable moving heavy ceramic containers from one end of our patio to another, squinting at the piercing sun with a cigarette dangling from her lips, and eating In-N-Out burgers and french fries that my dad bought her for lunch. But now I was dumbstruck to see her depending on others to change her adult diapers and hoist her onto her wheelchair so she could sit in the hallway with the other nonambulatory halmeonis.

Then my father called me in January 2006 to tell me he had colon cancer.

"I was feeling really tired but thought it was because I'm seventy. I went to the doctor for labs, and they noticed something was wrong with my liver. I had to do a colon cancer test at home and it came back positive," my father said calmly.

"Oh no, I'm so sorry, Dad! Do you need chemo or surgery?"

"Surgery. Scheduled for next week."

"Okay, I'll be there with Mom," I said, feeling sharp jabs down my spine.

I was wrapped by a tremendous sadness hearing this life-changing news that my dad had delivered so impassively. I had always thought I'd feel numb to any reports of my father's illnesses. It was the first time he had ever sounded humble, and I was surprised that I didn't want him to sound that way.

"After his stomach cancer surgery in Arcadia, his doctor told him to come back for checkup, but he never did," my mom said, sucking her teeth.

I wasn't sure whether there was a direct correlation between his stomach cancer and colon cancer over twenty-five years later, but there was something to be said about erring on the side of caution, which wasn't in my father's DNA. He came from a distant generation where mental fortitude guided one's fate. There were no annual preventative medical checkups to be had when you felt fine and when the power of pushing through any obstacles was paramount to physical, spiritual, and mental health. That was my dad's religion.

After the surgery my mom and I visited my dad in the

recovery room. Watching him sleep, I noticed the faint visible scars of sankapul surgery. I never got sankapul surgery, but my father did, when he was seventy. It was messed up, disheveled by dissociation, but I couldn't control my laughter over the irony during this sober situation so I ran into the bathroom. My mom forcefully shoved away air with the back of her hands motioning me to stop.

His oncologist pulled me aside to tell me that the cancer had spread to his liver. "It's stage 4. I think the best thing to do is think. Just really think," she said.

"How much time does he have?" I asked the doctor, who had the look of someone with a short fuse.

"Like I said, just think. I've seen people live three months, he may have six. The cancer spread to an organ that cannot be operated on," she said stolidly.

I didn't know what the doctor meant by *think*, she hardly showed she was softening the truth or making room for a white lie. It was code for my father was going to die sooner rather than later. *Think* about preparing for that eventuality.

I started calling my dad every other day, because he would have freaked out if I called every day. He became sweeter and more thankful for my weak suggestions to eat cruciferous vegetables, even though I knew he was running on borrowed time. My dad was in pain. I heard it in his voice even though he shielded me from what he was really going through. He was pleasant and optimistic when we talked, but I knew he was scared. I was moved that he was defending me from his suffering that I often cried when I got off the phone with him.

"My doctor told me to get a parrot as a therapy pet, so I did. I named him Charlie and he tells me, 'I love you.'" My dad laughed like he had no care in the world. His terminal illness suffused him with a vulnerability he had never showed us. But he was also determined to be hopeful, like he was making a deal with death to let him live longer since, after all, he was only seventy and thought he'd make it to ninety.

"That's hilarious, Dad. Did you name it after yourself?" I said with tears blossoming.

"I named him after me and because he looks like a Charlie."

A few days later: "The chemo has been making me crazy that I accidentally left my bedroom window open after I let Charlie out of his cage and he flew away. At least he's free now." He sounded disheartened.

"Oh no, Dad, can you get another parrot?"

"No, I'm afraid I'll do the same thing. The chemo is making me forgetful. I forgot my cell phone in my pants after I washed them. It's dead. I'm borrowing a friend's phone now. That's why I called you on this new number."

I assumed his "friend" was his mistress-turned-partner, a woman I finally learned the name of after all these years on her outgoing message: "Hello, this is Kim, we're out right now. Please leave a message." Kim was using her maiden surname.

"Thanks, Dad. I love you," I felt like a foreigner in my own body to say that I loved him. It might have been the third time I'd ever said those words to my father since I was in preschool.

"I love you, too."

"Wait, Dad," I interjected, "did you have sankapul surgery?"

"Yes." My dad chuckled. "I told my eye doctor I

couldn't see out of my eyes because they were heavy hooded, so I got it done. Medicare covered it."

"Good for you Dad, you look like a new man." I was impressed by his creativity and vanity that had compelled him to alter his appearance as a septuagenarian. He was Dad 2.0, wide-eyed and slightly unrecognizable.

A few weeks later my father asked me for two thousand dollars to put toward an experimental holistic treatment in Mexico that he said was proven to slow advanced cancer. The first round of chemo had been debilitating, and he didn't want to go through with the second. His acupuncturist told him about the Immunity Therapy Center in Tijuana whose cancer program was designed to stimulate the immune system to identify and eradicate cancer cells in combination with noninvasive, natural therapies. I didn't know he didn't have much in the bank except for his monthly social security payments, which he used to spend on golf, post-golf Korean barbecue lunches, and gambling. It explained why my dad had moved in with his wealthy lover because he was attracted to her money. His cancer was advanced, but as wary as I felt, I didn't want to give him false hope. So I told him I couldn't give him the money. I was a supporter of holistic health care, but I didn't see how it could eradicate his metastatic cancer. With every cell of my being I wanted to help my dad, but this sounded like snake oil.

A week later my mom called to tell me, "Your daddy called your bank to check your balance, he knows your birth date and social security number, and the recording gave him the amount. He said you have the money he needs for cancer treatment."

I felt violated. But I also knew he must have been desperate, afraid to die, to have checked my bank balance.

"You don't have to explain, I agree with you," my mom said. "How long does he want to live?" My mom was always pragmatic. She accepted her mortality. It was not that my mom didn't fear death; she just didn't resist it as she got older, and she certainly wasn't the type to turn to chelation therapy and coffee enemas in Mexico.

I twitched with irritation. "Dad, I know you checked my bank account, and I'm upset that you did that behind my back. I never said I didn't have the money, I told you I didn't want to give it to you for a treatment that could end up harming you more. How much do you need?"

"Ten thousand dollars. If you and your mom can give me two thousand each, my friend will give me the rest."

We agreed. My mom was put through the wringer even after their separation, but she still came out magnanimous when she owed my dad nothing. It also bothered me that he had a sugar mama, that he was using Kim, too. Within a week he was off to Mexico.

My dad returned from Mexico the week before Thanksgiving 2007. He'd already surpassed his oncologist's "maybe six months" prognosis.

"I feel great!" my dad exclaimed on the phone from LAX. "Thank you and your mom! I couldn't have gone without you both."

My mom had never had a colonoscopy before my father's colon cancer diagnosis; in the early and mid-aughts, the media hadn't yet deployed incessant PSAs about getting your colon scoped at 45 or 50. I rushed her to see a gastroenterologist and within a week she was in the procedure room.

"Hello, Shodey-a!" my mom greeted me giddily with a wide, toothy smile in the recovery room, no doubt relieved from the news that she had no polyps or cancer. I bear hugged her doctor as he turned to leave. She seemed serene, grateful for life, enveloped in the warm womb of ease and security coming out of a slow amnesia-suffused sedation like she was ready to unwrap the day like a present. When we got back to my mom's house, she didn't want me to remove the hospital bracelet on her wrist. She always loved the formality of hospital procedures, and the bracelet was a badge of honor, a souvenir of good colon health. The relief I felt triggered a breakdown as I bawled on the floor near my mom's feet.

"Mom, please don't die! Please don't die!" My father was dying, and the anticipatory grieving was wearing me down.

"I'm not die, I'm not die, I have a golden dong-ko!" she said as she swung her left hip to the side like she was clapping it against someone else's hip to emphasize her golden butthole. This was the rare moment I sensed her triumph over my father.

My father's condition fluctuated wildly for the next two months. One day he was deliriously happy, the next, sober and distracted. Then he got really sick again. The treatments he had gotten in Mexico weren't working, so my father's oncologist suggested one more round of chemo, after possibly sensing his desperation to live. This second course nearly killed him with nausea, delirium, vomiting, and dehydration. He was forced to start hospice within two weeks. The last time I talked with my dad, he sounded stoic but tired. "I stopped the morphine, it made me hallucinate. My friend told me I was crawling on my hands and knees in my underwear trying to find my car keys. I'm so embarrassed."

"Dad, just rest in bed and take the medication if it helps with the pain. It doesn't matter what it makes you do. I'm sure your friend doesn't care either."

"I still have a strong appetite. If you're dying, how can you be as hungry as I am? I also bought all these supplements from the health food store to boost my immune system."

"Are you okay, Dad? Do you need anything?"

"No, sweetie, I'm okay, thank you for calling me so much. Sometimes I forget." My dad hadn't called me sweetie since the time a skunk burrowed its way under the crawl space of our house eighteen years earlier in Yorba Linda, during a freak-of-nature cold spell. The skunk sprayed under the house, and we stunk for weeks as a result. When we saw the skunk emerge one night, my dad sealed the hole and said to me, "You're crazy like a skunk: when you smile you're a cute sweetie, but when you're angry you're mean and nasty like skunk musk."

"Don't worry, Dad, I don't want you to be in pain. I wish you weren't going through this. I'll pick up Mom so we can visit you soon. I love you." I knew I'd have to ask my dad to tell Kim to leave their house during our visit.

"I love you too, talk to you later." Dad paused for about ten seconds, then said, "Don't have a funeral for me. I don't want people to know I died. I was once so strong, winning all the golf competitions in my age group. Everyone will laugh because I got this sick."

"Are you sure? Don't you think your friends and family will be upset if I don't tell them? I think they'll want to know."

"No, it's embarrassing. Don't tell anyone."

I was spooked. I couldn't believe he viewed death as some sort of competition—a failure or embarrassment if you succumbed to it. Now that we didn't live together or see each other every day and the threat of terminal cancer hovered over us, I appreciated him more. My dad had provided. He was a product of atrocious circumstances like war, starvation, and his own fractured relationship with his own father. He hit the ground ambitious, sprinting when we came to the States, to fake it until he made it, to become successful and prosperous the way he believed things would turn out for people who worked like animals in the land of opportunities.

I clearly remember the moment I fully forgave him for everything. It was right after his colon resection surgery: my father waving and looking down at me from a high floor of the hospital when I pulled up to the front to pick up my mom after our visit. I had also wanted to show him my brand-new white Mazda hatchback, to which he gave a thumbs up and a heartbreakingly sweet smile. Even from the hospital's crescent driveway I noticed how his face had changed from age and sankapul surgery. I waved and felt the hollowness of knowing that someone you're estranged from might not be there in six months or a year from now. I felt that dreaded grieving for a father–daughter relationship that never was. I don't know whether he thought he needed to be forgiven; maybe he was too proud, or maybe he didn't care anymore about the past. But I realized he loved me when he shielded me from his suffering, and no matter how much I blamed him for my mom's depression or Johnny's and my fucked-up-ness, he was still my dad, both heartbreaker and protector. Seeing my once hard-to-love, robust father succumbing to cancer obliterated any grudges.

My dad passed away two days after calling me "sweetie" one last time, on March 9, 2008. I received a phone call at 8 a.m. from Kim's friend: "Sunny, your father's gone. He and Kim went out to dinner last night and when they came home he was up all night with a very full stomach and couldn't settle down. He'd sleep for a couple of hours then get up to use the bathroom. He threw up a couple of times overnight, then Kim found him unresponsive this morning. I'm so sorry."

His spirits were good when I had last spoken with him so the news didn't fit. The brightness of the morning sun belied the moment. I got off the phone and sat at my kitchen table and wailed like he had done for his father. This time, I wailed like I meant it.

My dad had said not to hold a funeral for him, but he didn't say anything about a memorial service. So, my mom, Kim, Kim's best friend, her best friend's husband, and I sprinkled my father's ashes on the shores of Huntington Beach, just off the path where he and Kim took their evening walks. Johnny claimed he had to work, and I wasn't surprised by his inability to grieve, no less with other people. We collectively held our own private services. Kim whispered something in Korean while staring at my father's cremains blending in with the sand. I could tell she didn't want us to see her cry, so my mom and I followed my dad's ashes knees-deep into the water and rushed to shore when the waves pushed them back. I had expected my mother to cry or say something she wanted to get off her chest to vindicate herself, but all she said was, "What a weird, funny life."

Kim was nothing like I had expected. She was polite yet reticent around Mom and me. Standing about five feet tall, she was built like a fireplug—stocky with a wide face. I don't know why I had thought she'd be extraordinarily beautiful and fancy, sporting Louis Vuitton handbags, 18K gold jewelry, and strong designer perfume. Instead she wore tennis shorts, a short-sleeved white shirt, socks that she rolled over twice to hit just above her ankles, and sensible Adidas. I wondered if she had toned it down for us. I was too overwhelmed by my own ungainly demeanor that I didn't think about the humiliation my mom must have felt when she and I joined Kim and her friends for lunch afterward.

"I'm so sorry you had to be with Dad's friends today, Umma," I apologized as I drove her back home.

"You have to show up so they know you're not feeling bad." My mom was always saving face. "Your Daddy's girlfriend want to call you. She want you to be her stepdaughter and told me your Daddy said he doesn't care if she stay in touch with you."

"Never, you're my mom! I'll never be her daughter." I glanced over to see her eyes were watering.

"I want *crimination*, too," Mom said. She wanted me to prepare for this, but I knew I was going to put it off for as long as I could.

I started practicing Ashtanga yoga after my dad passed away. My hour-and-a-half morning program gradually grew to three hours the further I progressed into the series. I was on dawn patrol, waking up at 5 a.m. to get through my entire practice before I started work. Spent and catatonic by the time I hit my cubicle, I had to take a couple of fifteen-minute naps in my car to make it through the day. I met people with all kinds of addictions in the yoga room because Ashtanga's austerity, discipline, and oftentimes impossible poses made people hang up their tired, old impulses and ironically replace them with this new compulsion, except it was deemed *healthy*.

So it was no surprise that I became addicted to the routine and linear structure of Ashtanga, which is meant to be practiced six days a week, except for the days of the full and new moons, and the first three days of a woman's period. When I tried to explain to my non-yoga friends how cool I thought this practice was for synchronizing with nature, they looked at me with sympathy. Our controlling minds and sinewy muscles were subjugated by masochistic yoga poses. The established sequence of postures from one pose to the next increased in difficulty, with the blueprint already laid out so I didn't need to think. I wanted to be in automatic mode following my dad's death.

Ashtanga was a style of yoga based on Hatha yoga poses that became popular in the U.S. in the nineties. Many practitioners got through the first three of the six-series method, and that was only if they didn't have a life or a job. Anything beyond the fourth series was straight-up dangerous with contortion-style backbends and anatomy-defying twists. Ashtanga was considered an intimidating style of yoga: arduous, repetitive, demanding, and what some chip-on-the-shoulder practitioners labeled "the real deal," whatever that meant. I thought many of the same practitioners were affected, and in the beginning, I was dumber than a bag of hair for believing their dogma. They put me off like Kool-Aid drinkers, which made me love the music but hate the fans. The most important aspect of the practice for me was the merging of breath with poses to create a moving meditation. Ashtanga replaced my anorexia with its inherent self-control, and it was also a time-sucking, high-maintenance distraction when my mom was aging.

Another distraction was my new boyfriend, Theo, whom I had met a few months after my dad died, at a software company in Santa Monica we both worked at. Theo was a program manager who was in charge of his division's product launches, and I was a full-time communications specialist who wrote marketing plans. I liked that he was sensitive and shy compared to the arrogant clowns who usually asked me out. Theo also liked the house music scene, which I had never gotten into but had fun at the parties he took me to.

Theo was a white guy from Portland, Oregon, who liked Asian women. He was extremely polite to my mom, but she was embarrassed to speak to him. "I'm sorry my English is so bad," she'd say each time she saw Theo, who'd always return a Duchenne smile and respond, "No, Yong, your English is very good! I want to learn Korean so I can speak with you." Then they'd laugh over the Korean food she prepared for us when we visited her.

"You get married to Theo! He's such a nice man. And if he like me as a mother-in-law, I move in with you and take care of your children." While my mother was no tiger mom, always too exhausted to micromanage Johnny and me, her wishes could range from gentle to heavy-handed.

I didn't tell her I'd often catch Theo flirting with other Asian women at parties. And I never brought up his nausea-inducing yellow fever to him until, after our one-year anniversary, I saw him almost kiss an Asian woman on the cheek at a bar. He stopped when the woman's drunk friend bumped into them. Theo predictably denied his actions, then asked me to move in with him to prove he was serious about our relationship. But I wasn't as inured to lies as my mom was. So I declined.

16

"Your mom keeps repeating herself. Have you noticed that?" Renee whispered to me as my mom untangled an electric-blue plastic wind chime we had bought at the ABC store by her house.

"I've noticed that too, going on for a few months," I responded. "I think it's normal age-related stuff, and she has OCD, which could be making her say things over and over again." This was something I was going to talk to my mother's doctor about.

"It's probably not a big deal then. Just keep an eye on it," Renee warned.

For Mom's seventy-first birthday, I took her on a trip to visit Renee on Oahu in January 2009. Renee had always wanted to move to one of the Hawaiian islands after a childhood vacation to Maui. After traveling for a couple of years and living in Jamaica and Turkey, she actually followed through and moved to Oahu to teach English to mostly Chinese, Japanese, and Korean high school students. I was impressed. She told me that she was only adventurous because she didn't have a mother to root herself in one place.

My mom always complained that my father had never taken us on trips, so I wanted to plan one before she got to a point where traveling would be difficult. Renee was already living with her then fiancé, Derek, her Singaporean high school sweetheart from the Bay Area, in a small house on a quiet part of the island away from all the tourist traps. I was worried that my homebody mother's attachment to her apartment would dampen the spirit of the trip, but the inertia of island life successfully sucked her into its vortex. Oahu's warmth and humidity cast a calming spell on her and was a tonic for both of us. For the week we were there my mom hardly expressed any of her usual concerns that a phantom thief was going to break into her home to steal her jewelry, money, and clothes. But she did keep asking me to call Johnny on my cell phone several times a day to make sure he wasn't gambling.

But what struck me as more out of character at the time than my mom's repetition was her frustration with Renee, "She is a grown woman now, how much money do I give her?"

"I don't think she expects any money. Don't give her anything. You've given her and Melissa way too much money over the years. I can give Renee some money for letting us stay at her house."

I saw my mom pull out four hundred-dollar bills from an envelope in her closet, fold them neatly in half, and stash them inside one of the interior pockets of her carry-on bag.

"Aish, that gijibae is getting married, with just her and her fiancé and no family there, so she needing this one." My mom shook her head.

It wasn't so much the understandable annoyance of feeling pressured to give thirty-five-year-old Renee money that hit me as strange, but that my mom carried on and on about it for thirty minutes in the car on the way to the airport; she normally never let anything like giving a gift to her niece agitate her to that extent.

The womblike warmth of the island eased my mom's arthritis and boosted her energy levels. We hit the beaches and hiked Diamond Head, a steep volcanic tuff cone outside of Waikiki. It was no small feat. Mom started panting and wheezing by the time we were halfway up, but she kept repeating to herself, "I can do it, I can do it." Then enthusiastically encouraged strangers around her like a Korean Tony Robbins, "You can do it, you can do it! Everyone Jalhaess-eo!" which was met with laughter and adoring nods. I was one step behind my mom gently pushing her butt up the steps while Renee held her hand in front of her as we ascended the volcano. We were a walking sandwich. When we finally reached the top, Mom let out a hurricane sigh and shouted, "We did it!"

Her hands excitedly grabbed her chest, which seemed to keep her body from levitating off the ground. "Whaaaa! Fat Johnny can never do this one! I told everyone *you can do it* just like when I was young in Girl Scouts in Korea."

I'd heard about my mom's 8-year-old Girl Scout days before, but Renee hadn't and looked bemused like *Really? Girls Scouts back in the day in Korea?*

We went to the North Shore to sit on the beach afterward. "I used to swim at the beaches of Incheon and Busan every summer. I was a really good swimmer," my mom said, her capri pants rolled up to expose her porcelain legs covered in varicose veins.

"Why don't you go in the water now, Mom?"

"Aigoo, I'm too old, I cannot swimming now."

Renee and I started reminiscing about the time she lived with us during high school in Yorba Linda. My mom asked, "You know your friend Ashley in high school?" The sunlight hit her glasses in such a way that projected a dreamy phosphorescent glow.

"Yes, the one with the big hair and stupid makeup?" Ashley's condescension still nagged, ridiculing Mom's accent and our tract house.

"I never liked her, she was so boring with no personality. Her mother was boring, too. That's why they put ugly makeup on their same-o, same-o bindaetteok moon faces." My mom opened her mouth wide, her laughter joyous like a jubilee.

This took Renee and me out. My mom's bitterness toward an old acquaintance sliced the air. We fell back on the sand laughing so hard about the mung bean pancake comparison that it startled the seabirds circling us for treats.

I looked down at my mom's blistered toes and heels from the rubber beach sandals I had bought for her at the CVS in Honolulu. They were too big. My mom hadn't wanted to take her good SAS sandals out of fear that they'd get dirty. She always saved her valuable clothes, shoes, and jewelry for the *right* occasion that never existed. In true fashion, she never complained about the pain. She didn't want to make trouble.

My mom insisted out of nowhere that she wanted to call Johnny, to check in, as if she were his sponsor.

"We'll call him later, okay? Let's just enjoy the beach." I hoped she'd forget about calling him, but it didn't let up, and her whining persisted even as we all left the house for dinner later that night.

"Why don't you let her call your brother? Just let her do what makes her happy," Derek said to me like I was a big bully. Derek was a dutiful Asian man who especially respected elderly women, even holding their arms when they walked together.

Chastened, I handed my phone to my mom. You have to learn not to baby Johnny because he uses you, he's thirty-eight! He knows you'll always help him when he gambles all of his money away," I said slowly for what felt like the millionth time in my life.

My mom grabbed my phone and frantically dialed Johnny's phone number, faster than the speed dial on her landline, while she and Derek walked arm in arm ahead of Renee and me.

I broke up with Theo the day after we returned from Oahu. I didn't want the stress of second-guessing his every move or word, which meant the tenuous trust between us had finally disintegrated. Brief island living had given me a reset to start fresh, sucker-free.

When I was thirteen I asked my mother why she never used the shower. She'd always squat down in front of the bathtub faucet with a small plastic bucket to bathe. "We never had shower in Korea when I'm growing up so I'm not used to them. Not even at mogyoktang," she said. I wanted to take her to a Korean bathhouse in LA to help her reconnect with something she had once done habitually, where there was an abundance of squat stools in front of bathtub faucets. The mogyoktang was like the agora, a gathering place where friends and family met to bathe, relax, and gossip. Some of the ajummas who scrubbed knew my mom and her sisters well so the public bathhouses were a family affair. My mom and four of her younger sisters were once met with excitement when an ajumma called out, "Oh bo-ji wasso!" *The five vaginas are here*! Spending time with her sisters and the ajummas at the mogyoktangs was a release from the malaise at home with Korean in laws who mounted a daily campaign of psychological warfare. The grime, dirt, and sadness sloughed off along with the day

A few months after we returned from Oahu Johnny drove my mom to my apartment in West Hollywood so we could spend the day together at Olympic Spa in Koreatown. Johnny seemed more amenable to do favors for us because he was happy with the same freelance IT job he had managed to hold on to for the past five years.

In South Korea women and men generally entered the mogyoktang naked, but the rules were laxer in the States and it was not unusual to see women in bathing suits sitting in the saunas or hot tubs. My mom was reluctant and shy at first about removing all of her clothing, possibly because something she had been used to doing so routinely had fallen victim to the strange distance time creates. She finally lost her reservations when she saw other ajummas and halmeonis strip down. The steam from the saunas relieved her undiagnosed mild asthma, and the heat from the hot tubs loosened the grip of arthritis from her joints.

We rinsed off before using the hot tub, and I realized that, at the age of thirty-seven, this was the first time I'd seen my mother use a shower. She jumped with surprise when the warm water from the overhead shower covered her.

"How do you like the shower, umma?" I yelled through the sounds and chatter of the spa.

"Doesn't make me feel clean like bath." We both laughed.

When we got into one of the hot tubs, my mom's facial tension disappeared as the jets beat against her lower back where the compression fractures throbbed.

"I have to get out, my heart is bumping, bumping," my mom said five minutes later. I saw the placard above her head that read, "Saunas and hot tubs are potentially dangerous for patients with hypertension and heart disease."

She drank a cup of cold water before she headed straight for the bathing area where some women were squatting on short plastic stools in front of the faucets. My mom was home. She vigorously washed her face while I used a long, Pepto-Bismol-pink Korean exfoliating scrubber, which is a million times more abrasive than the ones I've found here, and scrubbed her back and legs the way I imagined the ajummas had done for her in Korea. I scrubbed my mother's back trying hard not to scratch her thin, soft, impossibly smooth skin. She was right about the white rice.

After bathing, mom cleaned her bright yellow plastic stool and the wash area around her, something she did out of compulsion. In the dressing room I watched her slowly comb her hair, which was thinning and falling out due to her hypothyroidism. She adjusted her top and pants and checked herself out in the mirror, picking out any errant hairs and lint, then walked over to the other side of the counter space to throw away the debris in the trash. She flashed a fake smile to help guide her lipstick application, making sure it didn't stray outside the borders. She gently patted her upper lip and tapped the stain of lipstick on her cheeks for blush. I hoped she'd always care about her appearance.

We ate doenjang jjigae at a nearby restaurant afterward, then went to the Galleria Market to buy rice cakes, pears, and Korean puff pastries to snack on at home. My mom repeated her childhood stories again, but not to the point that I worried something was wrong. When we got home we went on a walk around my posh neighborhood, which alienated me because I wasn't posh. I didn't shop at the Beverly Center, buy expensive cold-pressed juices, or work out at the plethora of gyms on every square block of Santa Monica Boulevard between Fairfax and La Cienega Boulevards. The only refuge I found from the swank was the Bodhi Tree Bookstore that, by great luck, was at the end of my street. It was a beloved relic of a shop that opened in 1970 before the city became commercial, mainstream, and affluent—it was an aberration after the effects of massive gentrification. I couldn't believe I lived so close to a groovy living landmark that sold new age and spirituality books. I wasn't interested in all of the books, but I loved the store's ambience, stillness, and complimentary hot teas, and that it was an interloper of West Hollywood. As Mom and I walked by I realized that we were both tourists too, and I liked that.

We went to Pinkberry at the other end of my block. We weren't hungry after all we had eaten, but we ate it anyway because it was something to do.

"This is nice area, but you need to buy house. We buy together. And Johnny can move in with us," my mom said out of the blue as we left Pinkberry, reviving the same old discussion I was tired of having. We were stuck at a familiar impasse.

"No, Mom! Johnny won't help pay the mortgage. Remember what he did to you? You lost the condo in Rancho!"

"You don't have children. You don't know a mother's mind. Don't you want children?" she asked dejected, emphatically digging into her plain yogurt while the blackberries fell out the sides of the cup. We kicked them into people's lawns.

I felt tugged and torn in two directions.

As an eleven-year-old, filial piety, to me, applied to end-of-life rituals in our culture, the way my aunt had carefully groomed her dying father in Korea. As an adult I interpreted it as an excessive demand on grown children to get married, have kids, and move their parents back into their house to be taken care of. But I was also aware that the roots of duty had already been planted in my mom's early words, "This is all for you and Johnny," as she counted hard-earned money in the kitchen at Gate 4: she had made grand sacrifices for me so my responsibility was to repay her with my own, which, I assumed, included my independence. This ancient ideal in the modern world pressured me, momentarily pushing me back into a corner with the same old feelings of shame I had experienced during the throes of anorexia.

The guilt I had felt as a child for my mom's distress was bleeding into an adult regret for not being able to alleviate her sadness or fulfill her wishes. Even though I always felt secure in my mom's love, this pediatric burden made me question my self-worth on an endless loop because my identity was connected to making her happy and defending her from danger.

As we turned the corner toward an alleyway that was a shortcut to my apartment, my mom shrieked, "Look at the autumn leaves!"

It was a clear, beautiful fall day. The colors of the leaves were dulling, turning more rust and tan, which stained the world bronze, even for LA. Despite it all, my mom and I had a lovely day together. I was concerned about her repetition, but in that moment, her essence, the thing that made the world coherent, was still intact. And I wanted it to last forever. We locked arms and walked toward my apartment through another tree-lined street covered in glinting red-orange leaves. We looked like a billboard advertisement for a K-drama about an overly protective mother who supports her wayward thirty-seven-year-old daughter with a mysterious mental illness ironically pursuing a delayed PhD in psychology at Seoul National University.

"It's so pretty today, right? Did you have fun today at the mogyoktang? I wish you lived closer so we could go every week," I said, homesick for Mom's youth, feeling my crushing attachment to her.

"I had a very good time today. Gomawoyo," she said with a smile full of blackberries as she wrapped her arm around my waist and leaned her head into my chest like she were a child squeezing her parent. She had shrunk—the top of her head reached just under my chin.

"I love you, Mom. I love you so much it hurts." My happiness was sobered by the thought of her getting older. We walked back to my tiny apartment in a city we both found so strange.

"I love you more, more, more, more, more!" my mom said, laughing and kicking more felled berries into strangers' lawns.

Unremarkable, ordinary things like calling me every day, paying rent and bills, or requesting that I call social security and health insurance companies whenever she received letters that confused her started to slyly fade away under a sepia-tinted cloud that was once her memory. I couldn't pinpoint when these familiar, everyday events suddenly stopped, but it was extraordinary when my mother didn't call me on my thirty-ninth birthday. A year and a half earlier after we had returned from Oahu, I made an appointment with my mom's doctor, monitored her behavior, and listened for repetitive stories. My mom's doctor gave her a standardized Alzheimer's test, which didn't show anything remarkable but that she could tell time on a clock. She passed. Mom's CT scan revealed mild atrophy that her doctor called "age related." I still wasn't satisfied so I enrolled her in a full-day comprehensive memory exam at the Memory Evaluation Program of UCLA Geriatric Medicine, where they ran a battery of cognitive tests. And still, the specialists said she had age-related, short-term memory loss.

But the repetitive storytelling lingered. One day Johnny called me screaming that Mom was "stupid" and had lost his social security card.

"Why the hell would you leave your own important documents with Mom?! You're a grown-ass man and should take care of your own business. Don't ever call her stupid again, that's fucked up! You're forty, Johnny! You need to move out of Mom's and give her some peace. Your yelling is giving her stress and making her forget where things are!" I shouted.

"She doesn't want me to be happy. Mom keeps hitting her head with both fists saying, 'I'm so stupid, I can't remember where I put it.' I need the card for my job, they want me to become a full-time employee and I need to fill out paperwork."

Johnny was always pigeonholing himself as a victim. The fact that he blamed my mom for not wanting him to be happy was absurd.

"Mom's not doing anything to sabotage you. Find your own damn social security card! I'll call APS and the cops if you call her stupid again!" I knew I wasn't going to call anyone out of fear that it would upset my mother; the bluffing came so naturally in the way Johnny and I communicated that we both brushed it off.

I resorted to more clandestine warnings, like ratting him out to my mom's apartment manager for staying there longer than the two-week visitation period. Patricia had said she needed proof that Johnny was living there so I showed her his suitcases in the hallway closet.

"I never see your brother, so I can't tell him to leave. I can leave a notice with your mom reminding her about the apartment policies," Patricia told me in a singsong tone, the verbal equivalent of an eye roll. The thing about Johnny was that even though he was overweight and hard to miss, he had the lightest step and left the faintest trail, which managed to evade Patricia's radar. He was frequently chased down by debt collectors and the IRS so he became masterful at pathological lying and artful dodging. When the debt collectors couldn't get ahold of him, they'd call me and leave messages threatening lawsuits. Working long hours Johnny was usually gone from dawn to 10 p.m. so he didn't exist to seniors who went to bed by 8 p.m.

My paternal grandmother passed away in May 2010, two years after my father died. Mom was sad but detached and I was beginning to see distance in her eyes, the same distance I'd read about in cheerful senior health magazines scattered on tables in doctors' offices. There was always a sidebar that read "signs to watch out for" in the aging and memory section, and "distant eyes" usually ranked in the top ten. At some point during all the tests and screenings for my mom and wars with Johnny, Uncle Young Soo fell sick with the same liver cancer that had taken

Aunt Min Jee. He died later that year in December. Even though Mom and Uncle Young Soo had had a prickly relationship because of my father's carelessness, she was still undone by her only brother's death. The cancers that had taken three of my mother's siblings tormented me to no end that I fixated on chasing away any illness.

17

The official diagnosis of mild cognitive impairment was made in early 2012 by the same doctor who had said her short-term memory loss was "unremarkable, age related." I didn't think much of it at the time because I thought cognitive impairment meant forgetting to turn off the hallway light or the names of extended family, rather than the dementia that robs its host of their memory, cognitive functioning, and communication skills. Or the dementia that's a serious, terminal disease that eventually leads to a person's death. I was naive and in complete denial.

The memory of my mother walking me out of her apartment shortly after the diagnosis still haunts me to this day: her anxiety palpable and face grimacing as she said with a small quake in her voice, "Something is wrong." I felt powerless to stop what was happening. This was the first and only time she verbalized what she felt. The worry over my mom's repetitions, CT scan, and multiple memory evaluations by doctors and geriatric specialists at UCLA were now a self-fulfilling prophecy. They had all been tone-deaf to my concerns.

"There's no cure for dementia. You can only try to slow its progression with drugs," my mom's doctor explained. He came from a conventional medicine background that rarely reported on the miraculous stories of people reversing their dementia through diet and exercise.

"Why didn't you see this over a year ago?" I asked, betrayed.

"Because she didn't have the symptoms then. You just

said she was repeating herself, but she wasn't forgetting and refusing to take her pills like she is now. I'm also concerned that you said she recently stopped bathing and grooming herself, which is a symptom of cognitive impairment and probably why your mother is getting frequent urinary tract infections. UTIs don't seem to cause as much pain in seniors, but they can make them more agitated. Let's put her on a low-dose Donepezil for now and monitor how she does."

I recalled Mom's drawn-out agitation about giving Renee money on the way to the airport and wondered if that had been an unforeseen UTI. I switched her physician the next day.

I knew Alzheimer's was bad in the nineties because after Ronald Reagan was diagnosed with it, his political enemies even seemed empathetic by thinking twice about criticizing him. I had watched enough documentaries to understand that it was a disease you didn't want for yourself or your family. At first I had felt sorry for the families whose loved ones lost their cognitive abilities and memories; now, I was the person I had pitied.

The mild cognitive impairment was just that at first: a series of UTIs and bouts of hostility, anxiety, and confusion. My mom stopped taking her medication on her own, then suddenly refused taking them altogether when Johnny or I tried to give them to her. She'd shout then clamp her mouth shut, "I'm already eat them!" Mom also stopped driving to her favorite shops, cleaning her apartment obsessively, and cooking. But she wasn't incontinent, yet; that would be the tipping point.

I was disturbed that my mother stopped bathing and grooming since she'd always been fastidious about her appearance and hygiene. Dementia crossed so many lines that I needed a miracle. When I tried to coax her into the bathtub, she screamed, "You try kill me!" and shoved me away. The paranoia that accompanies dementia made her shut down in her bedroom with the curtains drawn. After sundowning, my mom relaxed into her natural honeyed state again. I was clinging on to hope that she would always be *there*. My most colossal fear was that my mom would forget my name, who I was to her.

My mom's new primary care physician, Dr. Khin, was much more hands-on than her previous one. She increased the dosage of Donepezil based on my mom's symptoms, asked in-depth lifestyle questions, and offered diet and activity advice. It was information I already knew, but it felt reassuring receiving it from a more involved, concerned doctor.

"I pray I don't get dementia when I'm older. I don't know what's worse, dementia or cancer. With dementia so much autonomy is stolen from you, and you don't know who you can trust with your life," Dr. Khin said casually in front of my mom and me as she was listening to Mom's lungs.

"They're both horrible," I said, taken aback that the doctor would say something so blunt in front of her patient. I whispered to Dr. Khin, "I know my mom has dementia, but I want to think she's still in *there* and can understand things, so can you please not say stuff like that in front of her?" I was hypersensitive to how people viewed my mom, and it was sad that I had to advocate for her in front of her own doctor.

"I'm sorry, I certainly didn't mean it to be insensitive. I meant to say both diseases are awful, but, in my opinion, dementia affects the patients' families in more devastating ways. It's heartbreaking when you can't think for yourself anymore. But you can also say that about cancer," Dr. Khin said, backpedalling. I knew dementia was a tornado heading toward our home.

My biggest fear since I was fourteen had been that my mother would die early of cancer like Aunt Min Jee and Aunt Soo Jin. As a young adult I scoured resources to learn about cancers that affected people of East Asian descent, then made it my mission to protect my mom against any and all kinds of cancer. But now I was blindsided by this entirely different yet equally harrowing disease that felt like a merciless joke from the gods. At least there was a chance of recovery with some cancers, but there was little to no exit out of dementia. The curse felt graver, more doomed. I myself had no idea which was worse: dying from a disease that slowly killed your physical body, or from a disease that slowly killed your mind.

"Umma, naega nuguya?" I asked my mom who I was throughout the day in Korean despite the fact that my Korean language skills were at a four-year-old's level at best, trying to catch her off guard to test her memory's elasticity.

"Sun Yong-ee, oori ddal," she answered. *Sun Yong, our daughter.*

"Umma, ireum moya?" *What's your name, Mom*?

"Song, Yong Cha," my mom responded with her maiden name. And that was how it would be from then on, not Pak, Yong Cha, her married name for over forty years. Dementia had whittled away at her short-term memory, leaving her long-term memory fractured but intact, glinting with indelible parts of her previous identity.

I handled dementia with frustration and trial and error in the first few years. Mom didn't understand when I told her she couldn't drive anymore. I took away her car keys after she took off for two hours one morning in 2014. She returned home before the police started a search for her. The fact that she remembered how to get home made me wonder how dementia could turn on and off like that, and I realized how lucky we were this time. When I called the police department to have them stop their search, they suggested I look into sending her to a nursing home, which I firmly refused.

"The police are right. Your mom needs more care in a nursing home environment," Aunt Helen told me a few weeks later. "It's not safe for her to live alone anymore. I know you love your mom, but you can't do this by yourself. She can die if she falls or gets lost next time. Please think hard about your mom's safety."

But Asians kept their elders home. I had learned that empirically, as well as from suggestions from family. It's what I wanted to do for her, to spite dementia. I was horrified by nursing homes and their reputations for poor care, negligence, abuse, and rape by staff members who were oftentimes paid less than minimum wage. *Why should they give a shit about your loved one?* I shook in terror imagining anything like that happening to Mom. I hadn't given her the grandchildren she had begged for and I hadn't bought a house with her because the threat of Johnny moving in with us repelled me, so I was determined to at least keep my mom safe in her home. I knew she wanted to live and die at home, especially after hearing her mother-in-law yell for us every time we visited her at her nursing home.

At least Aunt Helen cared. For someone who wasn't my aunt by blood, I respected her more than my mom's sisters because she actually showed up for us. I received limited help and understanding from Johnny, who had also urged me to place Mom in a nursing home since she wasn't going to be his safety net anymore after I took over her finances. The audacity of his suggestion was tantamount to a vicious slap on my mom's face because she had always lived for him. There was also silence from my mom's sisters who had stopped calling. Renee stopped calling, too, which was a blow since my mom had been like a mother to her after Aunt Min Jee died. Dementia is tragic in and of itself, but what makes it much more brutal is the apathy from the people you once thought cared. Dementia is intractable without adequate support from family or friends. Aside from Aunt Seo Yun, who called my mom once a month from Texas, the convenient disappearance of her remaining sisters, nieces, and nephews devastated me, because if the roles were reversed I knew my mom would have been there for them, without any doubt in my mind.

I drove to Mom's house once or twice a week to buy food and supplies, and as soon as I got home after a full day of errands and appointments, I'd plan for the following week. One day in between visits the new apartment manager, Maria, who wasn't as laid-back as Patricia, called me at work to tell me, "Your mom is downstairs at the clubhouse complaining she's hungry. We're not a nursing home, this is an independent living community."

"Can you or someone else buy her a sandwich and I'll pay you back?" I begged.

"Yes, but you need to do something about this. I've noticed she wears the same clothes every day now. What happened?"

"It's really none of your business, Maria. She has every right to live there." I was in full defense mode because I was paranoid she was trying to evict my mom for having dementia. I started going mad with unsubstantiated fears after this incident. Some of my mom's ignorant, scuttlebutt neighbors were treating her like a pariah, and their gossip was getting to Maria. I understood the backbreaking, emotionally draining work of keeping my mom safe at home, but I surmised Maria and the other hens knew it, too, and wanted my mom to be at a more appropriate facility so they wouldn't have to see it. *Over my dead, busted body.*

Johnny complicated the problem because he was too unreliable to take care of my mom when I couldn't be at her house. He'd eat all of the food and use all of the supplies I bought for her. He didn't understand that my mom couldn't just jump into the car to buy more; he was in resolute denial. Johnny wasn't helping to pay the rent, utilities, or food, either. It was like dealing with two parasites: dementia and my brother.

I turned to guilting him into doing the right thing. Sometimes it worked, and the times it didn't, I'd send Maria to the apartment for a bogus repair to fix while he was there. The fear of being kicked out finally knocked some sense into him to buy food for my mom, because that's all he could really afford. Johnny traveled a lot for work, but when he was with my mom he spoke and cracked jokes as though she were still the same person, and when she didn't respond to the humor she had once understood by going blank, so did he.

18

I had first met Abby in the summer of 2010. After a yoga class one day, a few friends and I went to Café Tropical in Silver Lake. It had been nearly two years since I'd broken up with Theo, which gave me time to reflect on my poor choices in men. I was holding my teacher's six-month-old son when Abby walked in and grabbed him from me. Literally sauntered in, set his messenger bag and bicycle helmet down, and quietly mumbled, "Can I hold him?" as he lifted the baby from my arms. Abby was known for his soft-spoken mumbling and was constantly being asked to repeat himself as people moved their ears closer to his face. But instead of speaking louder he'd respond with more inaudible mumbling. His lips would move, but upon closer inspection, it was like he couldn't be bothered to enunciate. This attribute made some adore him and others want to strangle him.

Abby disregarded my personal space and lacked any concern for my desire to hold the damn baby. My friend later told me he was checking me out while I was drinking my hibiscus juice while simultaneously giving him dirty looks. He found me on my barely used Facebook page. Then we started hanging out as friends for three months, and when I realized he couldn't lie to save his life, I loosened my guard. The inability to lie was a prerequisite I had for dating the men following Jamie and Theo. I was also getting tired of attributing my fear of intimacy to the hell of watching my parents fight all the time.

Abby was seven years older than me and a few years out of a poisonous fifteen-year relationship. He was a lighting technician for films, commercials, and TV shows, so he was always too physically exhausted to do more than fifteen minutes of yoga on his days off. It was a relief to find another person who was enthusiastic about Ashtanga yoga but didn't fall easily into the trappings of its cult-like tendencies: the obsession with poses and progression in the series; eating only vegetarian or Ayurvedic meals at prescribed times (well before sunset); and live for months in Mysore, India to practice at the main shala (school) trying hard to gain the attention of their guru. We both had jobs and interests outside of yoga, which we mostly considered a powerful meditation tool to help us get through the day. He had never gambled before, and like me, was too chickenshit to lose money to a rigged system. I waited six months to introduce him to my mom because I was still wary about any possible skeletons in his closet, and I was unsure of my own baggage that could have vexed our relationship.

When I first introduced Abby to my mom on Mother's Day 2011, they fell in love. Abby handled her dementia-triggered moodiness like a champ and disarmed her by explaining in unnecessary detail the reason he had bought her a bouquet of flowers from an independent florist in his neighborhood: to keep them afloat so a chain store wouldn't replace them in rapidly gentrifying Silver Lake. He knew my mom's memory was receding, but thought that not engaging her in conversation was condescending; the way it was hurtful to see other families throw neglect and avoidance at their loved ones with dementia. Instead, we leaned into talking her through. Abby genuinely liked my mom and made her laugh with his deadpan, droll humor. The fact that Abby was authentically kind to Mom sealed the deal.

Abby never knew my mom before dementia, which was the universe taking a piss on us: the vibrant, feisty, funny woman who enjoyed cooking elaborate meals; who dressed stylishly and wore gold, diamonds, and sapphires; who painstakingly applied makeup; and who drove around town buying food for people she loved. Abby never got to taste Mom's homemade kimchi, banchan, or jjigaes. He never got to hear her stories about growing up in Korea with an enormous family during peace and war. All of this invited a fresh grieving. Abby's parents fought a lot, too, and he didn't have a good relationship with his overbearing Jewish mother, so I desperately wanted him to know mine. Abby was an abrasive Eeyore and doomsday yaysayer, but he was mostly a goofy mensch with a heart of gold who went out of his way to save animals and the defenseless. He didn't have patience for phonies the way my mom didn't. They were both my mensches.

Abby and I were in a strong relationship, but we felt marriage could wait since memories of our parents' distant fighting still disturbed us. Any thoughts of having kids practically evaporated by this point because I couldn't imagine raising any on top of taking care of my mom. Life had simply taken a series of unexpected twist and turns, complicated by my mom's aging and my own.

In 2014, Johnny was thrown in jail for stealing someone's poker chips in Las Vegas while trying to make up the forty thousand dollars he had taken from my mom's safe deposit box. I had stashed the key to the box in her top dresser drawer under some silk scarves. Distracted by caregiving, I got sloppy and accidentally trusted a junkie along the way. The fact that he must have asked my mother what the key was for when she was cognitively impaired slammed me with blunt force trauma—Johnny had preyed upon his own mother. The money had actually been set aside for him anyway, he just didn't know it, which made the violation that much more untenable. It was an informal inheritance my mom wanted me to give to him piecemeal, after she passed away, so he wouldn't blow it all at once. But it was still her money, then.

Johnny once told me that casinos gave broke gamblers bus vouchers to get home so they could work to save more money to return and gamble again. He was right. His work friends bailed him out of jail and I picked him up at the bus station near Ontario. I called APS and the police, who documented possible elder abuse.

"Johnny, you're dead to me. You need to move out of Mom's house. You're forty-three! If you don't, I'll find a way to get you out. I truly believe you're the reason Mom has dementia. All the years of dealing with your gambling, the stress and anxiety, the high blood pressure, the strokes . . . she was always worried about you. You and Dad have ruined her life!" I lost it.

Johnny trembled as he attempted to defend himself and buy more time. It was like hearing a savant with arrested development promise something that was going to break.

"You have two months to find a new place to live, but in the meantime, I want you to pay back all the money you stole and pay all of Mom's rent and utilities."

Johnny dodged me as much as he could. Even when I took back my mom's house and car keys from him, he still found a way to sneak in. Dementia did not stop my mother from opening the door for her son. Johnny paid the rent, utilities, and Mom's meals on the weekends. He was setting aside money to pay her back, but I knew he'd never be able to make up all of it. He owed the IRS and the state over ten years of unpaid taxes. It was like watching a house on fire while we were still in it.

"Can I have Mom's car keys? I need to be able to get to work since my car died. The buses and trains are very slow from LA to Rancho," Johnny asked morosely over the phone as I was moving my stuff into Abby's house. I remembered when my father had asked my mom to open a joint savings account with him after he left the house. She had asked rhetorically, "Does he think I'm stupid?"

"No way. You're just going to hit the sad poker tables again. I'm selling Mom's car to help pay for caregivers in the future. I know I'm going to need more help soon."

"I'm doing the best I can to pay Mom back, I just need it to get to work. I won't gamble anymore," he whined. Johnny wouldn't even attend the local Gam-Anon meetings I found for him. I knew he was lying.

I worried about whether Johnny was treating my mom poorly or eating all of her food. But when I couldn't visit her, he always made sure she took her medicine and ate her meals. Johnny would give my mom her pills and make her breakfast before he left for work. She'd sleep during the afternoons and eat the prepared sandwiches and meals I made or bought her on the weekends for the week ahead. When Johnny got home he'd heat up her food or buy dinner, then give her evening pills. There was always plenty of fresh fruit, pretzels, popcorn, nuts and berries, and oatmeal cookies for snacks. My mom would even remember to go downstairs to get her coffee at the clubhouse and check her mail. She was still pleasant and happy most of the time, with the exception of the unpredictable sundowning, which was a misnomer because it reared its ugly head at any time of day.

Since dementia was slow-moving and mostly manageable for the first few years, I didn't want to hire strange caregivers to be alone with my mom when we were still able to take care of her. But that also meant I had no choice but to trust Johnny when I wasn't there because the demands of dementia were too great to handle alone. Johnny became a warped blessing. If he hadn't been broke and had had his own place, my mom would have been alone and left to her own dangerous will. She refused to stay with Abby and me in our small one-bedroom bungalow because she couldn't be away from her home for more than four hours. "People upstairs are going to come in my house and steal everything!" Paranoia was another symptom of advancing dementia, breaking already deluded thinking.

It was becoming harder for me to hold on to jobs. I hadn't worked a full-time job since the software company in Santa Monica in 2008 because I needed the flexibility of freelance work to allow me to help my mom during the week. Even so, a few of my employers still terminated my contracts because I was requesting too much time off to take her to emergency doctors' appointments on top of appointments to see her endocrinologist, optometrist, dentist, primary care physician, and cardiologist. I learned to cram a lot of Mom's appointments into one day. On the days I took her to the doctor, she'd remark on the number of cars on the street or freeway: "Oh my gosh, too many cars!" She'd stop and point at flowers, trees, children, trucks, what people wore, or my shoes, and always without fail, comment on how beautiful everything was. She was absorbed into the moment while my mind was usually racing down the list of things to do for her. But I knew these special moments were going to be taken away from me soon. In the rush of going from one doctor's appointment to another, I forced myself to slow down to describe to her every detail about our matching Vans and bucket hats, and I clung to every word she used to describe the food she was going to prepare for a picnic with friends on the mountains behind her house. Her young life in Korea replaced her new reality. And who dared to tell her she was confused with the past if it anchored her in the present?

Despite the exhaustion, the hour-long commute on the 210 freeway between Rancho and Los Angeles gave me an odd sense of peace to sit with the loneliness I felt about my mom's dementia that nobody understood. Not even my friends, who felt pity but also alienated when I didn't have time to hang out with them. With the sun sourly beating down on my face I held a helpless resentment for them because their parents had partners, or they had the full support of large families.

My mom and I were in muzzy liminal states, heading in two different directions. I mourned the loss of my mother's essence while she was still alive. It was a daily unmooring. She was still here but over there, with faraway eyes drifting farther and searching for a home in her new reality. She was still sweet, caring, and generous, but we had switched roles. I became her parent and she my child, and I was furious about that because I wasn't done being her daughter. Abby suggested I seek therapy, but I didn't have the time or energy. My life was in a constant non-ordinary state of anxiety, hoping that my mom would hang on to as much of her identity as possible.

The symptoms of advancing dementia eluded me in terms of their progression. They didn't reveal themselves in such an immediate or linear way so that I could gauge behavioral changes and try to equip myself with antidotes. Every day was unequivocally dynamic with subtle change. One day Mom would understand how to get her medicine out of her pillbox and take it when I called her, the next day she didn't know what the pillbox was. One day she picked up her water glass to drink, the next day she poured the water onto a spoon and sipped. The clandestine disease was crept up, erasing my mom's ability to comprehend anything when it crossed over into the moderate phase in 2016.

"Umma, take your medicine," I said handing her a neutral palette of eight pills and a cup of water as soon as I walked through the front door.

"Moya?" my mom asked. *What is it?*

"Put the pills in your mouth and swallow."

"Swallow?" she'd ask quizzically.

My mom was going back to the mother tongue, speaking less English and more Korean. *This is common*, I was told by her physicians, but I was beginning to think that they'd say anything to make sense of something that was never going to make sense. If there were a time for tidal regrets, complaining about going to Korean language school when I was a kid was high up on that list. I desperately wanted to communicate with my mother in the language she heard when it didn't occur to her.

I had come back from Seoul at the age of eleven knowing how to read and pronounce Hangul, but unable to fully comprehend conversational Korean. I couldn't figure out the honorifics so I spoke to my parents like they were my elementary school buddies. Conversely, Johnny came back understanding and speaking Korean much better than me, but unable to read Hangul. It didn't help that we'd respond in English when my parents spoke to us in Korean. They enrolled us in Korean school on the weekends, but we just complained about wanting that time to play, and they were too busy and exhausted to put up a fight. So, we stopped going.

When I was in my late twenties living in LA it suddenly felt fashionable to speak Korean, but it already seemed too late. I tried to deflect the blame and convince myself that my parents should have forced us to speak Korean at home. But my parents had probably wanted us to assimilate, so speaking fluent English at the expense of our dwindling Korean was the price that needed to be paid. My entire family was caught up in the "American Dream," which made us excited to grasp onto English to attain that elusive state.

I didn't call my mom "umma" until my late twenties, and even then, it was occasional and only to be playful. After she emerged from watching a K-drama, I'd deliver a wink as I enunciated "umma" with a plucky lilt on the second syllable like it was a question, imitating the intonations of the actors on screen. Sometimes when I needed to tell her something serious with conviction, I'd also drag out the second syllable in *um-ma*, as if I had mastery of the language. I never felt so Korean.

It was only during my early and mid-thirties and into my forties that I regularly interspersed *mom* and *umma* in regular rotation, a response to my desire to connect with my heritage that had confounded and also endeared me to its peculiarities and beauty. A longing to find ancestors and understand origins comes with aging; however, my mom was aging faster, so I needed to scramble with urgency to make up for lost time. She was losing her ability to speak English and I wanted to turn back the clock, to make up for my foolishness of the past. I leaned on *umma*, which was a doorway to our shared first language. In the smallest of ways, saying that single word helped me to access my Koreanness, even though I knew it was inadequate.

I always thought *umma* had a naturally affectionate quality to it, more so than *mom.* It sealed the person who said *umma* in their youth, perhaps because of the visual comfort that the palindrome brings, the two syllables beginning and ending in a vowel imitating the sound of a baby. In an uncanny way, I also thought *umma* sounded and felt similar to *om*, which was considered a sacred sound in Hinduism. The opening and closing prayers chanted before and after the Ashtanga yoga practice started with an *om*, which was said to contain the entire universe as it was the first sound heard at the beginning of time; it also contained the present and future—an appropriate metaphor for a mother's expansiveness.

Sometimes my mom entered a dizzying, blissful state of delirium and rattled off stories in Korean like she was eight years old, about visiting her beloved uncle's house as a child in the country where he had orchards on two acres of land. Unable to keep up, I simply listened, allowing the foreign-yet-familiar words enter and temporarily exist in me. Language united experience, memories, and emotions; it dilated context and truth. So this inability to communicate with my mom, especially in her new reality, surfaced larger feelings of cultural shame. I felt like it was all slowly slipping through my fingers.

19

I traveled to Mysore, in Southern India, to practice yoga for the month of February 2016. Jokes about the city's name came too easy among the insulated, injured Ashtanga yoga crowd. I paid one of my mom's neighbors, Nancy, to help administer pills, shop for food, and prepare meals everyday. I timed my trip to go when Johnny wasn't traveling or working long hours so he could take over the evening shift.

India was beautiful, filthy, isolating, and big-hearted. I still wasn't able to completely disarm and enjoy the experience of traveling to a wild place like India, even though the hamlet I stayed in was westernized and had running water, flush toilets, and vegan cafes that looked identical to the ones in Venice Beach. It was a miracle to have been able to travel at all because it took the energy and support of a lot of people to make this trip possible. I wanted an escape.

But when I got there I found it difficult to escape from the worries that tied me back to dementia because sometimes I'd call at 11 p.m. Mysore time to have Nancy tell me at 9:30 a.m. PST that my mom was still in bed, refusing to eat or take her medication. I had no idea whether other yoga students in their 30s or 40s were anchored by a parent's dementia or illness while hanging out in India. I was envious of those with the peace of mind that comes with an elderly loved one's good health.

I also couldn't hear another tale of privilege concerning the microscopic amount of food some malnourished students ate at 4:30 p.m. to fall asleep by 6 p.m. so they they could wake up at 2 a.m. to practice with the "senior, advanced" students and teachers. It didn't escape me that their obsession with food made my years of anorexia seem normal. Seeing healthy adults set rules around digesting food reminded me of my own disordered eating that I did the complete opposite out of repulsion: I started eating more. The food was delicious, healthy, and cheap in the small Western-influenced suburb of Gokulam that I became insatiable. I ate before practice, I ate after practice. I ate two hours later for lunch, then a larger dinner at night. Sometimes a thick, rich, vegan smoothie as a night cap. If anyone told me I'd have this new outlook on eating when I was in the throes of anorexia, I would have collapsed on my scrawny little ass.

Yoga gave me plenty of fantastic things like meeting Abby who didn't get sucked into yoga drama, but it also left me with two herniated discs in my cervical spine and a fully torn right rotator cuff by the time I completed the third series. Being in India was a life marker for me, but I became burnt out by the lemmings and nonsense of yoga politics. I thought the yoga I loved was supposed to root me into my self surrounded by the collective energy in the yoga shala, yet instead, I felt like an unsteady pariah. I was grateful for my brief hiatus in India, but was ready for real life again.

By spring 2016 Johnny and I couldn't handle dementia's daily demands by ourselves anymore. Living in a country that doesn't have solid long-term solutions to financially support employees who need to take time off to care for their elderly dependents is abysmal. It was impossible to help your loved ones in the way you needed if you didn't have a lot of money. At the time, the state of California under the Paid Family Leave program provided up to 60 to 70 percent of the salary for people who had paid into state disability insurance (generally full-time employees, not freelancers like myself). However, the PFL program was only meant to cover short periods of time, usually only six to eight weeks off from work, and employers were not always required to hold a job during this leave. The system was stacked against the aging population, creating blockers to meaningful care by family members.

I caved in and hired a caregiver, Belinda, a family friend of Nancy's best friend. Nancy was an ally who loved Mom, and I trusted her judgment. "Your mom has lived here for as long as I've been here, almost twelve years. I've always adored her, she's so smiley and sweet. Years ago before her dementia, I used to love watching her walk to the clubhouse to get coffee. She tapped her foot back and forth and jumped over cracks, spilling coffee all over the place!" Nancy laughed. It took Nancy to remind me on a random, average day that Mom had stopped doing her OCD walk for years, something I was suddenly homesick for. A mannerism evaporated by dementia that distinguished my mother from the rest, robbing us of her idiosyncrasies.

I felt the hot sting of tears in my nose. "Thanks Nancy, for always looking out for her. I hope she never wanders out of the house, we won't be able to come back from that."

"I didn't think this was a big deal, but two weeks ago I saw your mom outside the front gate as I was driving in. I asked her if she was lost, but she just stared at me. So then I asked her to get in my car and I drove her into the complex. I noticed she had her house keys with her so I figured she knew what she was doing."

"Nancy, you should have told me! If you ever see that again, please tell me. What if you haven't driven by to see that?!"

"She seemed coherent, just confused about where the entrance to the building was. I told Barbara and Sergio who live right by your mom and they promised to call you if this happens again. Their apartment faces the path to the gate, so they see everything," Nancy said, trying to calm my swelling anxiety. "Belinda is very good, just loud and opinionated. She has six kids and has plenty of caregiving experience."

Nancy was right, Belinda was an opinionated loudmouth who got her lips filled and face botoxed. She charged way too much for the very little time she spent with my mom and refused to negotiate on her rate or availability: eight hundred dollars for six hours a week, Monday to Thursday. She said she was "worth it." She worked an hour on Mondays and Wednesdays and two hours on Tuesdays and Thursdays. Johnny was paying her so I didn't think much about it until I saw how little she was actually engaging with Mom. I was a control freak about how I wanted my mom to be taken care of, and Belinda, though she cared about my mom, resisted my requests. However, she had a knack for getting my mom into the shower even when she kicked and screamed. One time my mom fought Belinda so hard about taking off her clothes, her next-door neighbors went over to do a welfare check. Belinda called me for help, but my mom grabbed the phone.

"She try kill me! It's too cold! I don't want to take shower. I'm already did!" my mom screamed at the top of her lungs in a pitch only sea creatures could hear.

"Sunny, your mom is having a really bad day. I don't

know how to get her in the shower without being hauled away by the police. Today's Thursday, can you bathe her tomorrow or over the weekend, and I'll make sure I bathe her next week?" Belinda shouted in the background.

"Belinda, she's sundowning, give her some space. She'll come around in ten minutes, she always does. Don't panic because your stress will rub off on her."

"She won't take her morning pills, either," Belinda added.

"Just finish what you need to do, then revisit the pills and bath before you leave."

I didn't budge on having my mom bathe at least twice a week because dementia brought on frequent UTIs when she wasn't drinking enough water or wiping correctly when she used the toilet. First the UTIs had come every two months, then it subsided to once every four to six months when I bathed her regularly and set cups of water in every room of her apartment: on her nightstand, near her rocking chair, on the bathroom counter by her toothbrush, in the kitchen by the phone, on the bookshelf in the hallway. Belinda wasn't going to sabotage my mom's record of being relatively UTI-free.

Belinda finally got a hold of the phone again because my mom had gone back to bed. "It just reminds me of the movie *The Notebook*, where the woman has such bad dementia she just screams all the time. I love your mom and it makes me real sad to see her like that character," Belinda said whimpering. She was losing it. I couldn't believe she had just compared my mom's illness to a fictional character's in a cloying movie like *The Notebook*. I wanted to burrow myself in the tiniest of holes.

"Can we be more serious here? She needs to be bathed

today. Gently bring it up to her in ten minutes. We're paying you a lot of money for you to rush out the door every day." I was losing it, too.

"Okay, I'll try my best, but I noticed your mom went poo in her underwear this morning."

20

An officer from the Rancho Cucamonga Police Department called me on a sweltering Friday morning in August 2018 as I was walking into physical therapy to rehab the herniated discs in my neck.

"Your mother was found wandering around about three miles east of her apartment. A Good Samaritan called us saying your mother looked lost. She kept chanting her home address, so I checked the utilities for her house and found your phone number. She has her purse and the only things in it are her house keys and two bananas."

"Is she okay?! Where is she now?! Can you give her some water? Thank god she remembered her address!" My heart pounded as the heat of stress stung me.

"She has her address written in her purse as well. That's good someone did that. I gave her some water on the ride back. She's quite happy. We're in front of her apartment now. I'm just going to do a quick check around her house to make sure everything's okay, is that alright?" the officer asked.

"Yes, of course. By happy, what do you mean?"

"She was beaming from ear to ear when I pulled into her complex so I saw that as a sign."

"My mom loves hospitals, firefighters, and cops. I have no idea why. Can I speak to her please?" My shoulders tensed, compressing the herniated discs some more.

As the officer handed my mom the phone, I heard laughter in the background.

"This man is so nice. Choego-ya!" Mom exclaimed, *number one*!

"Mom, you can't just leave your house! You could've gotten hurt or killed!" I shouted as though she understood.

"Aigoo, gwenchana," she said. In that second, I recognized my mother, the one who had her wits about her, the one who used to calm me down when I was upset and told me things were going to be okay. "Here, talk to the nice man again."

"I used her keys to open her apartment door and did a quick check. Everything looks okay. But please consider doing something about this wandering. I don't think something like this just stops happening. Have you considered a nursing home?" the officer asked.

"Thanks for your suggestion, officer. I appreciate everything you did to get her back home safely. My mom has dementia, but I have a system, and she has other caregivers besides me. Today was just a fluke. What's all that laughing in the background?" Dementia had crossed the Rubicon and I was still digging my way into the hole of denial.

"Your mom's neighbors are all out wondering why I'm here. I think she's in good hands, some folks are giving her coffee and cookies. But just think about what I said. Your mother is very sweet and trusting, it makes for a dangerous situation if she wanders off and ends up in the wrong hands."

I went back into the physical therapy office and told my therapist everything like a crazy person, to which he said, "bummer." I had been resisting this very moment for years, but now I didn't know how much longer my mom could live alone. I selfishly wasn't ready for her to be in a nursing home or an assisted living environment. I often heard about people becoming more confused living outside of their homes, which ultimately led to further decline. Up until that point Belinda had worked for us for nearly two years, with Fridays off. We had started to lock horns about how she needed to be better about showing up on time and spending less time texting me or her family when she was supposed to be interacting with my mother. We needed to do something differently.

The next day, Abby and I installed security cameras in Mom's living room and bedroom to watch her every move and catch her if she wandered off again. I let Belinda know about the cameras and fired her the following week. On Belinda's last day I watched her trim my mom's fingernails on the kitchen table through the security camera app on my phone. Belinda then applied bright electric blue eye shadow, hot pink blush, and red lipstick on my mom. She looked like a manic clown. I listened to Belinda sing-song: "Hi my name is Belinda and I love all my seniors!" while she held my mom's face next to hers in front of her phone. Belinda seemed to be exploiting my mom to promote her caregiving services on social media. I called Belinda and told her to remove the makeup and any online posts. I feared she'd be vindictive and hurt my mom so I left it at that and looked forward to erasing her from our lives.

I hired another caregiver through In-Home Supportive Services, a state program that offered and paid for caregiving services for seniors so they could stay at home. The program was a godsend. Because my mom qualified for extra hours of care due to her needs, Diane, the new caregiver, could work more and get paid decently for it. Diane was a tall, cheerful Black woman who, at forty-eight, shocked me when she said she had three grandchildren because she looked no older than thirty-five. Right out of the gate she talked about her church and faith. I suspected she wanted me to know she was on the straight and narrow and that she expected that of us, too.

"When you called me I worried about working with your family because I could tell you weren't Black. I've encountered a lot of racism caring for people who aren't Black so I had to make sure you knew who I was," Diane admitted on her first day on the job.

"I understand and want you to feel safe with us. Rancho is still kind of the Wild West at times. I just want someone kind, honest, and patient to care for my mom. I knew you'd be a good fit since you take care of your own parents. Can you bring your grandchildren over to meet my mom? She loves kids."

Diane worked three hours in the morning and two hours at night Monday through Friday, which was much more helpful compared to Belinda's anemic six-hour-a-week schedule. This gave Diane plenty of time to cook, clean, and bathe and groom my mom. Belinda had made me skeptical of future caregivers, but Diane restored my faith. She learned to give my mom space when she was sundowning, and directly interacted with her with conversation and singing. Diane was smiley like my mom and worked hard. I told her I had security cameras in the house to monitor my mom's activities, to which Diane laughed and said, "Good, I got nothing to hide!"

"You Are My Sunshine" was my mom's favorite song around this time so Diane sang along with my mom whenever she belted it out loudly, sometimes on an endless loop. It seemed to be the go-to song for people with cognitive impairment, though I had no idea where my mom had gotten it from because she had never regularly sung it to us as kids. Mom messed up the words at times, but Diane and I never had the heart to correct her when she sang so earnestly. When she got bored with it, she taught Diane Korean folk songs like "Arirang," the unofficial anthem of Korea. Diane texted me daily updates that they "got their sing on."

Most people are addicted to social media, but I was addicted to home protection products to watch my mother's every move. I was stuck in a continuous loop of worrying that something disastrous was going to happen, so Wyze Cam, the camera we installed, was a trusty confidant and tattletale. I depended on Wyze when my mom was home alone for an hour or more, which was the witching hour of dangerous dementia activity. Wyze let me know when Mom moved the perishables in the refrigerator to kitchen cabinet drawers or left the refrigerator door open, so I'd call her to close it and inform Diane or Johnny to move them back. Wyze let me know when she was about to open the door to a stranger, so I'd call to stop her. It was amazing my mom complied at all. Her doctors said she had "sweet dementia," the shallow diagnosis I regurgitated to people to emphasize that she was not violent or hostile. I slept with the Wyze Cam app open in case Mom opened the door to an imagined old friend at 3 a.m.

Wyze Cam was an illuminating portal to my mom's brain. It snitched and revealed that she only ate the small chunks of dark chocolate in the trail mix. I was relieved to see that one of my mom's eccentricities lingered even in the midst of advancing dementia: as she sat in her rocking chair, she'd pull at the bridge of her nose with her right thumb and index finger—the ritual of manually contouring her nose still poked through her memory banks. On hot days Wyze revealed my mother taking off her clothes except for her underwear and climbing on chairs to shut off the vents when the air conditioner blew too cold because she had forgotten how to use the thermostat. It was a careful dance. I'd wait until she got off the chair to call her so she wouldn't risk falling to answer the phone. Or I'd catch her bringing her shoes from the hallway closet to the front door to leave the apartment so I'd call her to redirect her, telling her I was going to be there in five minutes. It worked most of the time.

"No, I have to make breakfast for my children, they're going to leave for school soon!" my mom shouted in Korean.

"Umma, I'm your child. I ate breakfast, thank you for making it. It was delicious." I was a character making a cameo in her new reality.

"No, you're lying. I'm going!" And she'd take off. Besides cooking breakfast for her children, my mom also had to "meet her family in the mountains for a picnic," or she "needed to go home." Sometimes she'd put her shoes away and settle back in the house or sometimes she'd put up a fight for ten minutes, telling me she had to go to school and find her books. She was tormented with the anxiety of having to do something or be somewhere.

My backup plan was to call my mom's downstairs neighbors, Barbara or Sergio, who'd stop her from leaving the apartment complex. Barbara and Sergio were the paragon of human kindness. They loved my mom, and luckily, were always home. Sergio in fact volunteered at an Alzheimer's facility.

"Sunny, I have your mom here. I'm going to make her a cup of coffee, and Sergio is going to walk her back up soon,"

Barbara said.

"Thank you, Barbara! You're a lifesaver. I'd like to keep my mom home for as long as she can, but it's only possible because of people like you, Sergio, Diane, and Nancy."

Abby told me I needed a moratorium from my phone since I was on it so much, but my mom's life depended on it. I was a conditioned lab animal: each time the Wyze Cam app buzzed with a notification of detected movement, and if I didn't already have my phone in my hand, I'd nervously check the replay. I took my phone with me to the bathroom at gatherings when I couldn't blatantly stare at the live video stream in a room full of people. I slept with it, I pulled over when driving to check my mom's activities in real time. Wyze Cam was my co-captain.

Wyze also helped me monitor what Johnny was doing. I told Johnny once to heat up some japchae I had bought for my mom. He served her a portion, but I caught him eating the rest of it in the dark hallway. I called him immediately to tell him to stop eating the food meant for her when he was able to get his own. He was amazed I could see him eating in the dark; he didn't know Wyze had night vision! He swiftly put the remaining japchae in the refrigerator. A few weeks later I caught him shouting at my mom because she had eaten a few slices of his bread, then later for having an accident on the bathroom floor. I called the police who went over to do a welfare check. They asked for Johnny's ID and checked on my mom. She was napping but seemed to enjoy the company after the female officer woke her up to ask how she was doing. This scared the hell out of Johnny and he stopped raising his voice at her for at least four solid months. I became my mom's shrewdest advocate, especially when it came to protecting her from her own son. Johnny was forty-eight and still living with her, dismally broke from gambling debts, paying Mom's rent and utilities, and saving money to pay her back. He couldn't afford living in LA and wanted "to stay with Mom to make sure she ate and took her pills." I couldn't argue because he was helping her. And me.

I got twitchy when the Wyze notifications went quiet for longer than ten minutes. I noticed during what I considered to be Mom's late-stage moderate or early-stage advanced dementia moments of motionless staring into space, like all her attention was thrown at an infinite vortex. It usually happened at the bookshelf across the room from Wyze, which housed various souvenirs: the encyclopedia set my parents bought for us when I started junior high, a weathered globe my parents bought the same year, the kind that twirled on its axis and all that remained was its once vibrant colors that marked borders. Next to that, a miniature pair of hand-painted Dutch clogs I had bought from the Netherlands in 2002, and two mini wooden airbrushed surfboards that Mom and I had brought back from Oahu. She kept both souvenirs all those years. During her bouts of staring, I imagined she wondered what these mementos were, her hippocampus trying to organize data by some complex mingling of ideas and special connections, but sputtering. Instead of becoming flustered by confusion, she would startle out of her trance and shuffle to the bedroom, hunched over, hands clasped behind her back.

The other spectacularly ordinary thing I witnessed was that whenever she got out of bed to use the bathroom, she'd make the entire bed. Not just the crumpled corner she slept in, but the entire bed, just to walk fifteen feet to use the bathroom and return five minutes later to crawl back into that freshly made corner. Her true fastidious essence was still there, and it was heartbreaking to watch because everything else was fading.

Glued to a home security app on my phone with the glare of a 2.75" by 4.75" screen ricocheting off my face, I could observe a glimmer of my mom's old self, forty-five miles away. Right then and there I desperately wanted to tell her how much I missed our talks, arguments, laughs, regular trips to the Korean markets, and even her temper. I wanted to tell her how grateful I was to be her daughter and how much I loved her, before dementia took everything.

So I called her. "Umma, saranghaeyo. I love you, I love you, I love you."

"Oh yeah? I love you more, more, more, more, more!" my mom giggled.

"I want to take you to the Korean market to shop for food. We'll do that in LA, okay?"

"I want to see you, too. I'm going to cook dinner now. Thank you for you call me." I always loved "thank you for you call me" when we were about to hang up. It started happening right before she was diagnosed with cognitive impairment so those words belonged to her, not dementia.

I knew she wasn't going to cook dinner. Instead, she peered outside the blinds of her front window, swaying and chanting to herself for about five minutes, then walked to the front door to neatly arrange her and Johnny's shoes. Then she walked to the coffee table and pulled out all of Johnny's letters from debt collectors and organized them by size.

21

Things went well the first year with Diane on board. She'd show up with gifts like silk flowers that Mom put in a vase of water, and glittery cards that Mom opened and closed every day to catch a sparkle. I still stopped by once or twice a week to bathe my mom and drop off food and supplies. I took her to all of her doctors' appointments when health updates and medication changes needed to be directly communicated, and I let Diane take my mom for minor lab appointments. I continued to be a micromanaging control freak, but Diane was hardly the obnoxious know-it-all like Belinda was. I'd send Diane a long list of things to do; no two days were the same depending on whether there was laundry to do, blood to be drawn, urine to be collected, or groceries to be picked up. Monday and Wednesday were shower and errand days, Tuesday was shopping day, Thursday was laundry day, and Friday was cleaning day. After Diane left each day, I'd create notes for the following day and save it on my phone to fire off first thing the next morning like a dementia care missile. And even with the occasional all-caps instructions emphasizing importance and urgency, I'd still remind her of them, to which Diane would respond, "Are you referring to what you already put on the list for me to do today? In ALL CAPS?" I deserved her smart-ass answers; I had a difficult time giving up control and trust.

"Sunny, don't call me right now if you plan to," Diane shouted in hopes that I'd see or hear her on Wyze. I always did. I had a system of letting the app run while I had headphones on at work. I saw Diane's right hand on top of my mom's as she tried to maintain her grip on the handle of a frying pan. "Ms. Pak is not having a good day, she grabbed the hot frying pan from the stovetop when her Korean pancake was heating. She wants to throw it away. I'm trying to make sure she doesn't touch the hot pan with her other hand!"

I sat motionless and barely breathing watching the danger unfold on Wyze, while hearing my coworker typing furiously behind me. I was going into the office twice a week at my latest part-time fashion marketing job so I could see and feel the overpriced vintage apparel and accessories. Diane slowly walked my mom to the counter and placed the frying pan in the sink as my mom let go of her grip.

"I don't want to eat, I'm not hungry! Jibae-ga!" My mom screamed *go home* to Diane in Korean.

I waited until she was calm enough on her rocking chair to call Diane. "You're amazing, Diane! I don't know how you managed to do that without burning Mom or yourself!"

"She's having a really bad day and won't bathe or take her mornings meds. I'll check back in twenty minutes after I heat up her lunch. By the way, I keep forgetting to tell you: when I ask your mom to finish her lunch, she says, 'Lunchie?' Just thought I'd tell you that to lighten the mood. It's so cute."

"I grew up with lunchie," I laughed, deeply relieved and grateful that Diane was with us. "I'm so sorry, Diane, let's check back later so she doesn't feel pressured."

"I know this isn't my usual sunshine girl this morning. We all have bad days. I'll bust out 'Arirang' soon, ha!"

I complained to long-suffering Abby about my worry that

Mom's behavior was becoming increasingly unpredictable and dangerous. He thought she felt cooped up and wanted to take her out of her microcosm and drive her somewhere antithetical to Rancho Cucamonga—the ocean. Abby always had my mom's best interest at heart; he was her honorary Korean son-in-law. Since 2016 he had wanted to take my mom to visit Aunt Yun Hee and Aunt Young Soon in Torrance in case anything happened to her, or them. I was lucky he had the foresight because I was still bitter.

"It's shitty of them to stop calling their own sister or visiting her in Rancho, so we have to do the right thing and bring her to them," Abby said despite my complaints that it would take us nearly three or four hours roundtrip. "You have to do this for your mom . . . before anything happens. You'll regret it if your mom doesn't get this chance to see her deadbeat sisters."

Chance for what? I thought. Her sisters weren't the ones with dementia. They should have been the ones to go out of their way to visit or call their sister. But I wasn't betting on it. Aunt Young Soon's relationship with my mother was already strained from years of envy and competition. And since Aunt Yun Hee worked full-time as a manager at a Japanese restaurant at the age of seventy-two and was also Aunt Young Soon's primary caregiver, I couldn't be upset with her for being so flaky. Aunt Yun Hee, usually the happy-go-lucky one, had changed in the past four years. She was now short-fused, no doubt feeling her own mortality after sacrificing her entire adult life, out of duress, to care for her oldest sister. My mom told me years before dementia that Aunt Young Soon had intentionally scared Aunt Yun Hee's boyfriend away because she didn't want her younger sister to marry anyone; she wanted Yun Hee unencumbered so she could take care of her. I wasn't surprised but still stunned at how artful Aunt Young Soon's manipulation was. Meanwhile, she hesitated to pressure her own son, Steven, when it was Korean custom for the oldest son to take care of his parents.

Abby and I planned our road trip to Torrance two weeks later on the first weekend of May 2019.

"Oh my gosh, too many cars!" my mom exclaimed in the back seat as Abby and I laughed. She was so tiny, we could only see the top of her head from the rearview mirrors.

When we got to Torrance on a breezy morning, we stopped by the Korean Bell of Friendship in neighboring San Pedro. We hoped the enormous brass bell would rekindle some memories of Korea for my mom. But as we stood under the structure she stared at it in awe, then quickly remarked on the children playing around us. "Ba! Ba! Go-ma, ba!" *Look, look, look at the little ones!*

"Let's go up to them," my mom said enthusiastically, as though the children were small animals we could pet.

"No, umma, we can't just touch them. Their parents might get upset."

"Aigoo, gwenchana!" my mom said as she walked up to a toddler and waved hello. Their interaction became a two-minute back-and-forth of saying hello to one another. The little girl's parents laughed and told me my mom was adorable.

As we drove out of the park to head to Aunt Yun Hee's apartment, my mom pointed at the South Korean flags lining the exit and asked, "Igeo hanguk geoya?" *Is this Korean?*

"Nae, umma, hangug-eoyeyo." *Yes, Mom, it's Korean.*

Dementia was a series of thefts and surprises. I was used to the disease stealing my mom's vocabulary and language, as well as her understanding of how to do life. But I was stupefied by the things that sparked my mom's cognition or memory, like her profound love of children or her recognition of the South Korean flag.

But my mom didn't recognize her sisters when they greeted us outside their apartment building. "No, that's not Yun Hee," my mom said, visibly disturbed. This was one of the surprises. I was sure she'd recognize Aunt Yun Hee, her little emaciated three-year-old sister she'd carried on her shoulders to get more sympathy and food from the U.S. troops.

"Umma, that's Yun Hee, your sister."

"No!" my mom screamed and charged into the crowded parking lot.

I shouldn't have been disappointed. My mother hadn't seen her sisters in five years so how could she have been expected to know their aged faces?

"She would have recognized them if they bothered to visit," Abby whispered snidely as we followed my aunts toward the elevators to take us to their apartments. Aunt Yun Hee lived on the twelfth floor and Aunt Young Soon lived on the tenth. Their apartment was in a towering, ominous, tenement-style complex that overlooked San Pedro.

Aunt Young Soon could barely walk and refused to use a walker, so Abby stayed behind her in case she fell. My mom, Aunt Yun Hee, and I walked ahead of them.

"Why she lost her memory?"" I overheard Aunt Young Soon ask. I turned around to see her make a fist and motion to hit my mom on the back of the head.

"Why are you trying to hit her?" Abby asked.

"Because she lost her mind." Aunt Young Soon said to Abby. "She's always sad about her husband leaving her, it made her head crazy." This was the exact condescending pity my mom hadn't wanted to hear from her gossipy church friends about my dad leaving the house. I couldn't help but feel like Aunt Young Soon had schadenfreude about it, too. I was glad for a flitting moment that Mom couldn't understand Aunt Young Soon.

We all huddled in Aunt Yun Hee's tiny three-hundred-square-foot studio apartment. There was no inch of free space. Her bed touched the legs of her kitchen table, which grazed her armoire, which nestled up next to boxes of water and snacks from Costco. I felt a surge of smugness. My mom had searched tirelessly and secured a cozy, tree-lined apartment that her sisters always envied. I winked at my mom, who in turn flashed me a big, toothy smile.

We left to eat at a Korean restaurant while Aunt Young Soon stayed behind because her waddling was slow and painful. As we ate Aunt Yun Hee whispered to me, "I was so angry with your mom a few years ago. When I tried to pick her up to take her to Aunt Helen's house for Christmas, she refused to come even after we made plans."

"My mom has had dementia since 2012. Do you know what it is and what it does to someone's memory?" I glanced at my mom, who smiled politely as she ate and used the honorific generally set aside for strangers or someone older to offer Aunt Yun Hee some banchan. My mom had no idea who her sisters were, and I was beginning to think she thought Aunt Yun Hee was older than she was.

"She said her back was hurting, she didn't say she

forgot. Even then she should have come with me," my aunt insisted.

"Dementia causes anxiety, confusion, distress, and physical pain. I can't believe you made this about you. Is that why you stopped calling her?" I asked.

"No, I've been busy with work and taking care of your Aunt Young Soon. Now lazy Chan Mi is sick and she needs my help. I never have time for myself anymore. I wanted to call your mom. I'm sorry." Aunt Yun Hee looked away and changed the topic.

On the drive back to her apartment, I looked at my mom's resting smiley face through the passenger side-view mirror. I wondered when Aunt Yun Hee had given up on my mom. I had never had high hopes for Aunt Young Soon or Aunt Chan Mi, but I always thought Aunt Yun Hee would be different. I thought she would check in regardless of how busy and tired she was. Still, I was glad we had visited them. I would have regretted not bringing them together, even though the recognition wasn't there on either side. I suddenly worried if my mom had forgotten me.

"Umma, naega nuguya?"

"Shodey, na dongsaeng," my mom answered. *Shirley, my younger sister.*

"Mom, how old are you?"

"Sixty-five," she said, shaving off some years.

Asking my mom repeatedly what her name was or who I was allowed me to check in with her mind. It gave me a sense of comfort, the same comfort my mother may have felt doing her OCD walk. Sometimes I was her younger sister, sometimes I was her daughter. Sometimes I took it personally because I didn't want to be her younger sister, but most times it was heartbreakingly endearing.

"Umma, ireum moya?"

"Song, Yong Cha."

"Na umma ttal-ijana," *I'm your daughter, you know,* I said using my finest emotional K-drama tone.

"Oh yeah? That's good!" my mom said with a flourishing frisson.

"Umma, I love you, I love you, I love you!"

"I love you more, more, more, more, more! Oh my gosh, look at the cars, too many cars!"

22

A few weeks later, just after Mother's Day, I took my mom to lunch at the Cheesecake Factory, situated in a mega outdoor mall near Aunt Helen's house. Abby had a long-standing joke about making my mom a kimchi cheesecake. Every time he saw her he'd threaten to make her one: "Yong Cha, my lifelong dream is to make you a kimchi cheesecake, because Jews love New York–style cheesecake and Koreans love kimchi, so I want to combine both stereotypes. I'm going to start with a graham cracker crust, then add a layer of sweet cream cheese, then finally pour the spicy kimchi on it as the topping." Without fail Mom got the goofiness and laughed hysterically, saying how disgusting that sounded. So, Abby suggested I take my mom to the Cheesecake Factory for fun.

As we walked up the sidewalk toward the bright yellow Tenji blocks, the bright yellow tactile paving meant to help the visually impaired, I stopped to look for oncoming traffic. I usually walked arm in arm with my mom, but I needed her to stand in front of me to watch for the cars driving behind us. The second I let go of her arm, one of her Vans slip-ons got stuck in the Tenji block tiles. I heard a dense thunk as she fell hard on the right side of her face and wrist, the same wrist that had been surgically botched over thirty years ago. I felt my legs buckle as I landed next to her side, screaming for help.

An Asian woman ran up to us and dropped to her knees. She lifted up my mom's torso and leaned it against her chest and thighs.

"Are you Korean? I saw everything. I just called 911," the woman said.

"Yes, are you?"

"I'm half Korean, but I can communicate."

The woman asked my mom in Korean where her pain was, to which my mom screamed in English, "My arm!" My thoughts were scattered, but they homed in on the fact that this half Korean woman's Korean speaking skills were infinitely better than mine, and that she was communicating with my mother the way I should have been. That this kind stranger in the right place at the right time could speak so easily with my mom made me burn with regret. I couldn't understand the absurdity.

A young family with a toddler rushed over to ask if we needed any help, and in the midst of my mom's howling, she stopped, made eye contact with the little boy, smiled coyly, then went back to crying. It was surreal. In the middle of my mom's suffering, she had momentarily seen the joy of a small child. She was too good for this world.

The paramedics rushed my mom to a regional medical center, the only facility within a twenty-mile radius that could do a CT scan of her brain to make sure there were no clots or hemorrhaging. There were none. My mom had come through again. But her right wrist looked broken and deformed from the swelling. The ER doctor and nurse administered nerve blocks and pain medication so that they could manually reset her fractured right wrist. They wrapped her arm in a splint, but she wiggled out of it and pointed to her arm, yelling, "Sick!" They wrapped her arm three more times and she wiggled out again each time, until the opiates kicked in and she fell hard asleep.

I couldn't handle the allostatic load anymore. The driving back and forth between LA and Rancho, rushing to multiple doctors' appointments and exams, making nonstop trips to stores and carrying heavy bags of food and supplies, obsessing over Wyze, fearing disaster, fighting with Johnny. I was drained by both a mental and physical lassitude that depleted all of me.

Beyond the drawn cubicle curtain at the hospital, I heard a manic flurry of activity across from my mother's bed: equipment and oxygen machines were being shuffled around, and the frenzied footsteps of doctors and nurses running in and out of the ER intensified. I overheard a staff physician say a man's head had been hit by a car on the 15 freeway; not his body, only his head. The same staff physician then quickly excoriated a med student who was taking too long to administer the pain medication. I was indifferent about how this preposterous set of events could have unfolded as I solipsistically turned my attention back to my confused eighty-one-year-old mother. The room became quiet and still as I looked down at her frail, once knowing body. I wept. I wept so unreservedly that an ER nurse tending to the man's head across the way came over and peeped through our curtain to see what was happening. I brushed her off and wept some more.

Johnny had left just a day before for Paris to work the FIFA Women's World Cup. He was going to be gone for a month. So I planned on staying with my mom in Rancho for a few weeks during her recovery. On the way home that evening I stopped by CVS to buy a toothbrush for me and more elastic bandages in case my mom decided to peel off her hospital dressing again. She had a big blue blossoming bruise around her right eye and a chipped front tooth, for which I'd already made a dental appointment to get fixed at the hospital. We crashed on her bed almost immediately. At five the next morning I felt the bed stir. I looked over at my mom who had removed her splint again and folded the bandages neatly next to her. The splint was set perfectly straight on her nightstand.

"No!" I screamed, oblivious to the fact that it was five in the morning. "Why did you take the bandages off?!"

My mom was agitated. "Aigoo, waegurae?"

I had fallen asleep with my clothes on so I quickly dressed my mom and drove like a lunatic to the ER. One of the few benefits of Rancho and its surrounding cites was that they weren't densely populated, so wait times at hospitals could be astoundingly short. We waited only fifteen minutes. But instead of going to the ER, the staff took us to the main hospital where there was a gaggle of young orthopedists ready to assess my mom.

"We're going to try to reset the bone again, but if she keeps taking off the dressing we'll have to admit her for three days and send her to a rehab center where she can recover," a tall Indian doctor with braces told me. He was so young, I was worried if he was qualified for the job at all.

"Please help with the pain, she's making faces and doesn't understand why she needs to wear the splint. She has dementia," I responded.

I watched the doctor and his aides hoist her right arm up and hitch it in order to set the bone in its correct position, at least three times. My heart hit the ground as I watched my mom writhing in pain even with the help of a long-lasting nerve block and more opiates.

"Let's stop, she's in too much pain!" I screamed.

"One more pull," the doctor ordered, and I heard a snap. It was over. They wrapped my mom's arm again, but this time in a soft cast. "Let's see how this holds after a week. If the bone is out of alignment, she may need to have surgery. In the meantime, I think it's best to keep her here for a few days to make sure she doesn't remove her cast again."

Maxed out on stress, I surrendered to the unforgiving, unsympathetic gods and circumstances that were never going to offer me a reprieve from the demands of caregiving. Yielding, I felt some relief knowing Mom was going to have round-the-clock care at a hospital for three days so I could go home and rest for the same amount of time.

Instead, the next day, I called a memory care facility in Glendale and asked if they had any Korean-speaking residents, to which the administrator mewled, "No, but we do have a nice Chinese lady, and a Filipino man and his Japanese wife live here, too. I'm sure they'll all get along." A friend recommended I call some Koreatown doctors to get recommendations for the best Korean-speaking assisted living facilities in LA County that specialized in memory care. Each doctor's office hands down recommended an assisted living facility called Golden View Health Care, which was only six miles away from my house, not the forty-five to Rancho. Aunt Yun Hee even said some people at her church had family members living at Golden View who vouched for its quality of care. Golden View was also 100 percent Korean-speaking, which was critical if my mom needed to communicate any discomfort or pain. I visited three hours later and knew my mom would love its tidiness, Pergo flooring that Koreans adored for its ability to resist stains and messes, and smell of jjigae. Each bedroom was clean and bright, illuminated by warm, natural light, and had the capacity for two residents, maximum. The armoires were modern with a pine-colored finish that could only hail from IKEA. Their website boasted that each bed came with comfortable, firm futons that were turned each week. *Mom is going to love it*, I thought. I already did.

The owner, Jenny, had a short, severe, angled bob and looked to be in her early or mid-sixties. She told me there was a long wait list for admittance that would most likely take six months to a year to get through, but that she'd prioritize my mom due to the urgency of our situation since Mom lived so far away. When I asked about the type of memory care Golden View offered and described my mom's daily needs, Jenny unquestionably declared that her staff was well trained to care for her grooming, bathing, mental stimulation, and wandering. Jenny even mentioned that they had a special wing on the second floor that required key code access to leave for residents with wandering dementia.

The hallways didn't smell of urine and none of the residents were carrying dolls. In fact, I was told that Mom, at eighty-one, would be one of the youngest residents, while most of the halmeonis and harabeojis were in their late eighties or early nineties. Most of the residents were ambulatory or used sleek, fancy modern walkers that transformed into stools with a flick of the wrist, because their children were involved in their parents' care and bought them devices with design in mind. Seniors roamed around freely to socialize, but under constant supervision. It was like her apartment community in Rancho, just more clinical with nurses, med techs, and caregivers making their rounds. For the first time since the beginning of her dementia, I was thrilled at the prospect of my mother socializing with others with similar backgrounds, eating three nutritious Korean meals daily, and being cared for round the clock. I had never thought I'd ever be ready to send my mom to an assisted living facility until I saw Golden View. For seven years I had existed under a boulder of caregiving and worry, without a well-rounded understanding of what an assisted living facility could offer.

I knew assisted living wasn't going to be like home, and that the change in environment would confuse her more, but it fit the needs of who my mom was becoming. I was excited about the idea of living only six miles away from Mom, finally in the same county. I'd visit almost every day to spend meaningful time with her—time that wasn't rushed due to competing doctors' appointments or pressured by a need to find more work after losing freelance contracts. I'd pick her up to go to nearby Korean markets, restaurants, and movie theaters, or drive her to my house for dinners, walks, or to spend the night. But I was getting ahead of myself, remembering the six-month-to-year-long wait list for admittance. I put my mom's name on the list anyway.

"Your mom is having the time of her life in physical therapy, Sunny!" Diane exclaimed from the hospital as I was driving home from Golden View. "She's singing 'You Are My Sunshine' nonstop and cracking up the entire staff." I had felt bad asking Diane to visit my mom at the hospital on her day off, but I wanted to make sure she was doing well while I visited some facilities.

"Thank you for visiting her, Diane. We're driving over tonight to see her. She loves hospitals, and maybe the attention, too. The plan is to send my mom to a rehab center for a few weeks to help her with recovery. I was told her gait is off. She's going to need daily physical therapy for her right wrist and hip. The physical therapist at the hospital gave her a walker but she walks right by it, she doesn't know what it's for. I'll call you when we get closer to her release date to see if you'll be available, okay?"

Sierra Rehabilitation Center was ten minutes away from my mom's house. It was clean and smelled of mashed potatoes and Pier 1 Imports candles. Luckily, the marketing manager, Catherine, was a friendly, enthusiastic Korean-speaking woman who was able to communicate easily with Mom. She also happened to be fancy the way Korean women can be wearing a billowy, pleated nude-pink blouse, skinny designer jeans, and four-inch Balenciaga ankle boots. Her makeup was entrancingly applied using layers of dewy cushion foundation and hydrating face mists, along with lilting cat eyes, fanning eyelash extensions, and a perfect lip-stained rose pout. Her sable-colored hair seemed straightened using the Korean Magic Straight Perm because it didn't look fried with flyaways, just pressed flat like sheets of metal. She was glamorous in a K-drama kind of way, and had probably never been called "ajumma" before.

"Your mom doesn't even seem like she has dementia. She's very pleasant and takes direction well," Catherine said on my mom's first day there.

"That's why it's been difficult knowing whether I need to move her somewhere else where she can get more help. She's still the same person, but also different, if you know what I mean."

"I know what you mean. It's one of the hardest decisions, Sunny. My grandmother had Alzheimer's and it devastated us. We eventually sent her to a nursing home when she kept trying to leave the house. I can't imagine how you handle everything as her main caregiver. We have a huge family and still couldn't take care of her."

I wished I had the support of Catherine's large network. Instead I had an unreliable brother with a gambling addiction who sometimes yelled at his own mother when he was irritated, and an extended family who didn't call. I thought about what it meant to be filial, the virtuous duty my mom had instilled in me by telling me to buy a house and have children so she could move in and take care of them, so that I, in turn, could take care of her. To her, this was an honorable life. I was now caring for my mom, but hardly the way she or I had intended.

I stopped by the rehab center every other day. One morning I walked into their activities room as Eminem's "The Real Slim Shady" soared from the speakers. My mom was at the front, pumping both fists up in the air. Esther, the activities coordinator, was conducting the patients in a seated, choreographed upper body workout. My mom rolled her shoulders forward and backward, then looked over at me and flashed a big smile, which mollified the intensity of her bruised face and chipped front tooth.

I'd never thought I'd ever witness my mom enjoying herself in a senior communal setting at a physical rehabilitation center. Before my mom had gotten dementia, she wouldn't have been caught dead at a senior center where she was the only

Korean woman because she was slightly antisocial and very insecure about her English. She even stopped socializing at the Korean Presbyterian church she had attended for over ten years because she didn't like the gossip. But now with cognitive impairment, a bruised right eye, a chipped tooth, a fractured right wrist, and a sore hip, my mom was grooving happily to Eminem. If I hadn't seen it with my own eyes, nothing in the world would have made me believe it.

I took my mom to two orthopedists for opinions on surgery since her wrist was still causing her pain. The first one was an insensitive asshole who said, "Your mother is eighty-one with dementia, is it even worth it?"

The second surgeon was half the age of the first and much more ambitious. He said surgery was the only option because without it the bones in her wrist and hand wouldn't heal correctly, causing a painful deformity. Dr. Ahn was also Korean American and couldn't speak a lick of Korean, but it didn't matter because he was respectful and had a solid reputation. A couple of weeks later my mom had two small pins implanted in her right wrist to stabilize the joint. I was terrified of her undergoing general anesthesia at her age, but the anesthesiologist told me he would give her a larger dose of a localized nerve block and less general anesthesia. When she woke up in groggy good spirits, I wanted to hug the anesthesiologist like I had hugged her gastroenterologist after her successful colonoscopy.

I drove my mom back to Sierra Rehab Center and that evening several nurses stopped by her room before their shift to make sure she was okay. Mom was adored by the staff. When I called later that night to check in on her the nurses told me she was sitting at the front desk answering the phones, organizing stacks of paper and stray pens, and singing "You Are My Sunshine." I heard a roar of laughter in the background.

"Why isn't she tired?" I asked Eliza, one of the kindest nurses I had ever met.

"I don't know, but she sits up here with us until midnight sometimes. She thinks she's working, it's so cute. We love giving your mother our full attention, she's pure joy. I'm going to be so sad when she goes home."

"If she gets hungry, can you give her a snack? She didn't eat much today."

"Of course, we have peanut butter sandwiches, yogurt, and fruit for her if she gets hungry. Here's your mom." The laughter and clapping in the background amplified as my mom finished singing "Que será, será" with a flourishing *dun dun dun na.*

"Yoboseyo?" my mom said.

"Hi umma, how are you feeling?"

"I'm fine. I'm busy working right now. Thank you for you call me. Jeonhwa kkeuneulkkoya?" My mom had said she was going to hang up the phone in that peculiar way Koreans end phone conversations without ever saying goodbye.

Mom felt better almost immediately after the surgery. The cast took up most of her arm, spanning from just under her armpit to her hand so there was no way she would have been able to get through the carapace to remove it. Her walking and balance improved after nearly two months of physical therapy, five days a week. However, my mom's room was across from the front desk, so the chatter, alarms, and phones kept her up at night. She was exhausted and wanted to go home, nearly busting out of the rehab center on three occasions, but it was easy for the staff to redirect her back to the front desk where the nurses disorganized some pens and papers for her to reorganize. Eliza said my mom roamed around the facility and gardens, or joined activities during the day, and was rarely in the room she shared with a pleasant Black woman named Portia, who also had dementia. Every time Portia saw my mother and me together, she said, "It's so nice to see you again, my dears. Let's have tea together later today."

Mom was finally discharged in mid-July. Johnny was scheduled to return from Paris soon afterward, so I was relieved to be getting the extra help. I was still conflicted about any possible plans of moving her out of her home—it was never going to feel right for her, or me. On the one hand, I felt horrible for wanting her to stay at Sierra Rehab a bit longer because it freed up some of my time and energy. It was an unanticipated awakening that Mom actually enjoyed the activities and attention at the rehab center where I knew she was safe, well fed, and happy. On the other hand, fun activities were not the same as challenging caregiving and I was concerned my mom's agitation and confusion would increase with a drastic change of environment. I was also nervous about giving up too much control over her daily care needs. I knew I'd have to make difficult long-term decisions about her future sooner rather than later, but still struggled to seriously consider an assisted living facility, especially when Catherine told me how fervently my mom wanted to go home during her last few days at Sierra Rehab.

"Sunny, your mom was the darling of the show yesterday!" Catherine stopped to tell me on my mom's last day.

"Esther was having a sing-along, and all of a sudden your mom started singing this old Korean folk song I've never heard before. Everyone in the room literally surrounded her and when she stopped to look around, she lit up and smiled from ear to ear. I've never seen her smile so big. There were a couple of occasions this week when she fought with us about wanting to go home, but we still love her so much. I'm sad to see her go."

I'm sad to see her go, too, I thought. "Thank you so much, Catherine. She really had a great time here. It shows me that if I need to move her in the future, she may be okay with it."

"It's a hard decision, like it was with my grandmother. But we had to think of her safety first, and you have to do what's right for your mom." Catherine's impeccable eyebrows sloped with sympathy.

"By the way, how did my mom remove her cast? I was told she did."

"Her arm atrophied, and she removed all the cotton from inside the cast and slipped right out of it," Catherine chortled.

"That's my girl!" I laughed.

23

There was no adjustment period when we got back to my mom's apartment. She would always know her home and behaved like she had never left. After I bathed her she slept for nearly ten hours straight as I ran her errands, prepared her food, and cleaned. Rancho was always sweltering in the summer, so I bought my mom two cotton short-sleeved dresses at Target that she could easily lift up to use the bathroom since her arm was still sore. I also bought a few loose cotton capri pants and billowy tops that she could easily get in and out of.

Johnny returned from his work trip one day later and requested two weeks off so I could go home and rest before her doctors' appointments resumed the following week. I couldn't believe I was happy for Johnny to be back.

Johnny was more patient with my mom after her fall; he had also probably accepted that Wyze would always rat him out. Diane returned to work as well—things were officially back to normal. Despite being thrilled that my mom was safe at home again, the familiar anticipatory dreading soon started to clamber up my throat again. *What if Mom wanders out again? What if she falls again? What if there's an earthquake and nobody is there to help her evacuate?*

The summer flew by. Abby and I took my mom to see *The Lion King* because he was convinced she'd enjoy Disney animation brought to life by Dolby Surround and oversized, plush La-Z-Boy chairs in amphitheater-like movie theaters. A year before we had taken her to see *Crazy Rich Asians* where the

Singaporean cityscape, lights, gaggle of children, and beautiful people mesmerized her. When "Can't Help Falling in Love" played at a wedding scene, her deeply entrenched memories of her early twenties and Elvis opened the floodgates to her soul. She sang along loudly and completely out of tune with the movie while her elevated legs danced.

Before *The Lion King*, we took her to dinner at a clattery gastropub across from the theater, which she didn't seem to enjoy even with the onion rings and screaming kids that normally made her laugh. She looked anxious. When I took her to use the bathroom before the movie, I noticed her underwear was soiled with poo. "Shit!" I screeched, unamused by the pun. Her accident explained her agitation at dinner. My mom wasn't able to communicate her discomfort or frustration so it revealed itself with visible angst. I covered her underwear with as much toilet paper as I could so she didn't have to sit in her waste for two hours. I sat quietly in the theater watching Abby and my mom drift away to sleep, worried people could smell her accident. Luckily there was no trace of odor, and I didn't have it in me to care anymore. I sat in the dark theater lit up by talking animated lions, cubs, and hyenas in front of a vast African landscape, and I sobbed.

When we got back to my mom's house Abby waited for me in the car because Johnny was there. Abby had no respect for him after he stole my mom's money and didn't want to risk fighting in front of her.

"Johnny, Mom had a huge accident at the theater. I need your help," I said, panicked.

"What do you want me to do, aren't you going to get her in the shower?" he said, dissociating himself with chips and a

Big Gulp from 7-Eleven.

Mom resisted getting into the bathtub. Since 2016, she had gained about twelve pounds on her four-foot-eleven frame due to her cravings for carbs and sweets, which was a dangerous side effect of dementia. At the time, my mom was borderline diabetic. I read that diabetes in dementia patients may be caused by their predilections for heavier foods with intense flavor, like treacly sweets and greasy fries, mostly because they don't experience the same flavors as they age. This is caused by the atrophying of the frontal and temporal lobes of the brain, the parts of the brain responsible for self-restraint in our diet. The extra weight made her robust and strong, enabling her to forcefully yank away from my attempts to hold her hand. I wanted to burn her soiled underwear with a vengeance, but the vacant, confused look on my mom's face reminded me to defend her, even from myself. I was fueled by rage and determined to have no trace of dementia on any piece of her clothing. So, I detached the showerhead and power-sprayed her underwear until most of the feces was gone, then I got down on my knees and handwashed the underwear until the large stain disappeared. I defused my mom's agitation with a reliable inside joke—similar to kimchi cheesecake—we'd make to ease the moment: "Umma, your bo-ji is dirty, so we need to wash it. A clean bo-ji is a happy bo-ji." My mom erupted in celebratory laughter because the word *bo-ji* cannot be said without barreling over. It was the one word that my mom lost control over. I even taught *bo-ji* to Diane, who used it to try to disarm my mom when she refused to bathe; it always worked. After she surrendered out of fatigue, I quickly bathed her and put her in bed.

Then I took my roiling fury at dementia out on the bathtub, scouring the bottom, sides, and railings with Clorox disinfecting scrub. I moved on to clean the bathroom floor until it was as bright and white as the bleached teeth in West Hollywood. *Don't waste one grain of rice.* I heard my mom's once coherent lesson in my head, which I thought would tickle her to have engraved on her headstone, as I punishingly sanitized every surface. I threw her clothes and once soiled underwear in the laundry machine, not to be wasted.

The last few months of 2019 flew by. Johnny usually traveled for work during the holidays, so my mom stayed at our house during the weeks of Thanksgiving and Christmas. It was fun spoiling her with big breakfasts at home, taking her out for resplendent dinners at Pace in Laurel Canyon or Korean restaurants in the belly of K-Town, and meandering around the Hollywood Farmers' Market where Mom jauntily walked up to fruit and vegetable vendors and pounded on their tables, "Hey, hey, hey, I know you!" The vendors, charmed by her ebullience, never stared at her with their mouths agape like she had four noses as some Korean people did when she walked up to them to say hi to their children. I noticed she didn't fight us to go home as she usually did in the past when she spent the night at our house. Her paranoia dissipated while her curiosity grew. Dementia brought out people's true natures, and my mom's was full of wonderment and light.

"Sun Yong-a, let's sing 'I Went to Your Wedding!'" my mom said in Korean after breakfast Thanksgiving morning.

Abby found the Patti Page version on YouTube and put headphones on my mom so she could listen in hi-fi. My mom mispronounced some of the lovesick lyrics, but she crooned loudly with an extravagantly tender facial expression, stressing and elongating the wrong words, and humming some of the lines she forgot. She sang completely out of tune with such earnestness that nothing else mattered in that moment. Abby and I sat next to her on the couch, giggling gleefully. She was oblivious, lost in the past.

For lunch we stopped to get tteokbokki at a neon-lit restaurant before catching *Frozen II* with Korean subtitles at CGV. We didn't intend to infantilize my mother with more PG-rated Disney movies, we just thought she'd love the animated musical fantasy film with its cheekiness and charm. It was cold for LA so I swaddled my mom in leggings, two sweaters, a down coat, thick wool gloves, a wool beanie cap, and a long wool scarf that wrapped around her neck at least three times. The plush hood on her down coat that covered her beanie-capped head took me out. She looked like Kenny on *South Park* and even walked with her arms slightly extended out to the side. She lost her taste for tteokbokki, which had once been one of her favorite food groups. "My tongue say too jjah," she said. *Salty*. So I ordered white rice to offset the saltiness and spiciness of the fat finger rice cakes. My mom gingerly scooped small spoonfuls of spicy sauce onto her rice and ate it without complaining. White rice had been a constant throughout her life, the slightly sweet, chewy backbone to her daily Korean meals, the one thing she remained loyal to during the tumult of her disease. It was her lifeline.

A middle-aged couple sat down at the table next to ours as we were leaving, so my mom said in Korean, "It's nice to see you again. Where have you been?" The couple stared at her blankly, breathing out of their mouths.

"I don't know what you're saying. Do I know you?" the woman asked in Korean, eyebrows quizzical.

"Yes, you came to our house last year with your family," Mom said cheerfully.

"We've never met you before, you're mistaking us for someone else," the man said with the same eyebrow action, but with disdain in his voice.

"Why are you making sour faces at my mother-in-law? Just go along with it, it's funner!" Abby snapped as we walked out. Koreans don't do mental health issues, let alone cognitive disorders like dementia. It isn't the tidy, orderly demeanor they're used to seeing in public. The easily annoyed couple with nimble eyebrows didn't know our circumstances, but god, I loved my acerbic mensch. The anger departed my body as I watched Abby confront this couple who had stared down my mother like she had six arms and an elephant trunk. I thoroughly enjoyed their public shaming in front of other customers.

To play along with an innocuous storyline my mom weaved instead of fighting it was easier for everyone. At the beginning of dementia Johnny and I were short with Mom when she told incoherent stories of meeting her friends at the beach or being late for school, but once we understood that her reality had changed shapes, we saw the beauty of these intimate microcosms only she understood. I hated when her doctor recklessly referred to them as delusions, which connoted a breakdown in judgment, because my mom's creative worlds were much more complicated than that. Her stories were a collection of experiences and images from her past that she linked to make sense of her new context when everything else was vanishing.

We slept through *Frozen II* then went home for Thanksgiving dinner. Abby and I had become more vegan-ish over the years so we prepared a vegan lentil loaf, gravy, cranberries, mashed potatoes, and grilled Brussels sprouts. We bought some sourdough bread from Bub and Grandma's and rounded out the meal with a side of kimchi. Earlier in the day we had also bought my mom two turkey legs from Gelson's, but she seemed to enjoy the vegan lentil loaf more. Dementia changed my mom's cravings; she wanted less salty, savory foods and desired more sweets. But she still ate all of her food, along with the blueberry and pumpkin pies.

My mom and I slept on the bed while Abby took the couch with our tripawd cat, Molly, whom Mom referred to as "gae," which means "dog." My mom was semi-incontinent, having accidents mostly overnight, but she still got up to urinate for what seemed like every fifteen minutes due to the diuretic side effect of some of her medications. I accompanied her each time because she was a fall risk and the furniture in our house had lots of right angles with pointy corners; and also because I had started wiping her a year before because she had forgotten how to or she couldn't reach. I was glad she still had the urge to use the bathroom instead of just letting go in her adult underwear.

"Ohmuhnah, gomawoyo," my mom said, surprised and appreciative after I helped her.

"Gam-sa-ham-ni-da, umma." I returned a thank you with a flourishing honorific.

"Oh yeah? Jalhaess-eo!" My mom said I had done a good job.

She often forgot to wash her hands after using the bathroom at her house, so Diane or even Johnny would help her, which amazed me because most male children would rather die than help their mothers navigate their bathroom behavior. There were no Wyze cameras in the bathroom, but on one occasion I opened the app to hear laughter erupting from it. Diane called me ten minutes later to say, "Your mom just tapped my shoulder to follow her into the bathroom where she pointed to a diaper clogging the toilet. She must have put it there thinking it was toilet paper. Your mom looked at me like a sly child sharing a secret. I didn't know what to do so I laughed. Then she laughed."

Then I laughed, because if I hadn't, I would have cried.

As I put my mom back in bed with her back facing me, I settled in. I wanted to spoon and hold her like I had done as a child when my dad was out gallivanting, but I couldn't. Something stopped me. I was afraid my adult-sized body would squish her petite frame, but mostly, I didn't want to realize the anticipatory grieving of losing her one day. I couldn't hold her out of fear I would be accepting the fact that this might be my last chance, I wanted to push back that final time. It was illogical and supremely selfish. I had an extraordinary love for my mom and had been obsessed with her health and happiness my entire life, but I couldn't envelope her in my arms in this moment because I didn't want to suffer the ineffable sorrow this gesture would imprint in my heart, one whose memory would be too unbearable and unsurvivable after she was gone. I was protecting myself from a sign of love I'd be left alone to mourn one day.

As I laid next to her, facing the back of her head, I

gently placed my hand on her back and said, "Saranghaeyo, umma," *I love you, umma*, to which she sleepily responded, "Oh yeah? I love you more, more, more, more, more."

24

The COVID-19 pandemic was a blessing and curse. I exhaled a sigh of relief when the world came to a screeching halt and we were forced to slow down all aspects of daily living. But this screeching halt put a hold on important exams for the vulnerable. The world was understandably worried about COVID's disruption to the medical system.

A few years earlier Dr. Khin suspected my mom had a mild case of asthma and prescribed her an inhaler to use as needed; however, over the years her wheezing became more intense and breathing more labored whenever she walked to the clubhouse downstairs, so I wanted to know if my mom needed more medical attention. I had no idea of the shit show that was about to ensue around early 2020.

The dog and pony show of going through diagnostic tests when I already knew Mom was asthmatic, after years of living in the Inland Empire where the air quality was notoriously atrocious, was gratingly frustrating. I was anxious to get an official diagnosis in case anything happened. I took Mom to see a pulmonologist to be officially screened for asthma right before lockdown in January 2020. The chest X-ray taken at the office showed an incidental small hiatal hernia that the doctor said was unremarkable and didn't require surgery. He scheduled her asthma screenings for mid-April, but nobody was prepared for the interruption of life COVID would impose and lockdown put a temporary hold on it because the facility closed for months. I was left with Dr. Khin's unofficial diagnosis and my frayed nerves.

The media and CDC told everyone to "shelter in place" and not to visit friends and family who might be vulnerable to the virus. I may not have held the official title, but I was an "essential worker" and needed to care for my mom who had hypertension and dementia, and undiagnosed asthma, which was a triple threat of preexisting conditions. Luckily Johnny got to work remotely, so he (and Wyze) made sure my mom washed her hands, didn't touch her face, and was safe at home when I couldn't be there. We still needed Diane's help, but I was worried she would inadvertently bring COVID to my mom since she occasionally helped her son at the gym he owned and saw her daughter and grandchildren every day. So she kindly refrained from unnecessary visits with her family. I trusted Diane, and without saying anything to her about safety protocols, she showed up double masked, wearing gloves, and staying at least ten feet away from Mom. Diane was always a thousand steps ahead.

Johnny sanitized and wiped down every high-touch area like light switches, doorknobs, and handles to counter spaces, the toilet, and phones. COVID was a piece of shit, but it forced us to cooperate because my mom's health and safety depended on it. She was such a high risk that we didn't take her outside for walks until a month after lockdown when she started getting island fever trying to leave the house every ten minutes in shorts and a short-sleeved T-shirt when it was fifty degrees outside. Nobody knew a goddamn thing about the coronavirus, but we were determined it wasn't coming into her apartment.

During the first few months, when hospitalizations and deaths were at their peaks and the world was deranged, my mom's house was an oasis of calm and stability. I was surprised to be at ease, even with Johnny around all day. It was the first time in over eight years I could work remotely without any worries that my mom was in a dangerous situation. But I knew it wasn't going to stay this way. Johnny was applying to be transferred to a new position based in Arizona once COVID restrictions lifted, and I felt the pressure of planning for a long-term situation for my mom, especially since her dementia was causing her to do more terrifying things, like abandon her apartment in the middle of the night while Johnny was there, under the spell that she lived elsewhere.

I had resisted my family's and friends' suggestions to place my mom in a nursing home for years. A team of people had managed to keep her safe at home for nearly ten years with dementia, and I wanted to keep it that way. But my options were diminishing along with her cognitive abilities. Either I would have to move into her apartment, or my mom would have to move in with Abby and me. I couldn't bring myself to live in Rancho, and moving her into our house was unsafe because she sometimes tried to take off when we were sitting right next to her on the couch. We'd still need twenty-four-hour care for her.

By mid-April 2020, Johnny's relocation was approved and he planned to move to Arizona on June 1. He was burnt out and no longer wanted to do the long commutes between LA and Rancho using trains, buses, and Ubers. In Arizona, he'd only have to take a twenty-minute bus ride into work once COVID restrictions lifted. He was also exhausted from taking care of my mom on the weekends or when I wasn't there. Johnny finally realized the severity of Mom's condition when she frequently forgot to turn off the water in the bathroom sink during the middle of the night, or when she asked when to spit out the toothpaste as she was brushing her teeth, or when she poked at her hamburgers and sandwiches because she blanked on using her hands to pick them up.

With Johnny's imminent move, I buckled and called Jenny, the owner of Golden View, the Korean-speaking assisted living facility in Koreatown, to see whether there were any openings on the six-to-twelve-month wait list—it had now been eleven months since I last saw her. I wasn't totally insane; I only contacted Jenny after I found out that Golden View had zero COVID cases since the beginning of the pandemic due to their rigid, medieval-like safety protocols for the staff and residents. Golden View had nearly 126 residents, with about 30 living on each of its four floors. I remembered that when I had first met Jenny, she said she'd prioritize my mom's admittance.

"Two residents—a married couple—are moving to a skilled nursing home next month, so we have some space. There are a few people ahead of your mom on the list, but I know you've waited for almost a year and she lives far from you. Are you sure your mother is ready to move out of her home?" Jenny asked over the phone. "It's very difficult to change environments."

"I don't think I'm ready for it to be honest, but no, she can't live alone anymore. It's not safe for her. My mom is very pleasant and sweet but needs help with bathing and grooming, and sometimes she tries to leave the house. But she's easily redirected, for the most part. You said you can help with that, right?"

"Yes, and our second floor is dedicated to more advanced dementia, as well as residents who can't walk. I want my administrator to meet your mother, so please bring her next week for an interview. Also bring a negative COVID test result for your mom and yourself."

The interview went well. The administrator, Tina, who was also a registered nurse, was no-nonsense and tough, but I could tell she liked my mom who told Tina she was a "good student."

Within three weeks, my mom was accepted at Golden View with a move-in date of June 1, the same day Johnny was leaving for Arizona. It was kismet. But I thought it was odd at first that Jenny and Tina wanted to place my mom on the fourth floor, reserved for more independent-living residents, and not the second floor for wandering residents. Tina said, "Your mom is calm and agreeable, she'll be fine with her new roommate on the fourth floor. You have to trust us and give it a month or so for her to adjust."

The risk was high placing my mom in a facility during the height of COVID, but Golden View maintained rigid restrictions for visitors and staff. Visitors weren't allowed in and residents weren't allowed out, unless, upon return, residents agreed to quarantine for a week. The staff was tested for COVID once a week and required to wear masks, gloves, and face shields, going above and beyond what other long-term residential facilities mandated. If staff failed to abide by the rules, and garroting was an option for punishment, Jenny may have considered. With their zero-COVID infection rate in sprawling LA County, Golden View was an outlier.

Depression and guarded relief slammed me all at once. I was overjoyed my mom was finally going to be able to socialize and speak with other seniors in Korean. My mom was leaving her independent-living sanctuary of sixteen years and moving to a communal-living residence where she'd be monitored twenty-four hours a day. The life change would be enormous. The smells, sounds, furniture, trinkets, and nooks of Mom's home were extensions of her heart and psyche. She even enjoyed the sunlit projections that produced dust fractals in her living room.

The disruption that dementia had caused in my mom's daily life was a massive displacement of patterns and routines, which I mourned for her and me, because her life conducted the trajectory of mine. She was my creature of habit even when she forgot. I'd lose control of every detail of her life: what she ate, when she took her medication, how she bathed and groomed, and what she wore, all of which were so ingrained into my brain that I started to go through premature withdrawals. I would continue to go through the motions of caregiving in my muscles, in my dreams. Taking care of my mom was like breathing for me. It affirmed life, it became purpose. It took me nearly ten years to admit and say out loud that I was my mom's professional caregiver; my official title was Full-Time Caregiver for Umma, Part-Time Writer of Corporate Bullshit. She was every day.

Saying goodbye to Diane was difficult and strangely anticlimactic. She had been our kind friend and patient health care provider for the past year and a half, everything I wanted in a caregiver, a true senior advocate. I would miss seeing her pray with my mom before she took her medication, via Wyze. Diane seemed relieved that my mom was going to move to a place where she'd receive more care.

"I love you like a sister, Sunny. I know this decision was hard for you to make, but I see your mom in person five days a week, and she needs a lot of help. She spends a lot of time sleeping or lying in bed, and I think this Korean-speaking place will motivate her to do things. I always pray for Ms. Pak's health, and honestly, I think she's going to make it well into her nineties, she's so strong!" Diane said as we hugged one last time.

Then she turned to my mom and said, "I love you, Ms. Pak. Thank you for letting me take care of you. You are my sunshine!" With that, we all got our sing on one last time together.

"You are number one! I love you too!" my mom said to Diane, with no idea about the finality of the situation. My heart ached completely.

25

My nervous system had fried during the first week Mom was at Golden View from moving all of her belongings out of her apartment and donating or selling clothes and furniture that she had once protected with a vengeance. Jenny called the first night, saying, "Your mom used the emergency doors and walked down four flights of stairs to the subterranean garage."

"Why didn't the alarm go off? She could have fallen or found a way out of the garage!"

"We never had a reason to turn it on since nobody had done that before," Jenny said tepidly. "This is the first time this has ever happened."

"You need to put an alarm on the doors, this is a safety issue for everybody."

"We'll turn it on tonight, but your mother needs a lot of help."

I didn't know what Jenny meant or was getting at since I was in the throes of moving when I received the call and couldn't deal with the ambiguity. I still wanted to know why Mom wasn't moved to the second floor, but I was too distracted. I planned on asking Jenny after the move.

The June heat in Rancho melted my thoughts as I gave away things I'd never thought I would, like clothes, birdhouses, wind chimes, shoes, appliances, bowls, and coffee mugs. My mom had seven rice cookers, three of which were the big, old school, vintage Zojirushi ones from the eighties. I wanted to keep all of them, but we already had two rice cookers at home. I gave them to her Korean neighbor next door who graciously accepted.

They were just things; things my mom had moved on from or forgot about. I knew moving her out of the house she had lived in for sixteen years would be daunting, but the amount of stuff overwhelmed me to the point that I whimpered to strangers. I whimpered the most when I saw one of her most prized possessions: a large Italian mahogany chest of drawers that she had bought at a Korean-owned furniture store in Anaheim in the late nineties. It probably cost a couple grand, maybe three, but I gave it away capriciously to an old woman who was a friend of one of my mom's neighbors. She kept staring at it as she passed by while we were unloading boxes and furniture outside the house. It was her lucky day. My mom would have wanted me to have it, but I didn't have space for it in my house or garage, so I simply let it go. Just like that. I was under duress, stunned by having to go through years of never-ending paperwork that was piling up in the middle of the living room. When is anyone ready for such a large-scale emotional move like this? Luckily, a friend lent us her garage to store my mom's tea cabinet, kitchen table, china, and crystal and silver platters. There was a limit, my mother would have been pissed if I had given away too much.

Abby and I were pummeled by the enormity of everything. I was weepy from riffling through old mortgage agreements, credit card approvals, social security cards, passports, and family photos; depressed that the documents were a paper trail of the mother I once knew and that the fond memories they triggered didn't provide sustained succor because there were higher mountains of things to review in the other room. My mom saved everything. I saw the heaping stack of old power, phone, and gas bills from 1985 when we lived in our first house in Yorba Linda, whose fate awaited them at the commercial shredder by our house. I saw clothes that I had outgrown folded neatly in the back of her closet. They smelled of dust and Mom. I found never-used blankets and pillows, as well as plastic covers and empty boxes that once housed clocks, toaster ovens, and handheld appliances that became flotsam in the E-waste pile outside the apartment door. Her scuttlebutt neighbors sorted through the wreckage, but I saved all the good functioning items for Barbara, Sergio, and Ron, my mom's autistic neighbor upstairs. Ron was a prize who had always escorted my mom home from the street and clubhouse when she looked lost.

I found weathered and wrinkled fashion magazine clippings and photos of women in the latest styles of the sixties and seventies taped to random bills or letters in a drawer of her nightstand. I was choked by affection for my mom that she wanted to emulate the American fashion of the day. As I was making my way through her bedroom closet while wiping back tears in what seemed like an infinite stream of clothes, dust-covered boxes of crystal stemware I'd never seen before, and car loan and title documents, I thought about how inspired she must have felt to deliberately find a pair of scissors and cut out fashion photos that excited her. It felt impossible that the woman who had once thought like that was no more. It revealed my mom's humanity and positive intentions, just like all the other young women of the day who planned for the future and wanted to save money to buy nice things for themselves. My mom had big dreams, and the ocean-sized magnanimity of that broke my heart wide open.

I found small pocket address books marked up in my mom's writing. The old school ones with cascading alphabetized letters down the side and a ribbon page marker. I always loved her handwriting. Her Hangul and English were thoughtful, symmetrical. She wrote in cursive, something I had stopped doing and decided right then and there I was going to pick up again when this move was over. The circles, lines, and squares of her Hangul were the first I'd ever seen as a child, an indelible pattern in my memory, so every time I attempted to write birthday cards to her in Korean I tried to copy the same shapes and angles. I saw listings for my Korean family, my mom's sisters, her acupuncturist's office, and Golden Auto Body Shop in Garden Grove where we took the old brown Toyota Corolla for repairs because the owner always cut us a deal. I found my father's cell phone number, the one he had before he died, and I saw my name, Sun Yong and Shirley, next to several iterations of phone numbers and addresses over the years. I noticed my mom put "Sun Yong home number" in quotes for my old Pasadena apartment when I worked at The Huntington Library. I found the quotes to be delightful. I wasn't sure if she had intended them to signify something old, new, special, or important. Or if she had just used them incorrectly. I enjoyed the mystery. I found old birthday, Christmas, and Mother's Day cards that I had given her over the last twenty-five years stored in a medium-sized nondescript box in her closet, next to a large holiday Danish cookie tin that she and so many in her generation used as a repurposed sewing kit. I remembered she used to give me birthday and Christmas money stuffed in cards that I saved somewhere, and I remembered one in particular that read,

"Dear Sun Yong/Shirley, I hope you have a nice birthday. I hope your dreams come true. Love, your mom."

Then I saw it, the brown plastic urn containing my paternal grandmother's cremains under the bed, wrapped in a clear plastic bag worn thin with age. It was shaped uncannily like one of the fourteen Korean Bibles my mom owned. I had had no idea where it had been since 2010 and felt horrible to have found it under my mom's bed. I held up the urn, stared at it intently, and apologized profusely. I placed the urn in my car immediately.

During the first week of moving, I still stopped by Golden View to visit my mom through the glass window facade to drop off watermelon juice and snacks for her at the reception area. Golden View was in the middle of a concrete jungle in Koreatown, surrounded by apartments rented by hipsters and old homes owned by boomers. The barometer of gentrification was the Korean-owned coffee house down the street where I bought chocolate croissants and decaf oat-milk lavender lattes for my mom. Each frustrating visit with my mother entailed screaming at each other through the thick full-length windows, so naturally she'd try to open the front door to let me in. The receptionist explained to her that visitors weren't allowed in the building, but that just made her feistier, pushing the receptionist away. The concept of not being able to speak with family in person didn't exist to my mom, and it shouldn't have. She couldn't comprehend what was abnormal or unbelievable in a dystopian world.

"Umma, darree apa?" I asked my mom if her legs hurt after seeing the swollen bright-purplish-red rash on her calves poking through the capri pants I had bought for her. I couldn't believe it had been a little over a year since Mom had fallen in the parking lot of the Cheesecake Factory.

"Ahni, anh apa." My mom said it didn't hurt, with a smile. Even with dementia, I knew she didn't want to cause trouble.

I called the administrator, Tina, on the intercom.

"Tina, my mom has a big rash on both of her calves. What is that?"

"It could be deep vein thrombosis. I'll make sure she gets an ultrasound this week. Your mom walks all over the place. She just needs to elevate her legs since she walks so much."

The caregivers at Golden View didn't speak or understand English, but some of the med techs, nurses, and Tina spoke fluent Korean and English. Tina was honest and intimidating in a benevolent way. She knew I was a nervous wreck about my mom's care and that I was the only family member who called after 9 p.m. each night when I worried that my mom was having trouble sleeping. Tina was in the trenches with the residents and had a more solid understanding of dementia than Jenny.

"I know you've been calling to check on your mom since she arrived. Some of the caregivers think you don't trust them. Like I said earlier, you have to trust us, at least for the first month. Let us help your mother settle in. The change is difficult for everyone. You're the most Americanized family member we have so I feel like you expect a certain level of customer service from the staff, but I want you to know we're caring for your mother like she's our own. The Korean caregivers work hard with their heads down and don't advertise how much they're doing for your mom. They don't like to brag like Americans. It's a cultural difference," Tina said sternly.

"The staff is required to inform me of my mom's condition anytime I request it since I'm her power of attorney," I said, flexing the knowledge I had gained after reading pamphlets from the long-term care ombudsman's office. "Mom doesn't answer her phone since her roommate picks up for her. I think she thinks my mom's phone is hers. It's not that I don't trust your caregivers. I'm concerned primarily about my mom's wellbeing. They also sound angry when they respond to my questions."

"They're not angry, it's just Korean," Tina said what I already knew about the impatient tones of the Korean language. But this wasn't the same.

Abby and I sluggishly navigated through my mom's belongings during the second week of moving when I received a call from Tina.

"We don't have the ultrasound machine to screen for DVT so the doctor wants to send your mom to the hospital just to be safe in case she has a clot. The rash doesn't look too bad in person, but it may look worse in the photo I just sent you. When she gets back we'll have to quarantine her for a few days in her room." Tina sounded rushed. "I'm driving her to the ER myself since you're not close by."

My mom's calves were swollen to the point that her ankles had disappeared into one big bright purple mass.

"How did this rash get worse if you were keeping an eye on it? She just moved in a little over a week ago."

"I have to go, I'll call you with updates." I could tell Tina felt guilty for not seeing the rash first, or for not taking me more seriously. *This is why I'm overbearing with Mom's care, this is why I'm hyper-vigilant, this is why I'm annoying to their staff,* I thought bitterly.

Tina called me two hours later. "Your mom has cellulitis. She has to be on antibiotics for seven days and needs to keep her legs elevated. I hope we can keep her in bed, but she's restless and likes to walk all over the place, and into other people's rooms, too."

"Cellulitis?! Isn't that a dangerous bacterial staph infection? How did she get it if the caregivers are supposed to be helping her with hygiene?"

"There's no one-on-one care here, or even in nursing homes for that matter. That would be impossible. We have two caregivers per thirty residents. She may have had something under her fingernails and scratched her legs, and since her skin is tissue-paper thin, she could have contracted the bacteria that way. I don't know for certain, but we caught it in time and now it's under control. Luckily she doesn't have DVT, either. Don't worry, she's fine now."

I had known my mom wasn't going to get the same one-on-one care, but I believed the benefits of regular socialization, activities, and home-cooked Korean meals outweighed the risks of further decline from lying around all day at home. I had also thought that Golden View, after everything they said about their quality care, wouldn't have dismissed my concerns and let my mom's cellulitis slip through.

I was in complete disbelief but not shocked that I had sensed something was wrong after only five minutes of visiting her through a window. I knew her best. I mourned that I couldn't depend on Wyze anymore. I was sick with anxiety, going from being 100 percent in control and knowing what she was doing every second of the day to having zero insight and access. During the pandemic, all assisted living facilities and nursing homes were required to offer "robust visual communication" via FaceTime or Zoom for residents to communicate with their families, but because I visited through the window every other day and called at least three times a day, I didn't want to push it with FaceTime. It was the least I could do. But I had to increase my advocacy for Mom while she was under someone else's care. Tina had told me multiple times to put my trust in them to care for the most important person in my life, but the pandemic and Golden View's neglect built a wall of distrust. It was also getting more challenging with the bad attitudes I was receiving from some caregivers.

"Do you know what time it is? Everyone's sleeping," a caregiver said when I called at 9.30 p.m. one night, in a tone reminiscent of Aunt Chan Mi's whining.

"My mom's not picking up the phone. I doubt she's sleeping right now. I'm calling to ask you to walk over there and have her pick up. Isn't that your job?" I barked.

The irritated caregiver sighed, "Aishhhhh." She slammed down the phone to return five minutes later. "I told her to pick up, you can call her now." The caregiver abruptly hung up.

"Mom, why don't you pick up the phone when it rings?"

"Because it's Ms. Chang's phone," my mom said while handing the phone to her roommate, who was incoherent and laughing at whatever was on TV. I asked Ms. Chang to hand the phone back to my mother. "Mom, it's your phone, not hers. Please pick up when it rings so I don't have to bother the ajummas there. What are you doing?"

"I'm waiting for someone to pick me up to go home,"

she responded in Korean.

26

We finally moved everything out of my mom's apartment by the third week of June. I had more time to visit her through the absurdly tall, full-length windows because we weren't driving back and forth to Rancho every day, and Mom was finally back in action by her fourth day on antibiotics.

Tina spontaneously quit within a few weeks, with no announcement. Jenny initially told me she was on vacation when I asked to speak to her, then admitted Tina had quit when I straight up asked where she was after a couple of weeks went by. I didn't understand why some Koreans dodged the topic of employees quitting. Was it to save face? My dad had done it too when Lysa quit GCU, telling me he wanted to cut down the size of his staff, but she had left because she wanted to devote more time to her music career. I was left to communicate with Jenny who was tone-deaf to dementia. I didn't understand how she could operate a memory care facility without the soft skills required to communicate and work with the very people afflicted with cognitive impairment. She seemed to want perfect little senior robots who didn't make trouble, noise, or a mess while living with a disease that was disastrously messy.

Some of the senile Korean halmeonis were cantankerous and mean, to the point that they began to antagonize my mother. They got pissed when my mom walked into their rooms and took little trinkets or shoes and stashed them in her room, or they were annoyed when she'd take a pillow from the communal TV room at night, which sparked outrage from the territorial halmeonis with seniority. My mom wasn't stealing; dementia was. At home she'd squirrel away the remote controls in her chest of drawers, or she'd take Diane's eyeglasses or cell phone and hide them in the bathroom while Diane followed behind, laughing. I learned from an amenable med tech that some residents walked into my mom's room and took her clothes, which were returned on laundry day when the caregivers noticed Mom's clothes, with her name marked on them, in other people's hampers. My mom's roommate, Ms. Chang, used my mom's landline phone to make long-distance calls, for which I had to foot the bill at first until Ms. Chang's son reimbursed me for the charges. I wasn't upset because I knew Ms. Chang's dementia had clouded her judgment the way it did my mother's and the other residents. The kicker was that the family members of my mom's neighbors wanted her moved to another floor. Right then and there I knew I'd have to have my mom moved to the second floor, where she was supposed to be in the first place before Tina changed her mind. But my gut instinct impelled me to look for a new facility.

Even though Jenny had said Golden View was a memory care facility, nobody there seemed to be trained to run that kind of community. I soon realized they had dealt in bad faith and didn't actually offer the memory care they advertised as having. I was appalled to find out that there was actually no system in place to redirect residents when they walked into other people's rooms or to recover items when they went missing. When I called the ombudsman's office and Community Care Licensing—a division of the Department of Social Services that licensed (and unlicensed) assisted living facilities—to complain, both state agencies opened cases to investigate why Golden

View was licensed as a memory care facility yet didn't have the traditional protocols to operate as such. After almost two months, I was back to square one, scouring LA county for a better fit for my mom.

On one of my visits to see her, Jenny asked how long Mom had lived in the U.S. I told her forty-four years, about half her life. Jenny seemed shocked that my mom had lived here for so long, her mouth ajar, releasing a protracted, "Ohhhh, she acts soooo Korean," with her big head blending into her neck to choke the glimmering gold cross she wore to bare her hypocrisy. I didn't understand what Jenny was insinuating: whether my mom's Koreanness came out with dementia because she'd spent more time in Korea, or whether it was because Koreanness deals in a specific kind of trauma, whose side effects lead to dementia. I surmised Jenny meant a bit of the latter, that dementia and all of its annihilating attributes were commensurate with my mom's cultural upbringing—to be Korean meant to have had endured tragedy, war, and a concatenation of colonialism that produced generational and intergenerational traumas, all of which manifested in dementia's merciless and wild symptoms. Conversely, to be more culturally American with its forced sunny disposition and plundered plenty would never produce citizens with untidy, savage dementia. I recognized that glint of self doubt in her question because, as a kid, I had also dismissed newer Korean immigrants, the ones who stuck out, the "FOBs" who often smelled of dank stews. I was only able to get over this once I learned that my perspective of them, and myself, was total bullshit.

I was concerned it was cultural: that Korean caregivers lacked the interpersonal skills, awareness, and patience to deal with those with advanced dementia, and that they would mistreat or discard the vulnerable as a result, out of fear it was contagious. It reminded me of the middle-aged Korean couple at the tteokbokki restaurant who frowned at my mom. Her incoherence disrupted their orderly lives. I started to realize that Jenny was intimidated by my mom's dementia due to her own ignorance of the disease, and this nescience seemed generational since I noticed the same cluelessness in my baby boomer aunts. They didn't have a modern understanding of dementia. Or perhaps my aunts just didn't want to watch what could become of them.

Abby and I wanted to bring Mom home, but he was working full time as a set lighting technician on a new cable TV program and we were worried he'd bring COVID with him. We didn't know anything and were ruled by fear. I frantically searched for a new facility with an excellent reputation and real memory care. Even though COVID infection rates were dropping, many facilities in LA County were still closed to new admissions. Meanwhile, Jenny refused to move my mom to the second floor, claiming she needed to keep the remaining three beds vacant to quarantine residents who returned from the hospital. I told her I needed more time to identify an appropriate facility for my mom so she wouldn't have to endure the same confusion and trauma of moving again.

On August 5, 2020, I received a call from a "staff psychiatrist" at Golden View. I had never heard of him before and he did not speak Korean.

The doctor requested that we FaceTime. "Wow, you look Korean," the doctor laughed. I saw Jenny cowering behind him. "The overnight nurses caught your mother walking around without pants on three nights ago."

"If this is urgent, why did you wait three days to tell me? It's not uncommon for people with dementia to forget how to dress themselves. She's in a new environment. And I was told by multiple nurses that the thermostat is set to seventy-eight degrees overnight. That's too warm for anyone especially in the summer!" I snapped.

"Your mom has been looking sexy these days walking around without any pants on," The doctor snidely giggled.

"What did you say?" I wasn't sure I had heard correctly.

"Your mom has been looking sexy lately," the psychiatrist repeated less cavalierly this time.

I looked over at Abby, who had heard the entire exchange, then turned back and shouted, "She's eighty-two with dementia! You disgusting, sick pig!""

The doctor hung up. My blood boiled. I didn't pick up the phone when he quickly called back. Jenny called me on her cell phone five minutes later to inform me that they were sending my mom to a psychiatric hospital on a 5150 if I didn't immediately pick her up from Golden View, which she wasn't even allowed to request without a thirty-day notice. I sensed that she and the psychiatrist were colluding to illegally evict my mom. On the way to Golden View I called the police to do a welfare check.

When the police arrived and assessed my mother, they told me she wasn't a harm to herself or others. "Your mother's doing fine," one of the Korean-speaking officers came outside to tell me. "I don't think any medic in their right mind would pick her up on a 5150 either, and if the owner of the facility is serious, she can hire her own private ambulance. In the meantime, I'd recommend finding a new place for your mother." The officer filled out the police report.

I called Jenny to tell her she didn't have my consent to unnecessarily send my mom to a hospital where she risked getting COVID. I called their bluff because they had no basis for a bogus 5150 on an innocent woman with dementia who had allegedly walked around without pants on. I called to speak with my mom at nine the following morning, but she was sleeping. I called again at eleven, and a nurse sheepishly told me she had been taken to a remote hospital in Orange County, about fifty miles away from Golden View.

"I told Jenny she didn't have my permission!" I shouted.

"Jenny didn't tell you? I thought you knew," the frightened nurse's voice quivered.

I called the psychiatric hospital to speak with my mom and the first thing the nurse said was, "Your mom is so cute, she's confused but very cooperative and sweet. We're required to keep your mom for seventy-two hours, but if it were up to me I'd release her right now."

"Is she scared? I'm worried she'll get COVID."

"She's just pacing back and forth in her room, but responding to questions and taking direction. Don't worry, she tested negative for COVID. And she's in a non-COVID building. She just told our Korean translator that she hopes to go back home when she can."

On August 8, 2020, the last day of the psychiatric hold, a social worker from the hospital called me: "A belligerent psychiatrist from Golden View just called. He threatened to sue the hospital if we discharge your mom." They were refusing to pick up my mother to take her back.

"It's totally obvious now that Jenny and this corrupt psychiatrist have colluded to illegally evict my mom! They sent her out on this phony 5150 and they know they can get away with it because it's a systemic problem nobody wants to fix!" I yelled. I was repeating the same words over and over again out loud to anyone who would listen. "They're obviously trying to dump her there!" I stopped myself. I had always hated the word *dump* whenever I heard stories of patient abandonment at hospitals. Never in a million years had I believed this would happen to my mother. "I mean *abandon.* The residents at Golden View speak only Korean, so it's very strange for Jenny to hire an English-speaking psychiatrist." I was sick of my cyclical thoughts. "I'm sure she paid him a shit-ton of money."

"I've already notified APS, and LAPD will be calling you to report the sexually inappropriate comment he made about your mom. Have you reached out to the medical board to report this guy?" the social worker asked.

"Yes, the same day he said it."

Abby and I drove to the Orange County hospital to pick up my mom. Our colossal relief to bring her home outweighed our concern that she'd catch COVID from us, at least for a little while. On the way there I received several phone calls from an unknown number that I ignored. I finally received a text message as we pulled up to the front of the hospital asking me to pick up a call from a Riverside nursing home administrator named Andrea.

I reluctantly picked up, but I was curious to see how this increasingly convoluted situation would pan out. I wanted to fuck with them.

"Hi Sunny, I know you don't know me but I'm begging you to take your mom back to Golden View. What Jenny did was wrong. It's against the law to leave your mom at a hospital after a transfer—Jenny was required to pick her up. I've never met Jenny, but our mutual friend briefed me on the situation and I'm just calling to do my friend a favor. I'm Filipino myself, but I've noticed that some Asians don't understand the laws of elder care here."

"You're right, let me drive my mom back there right now so she can live under hostile conditions with pissed-off grandmas on the loose. And so that the creepy, predatory, piece-of-shit psychiatrist can continue to sexually harass her, then send her out on another bullshit 5150 to an even more remote hospital during the middle of a pandemic!"

Andrea was silent.

"Do you know it's a violation of HIPAA privacy laws for you to be privy to my mom's medical information? Do you think I trust you or any of those idiots at Golden View? This is elder abuse, and if you're smart, you'll stay the hell out of this. It's too late for you to intervene anyway, and I know you don't give a shit!" I shouted.

Andrea was still silent. I hung up.

"Such good weather," my mom said as she was wheeled out of the hospital with both legs elevated straight ahead, her feet clapping like the time she watched *Crazy Rich Asians* on a plush La-Z-Boy a couple years earlier. The weather was lovely. It was the first time my mom got to feel the sun on her face in two months. In the mess of her suffering, my mom still chose to find beauty.

27

Even after being dragged through the system, Mom was still funny and loving, albeit more confused and swollen: her face was turgid from water retention, a side effect of one of the new medications the resident physician at Golden View had prescribed for her nonexistent DVT. He had also prescribed an antidepressant, which she had never taken before to help her sleep. I found out later from a state investigator that the caregivers had tried to keep my mom in her room so she wouldn't wander down the stairs or into other people's rooms. The antidepressant had probably been used to medically sedate her.

Mom also started to chant, an involuntary, audible tic brought on by advancing dementia. It had already started inconsequentially the last year she lived at home in Rancho when she'd quietly murmur, "huh, huh, huh," at random times throughout the day, when she got out of the bath, after she ate, as she walked to my car. When we brought her home from the hospital, the low, indistinct sound was louder, a more commanding *huh*, as if the drastic change of environment had established an indelible dementia marker. I wondered if the maundering sound brought comfort like a mantra, or a cat's purr. I wanted to chase down her consciousness and ask, *what do you want to tell me?*

My mom spent the next two weeks with us in our small hundred-year-old one-bedroom, one-bathroom bungalow with no central air conditioning, creaky floors, and doors that didn't shut properly, which drove her bonkers. We had window unit air conditioners in our bedroom and living room, but the assertive summer heat seeped through the pores of the old house, negating the earnest efforts of the air conditioners. In the bathroom I saw her slamming the door to close it completely through the one-inch gap between the door and the frame. "That man will walk by and see me!" my mom emphatically whispered in Korean, referring to Abby.

"It's okay, umma, I'll block it." I stood in front of the door, which appeased her.

It was just like Thanksgiving and Christmas a year before: my mom and I slept on the bed, while Abby and Molly, the cat, took the couch. And just like before, we were just as enthusiastic to spoil her. I gave my mom her morning pills as soon as I woke up, then prepared her breakfast by 9 a.m., which consisted of half a sprouted wheat bagel with thinly sliced figs or bananas atop a layer of almond butter, a cup of oatmeal, or cold cereal with nuts and berries. She was immersed in the present moment of eating slowly and deliberately while my mind raced, worrying whether we would bring COVID home.

"Sun Yong-a, let's sing 'Oh! Carol,'" my mom cheerfully suggested. Abby, the resident DJ, found Neil Sedaka's spirited version on YouTube and put the headphones over my mom's ears. Mom forgot the chorus, but sang the beginning of the song over and over again with her head nodding to the beat, feet tapping the floor, both hands in front of her waving from side to side like the fans of a nineties K-pop routine. The pluckiness and excitement of the song's melody belied the sadness of the lyrics that it was ironically twisted in all the right places.

"Umma, naega nuguya?" I asked, checking. *Mom, who am*

I?

"Sun Yong-ee, na ddal." *Sun Yong, my daughter.*

"Umma, ireum moya?" *What's your name, Mom*?

"Song, Yong Cha," my mom responded with her maiden name again.

"Umma, chaego ya!" I exclaimed my mom was the best.

"No way, you are number one!"

After breakfast, we put on the Korean YouTube sensation, *The Return of Superman*, where celebrity dads were left to care for their kids without the help of their wives or anyone else. The show enthralled her for hours with mischievous toddlers wreaking havoc left and right. It was a scorching August so we made plenty of gazpacho or cold pasta dishes with fava beans. I brought a bowl of blanched fava beans into our air-conditioned living room and sat down next to her to shell them. I told her it was like taking the tails off of kongnamul bean sprouts, but not really. She knew to peel the outer supple layer of each bean as if it were automatic, like breathing. Surrounded by the sound of screaming children in the background.

All assisted living facilities and nursing homes had staff members who handled a myriad of tasks. The nurses assessed medical needs; med techs and caregivers helped with passing out medication, bathing, grooming, or feeding; and the activities staff kept residents busy with games, puzzles, singing, and exercise. One person usually didn't have to do all of these tasks by themselves. Abby put me in touch with an Alzheimer's Association counselor (my mom didn't have Alzheimer's, but it fell under the general umbrella of dementia) because I was burnt out trying to fulfill all of these roles. I spoke with a soft-spoken counselor on a quiet afternoon that made me groggy yet ruminative.

"Your mother is of a generation that generally stopped having more than one or two kids, as opposed to the eight children your grandmother had, which likely increased the probability of at least a few of those children turning out to be dependable enough to divide the work to care for your grandparents." The counselor shared an obvious point I had missed over the years.

"Huh, interesting," I mumbled numbly. "My mom had seven other siblings, three of whom took turns taking care of my grandmother when she got older, my mother included."

"You said your brother checked out a lot but helped when he needed to, leaving you to do a lot of the heavy lifting with the occasional help of some hired caregivers later on in your mother's dementia. I'm saying don't be too hard on yourself. I sense your guilt for placing your mother in assisted living. Children can only do so much."

I wondered what I could do with this information because we were now in assisted living limbo. And I was more pissed than ever that my mom had been exploited. I was thankful for the counselor's insight, but how was this going to help my mom? I lived in a solipsistic universe governed by dementia that blurred everything else out of focus.

Abby was still going into work every day while I worked from home twenty hours a week at my fashion marketing gig. I needed to plan for when I'd have to eventually return to the office, so I researched more long-term residential care facilities that specialized in true memory care with the best reputations in

LA County. This placement would be temporary because my goal was to find a bigger house for all of us by early 2021, or a small senior community near my house where I'd hire a full-time caregiver during the day when I was working, then I'd stay with Mom during the evenings.

A few Koreatown doctors' offices and Aunt Yun Hee's church friends whose loved ones lived at Golden View had confirmed their "excellent reputation," so I trusted them. This time I did a deeper dive for authentic, nothing-to-lose recommendations from credible specialists in the assisted living industry. I didn't trust Medicare reviews, which were notoriously flawed because they covered up egregious problems. The Assisted Living Waiver program's administrator and some registered nurses and social workers recommended a memory care facility called Sycamore Hill in Claremont, a city right on the LA County line that marked LA's end and the beginning of sprawling San Bernardino County. It was mockingly ten minutes away from Mom's old apartment in Rancho, but they were accepting new residents. I also researched complaints made by family members whose loved ones lived at Sycamore Hill on the Community Care Licensing and Department of Social Services website, but nothing remarkable turned up in the past two years.

Sycamore Hill was much more intimate compared to Golden View, with a capacity for about fifty-eight residents. It looked like a home and less like an institution, with no flights of stairs to risk falling on or elevators to take and a brand-new residential wing where my mom would live. Most importantly, it had very little clutter to irritate her. A big backyard with only a towering sycamore tree created a shady, spacious area where residents could walk around. My mom, powered by a busy mind, couldn't sit still, so I envisioned her enjoying the outdoor space, picking up fallen leaves and debris from the ground like she did in Yorba Linda. Sycamore Hill was situated in a residential area that could have been Anytown USA, lined with various tall, mature trees. The nearby colleges gave the area a pulse. I was already planning to take my mom to one of the neighboring cafes once COVID restrictions lifted.

During my Zoom meeting with the administrator, she said there was a healthy ratio of staff members to residents, and one of the activities included gardening. It had been nearly twenty years since my mom put her hands in soil. I was vexed by the long drive should an emergency arise, but this was only temporary. *Sycamore Hill is just a stopgap until I can find a place near me*, I chanted over and over again to myself, evocative of my mother. We planned a move-in date of August 20, 2020.

The night before her move I put Korean face masks on us, the ones I had bought during one of our shopping trips to Koreatown the year before but had forgotten about once we got home. I blanketed my mom's face with the cool sheet and poked out the holes for her eyes and nose. We both laughed out loud at each other. The coolness of the mask's serum relaxed her almost instantaneously. "Shi-won-ha-da," Mom said. *It feels refreshing.* We laid in bed and couldn't stop giggling at our drooping masks while watching *The Return of Superman.* A dense weight knocked me down; this would be our last evening together for a while.

We both fell asleep with the masks on until something startled my mom. She got up quickly to leave the room. I chased her into the living room as she opened the front door to leave. Abby jumped up from the couch and put on his shoes. "Umma, where are you going?" I asked, trying to stop her.

"I have to go home and feed my children. They're coming home soon!" she yelled in Korean.

"It's 10 p.m., and very dark out. You can make me something now, I'm your daughter!"

"Let's take her for a walk around the house," Abby said, following her out the door.

We took my mom for a five-minute walk around the house and down the driveway. She started panting so we had her sit on our patio chair. Out of breath and redirected, she was less fixated on going *home*. "Where's the trash can?" she asked in Korean. Abby and I smiled at her with sleep in our eyes. She bent over to throw away a napkin in her pants pocket—which she had rolled up into a tiny compressed ball the size of one of the fava beans we had just cooked—into our Gainey pot. It stayed there for months after she left, until the first rain carried it away.

"We're home now, umma, let's go to bed," I said, looking into my mom's faraway eyes.

"Hodey apa," my mom said. Her back hurt.

I gave her a pain reliever and put her in bed. As I crawled in next to my mom, not wanting tomorrow to come, I was pained to spoon her like I had wanted to the previous Thanksgiving and Christmas, but couldn't get myself to do. I was intimidated by her power, which was like orbing around courage and fortitude wrapped in magic, something sublime, knowing she had endured the debilitating confusion and physical pain of dementia for nearly ten years without letting it completely win. Once again I didn't want to do something that would make me miss her to the point of madness after she was gone, a trauma of missing so intensely that it clung to mind and body, reminding me of a life that would never be again. I placed my right hand on her back and stroked it. Then I finally surrendered to the grief of dementia and my profound affection for my extraordinary mother by gently wrapping my arm around her waist like I had done when I was a child, and spooned her.

"Gwaenchanh-a?" My mom asked if I was okay.

"Nae, gwaenchanh-ayo." Tears flooded onto my pillow. In that singular moment I was stunned by the most capacious gratitude that my mom was with me.

28

I went back to driving on the 210 freeway heading east, this time to visit my mom under a sycamore tree once a week. I also called two to four times a day. The quiet mornings brought back bittersweet memories of my mother living in her apartment she felt she had won in the lottery, in a city that had given her refuge after my father left. Visitors weren't allowed inside so Mom sat on a lawn chair inside the property while Abby and I sat on the grass just outside the gate. I was comforted to see and hear her in person without having to shout through a tall, inhumane window.

The staff instantaneously fell in love with my mother. The receptionist and activities director said she was their favorite, even when they "weren't supposed to have any." My mom seemed to enjoy the pizza-making, gardening, and chair yoga. Coming off the burn of Golden View, I homed in on the tedium of her mental health and day-to-day care. I made enough in-person visits and calls to see that she was doing well, and to let the staff know I was watching.

"You're supposed to allow for daily visual communication," I told Lisa, the acting administrator, who seemed flustered and had said no to the Amazon Echo Dot I wanted my mom to use. It was a different side to her than the one I had met during the virtual admission interview.

"If we hooked one of those up for everybody we wouldn't be able to get any work done. Also, we don't have a tablet so we'd have to use my phone and I can't offer that every day. Can you bring her a cell phone?" Lisa said peremptorily.

"I'd like to bring the Dot that works just like a landline with no video capability so I won't be able to see anything, if you're worried. The Alzheimer's Association recommends it for dementia patients because you can drop in and out without having them do anything. My mom doesn't know how to operate a cell phone so I can't bring that."

"That goes against our HIPAA policies because you can still hear other residents." Lisa gave a canned response.

"That's a bit of a stretch to use patient privacy to refuse non-visual devices. I won't be able to see them, and if you're not doing anything wrong why does it matter? My mom will lose any portable device I bring her anyway, or it may get misplaced. The Dot takes the work out, it literally drops in and let's us start talking, then drops out."

"I don't make up the rules, Sunny. I'll make sure you get enough FaceTime, and our receptionist can connect you to your mom anytime." Lisa's regurgitation of HIPAA rules didn't make sense, and I worried they were being exploited to absolve Sycamore Hill of any wrongdoing or liability.

I used to chuckle with acknowledgment when Mom's primary care physician, Dr. Khin, referred to me as a "helicopter daughter," always hovering. I was sometimes flattered by the backhanded compliment. I showed up at Sycamore Hill with donuts and cakes for the staff so they'd take good care of my mom, and also because I feared retribution for the hovering. My mom's clothes frequently went missing after laundry was done, so I had the receptionist send me daily photos of her closet so I could keep tabs on her inventory. If anything was missing, I'd make the staff go on a hunt for them.

I noticed my mom's face was more swollen during our once-a-week FaceTime calls I had to aggressively push for. She gained 9 pounds her first month there, weighing about 135 pounds, which was substantial on her petite frame. She was already borderline diabetic so I requested a modified diet that excluded the daily Otis Spunkmeyer chocolate cookies, sugary fruit juices, and rich desserts that were being served with each meal.

"You're body-shaming her . . . just kidding!" Lisa said, trying to make me feel guilty about escalating this to the staff nutritionist, in a whiny, sneering tone reminiscent of bitchy high school girls. Lisa reminded me of a skeezy car salesperson who had been compensated handsomely after my mom was admitted.

"I don't need my mom to get diabetes just so she can go in and out of the hospital during a pandemic. Please put me in touch with the nutritionist. I've heard the meals are rich."

The staff nutritionist agreed to a modified diet and allowed me to bring nuts and berries, popcorn, and whole-grain snack bars that I had bought for her when she lived at home. She dropped a few pounds within a couple of weeks. The knots of anxiety I felt while my mom was at Golden View with their "twenty-four-seven care" revisited me. I needed Wyze.

I FaceTimed my mother one morning before Halloween and saw her putting a doll on the table next to her.

"Umma, who gave that to you?"

"I don't know, it's scary. They keep giving it to me, and I don't like it," my mom said in Korean.

I called the wellness director, Yolanda, to ask why they were infantilizing my mom. "Memory care doesn't have to mean babying the residents. Look around the room to customize each person's needs. My mom likes to sing and organize things, not play with creepy baby dolls."

"The doll belongs to her roommate, who gives it to your mom," Yolanda said unhelpfully.

"Please, just stop the baby dolls," I implored.

Before Thanksgiving, the media warned about a potentially dangerous COVID spike right after the holiday. I asked management what their plans were to prevent staff from bringing COVID to the residents.

"We can't force our staff not to visit family or friends. But I've put up a stern note urging common sense to keep the residents safe," Stacy, Lisa's supervisor, claimed. I had started going over Lisa and right to the source. Sensing the same wall of distrust that COVID had built at Golden View, I planned on bringing my mom home permanently during Christmas week when Abby would go on hiatus, decreasing his risk of bringing COVID home from work. I was determined to meet the goal I had set to find a bigger house for all of us by early 2021.

The Monday following Thanksgiving, six staff members and seventeen residents tested positive for COVID. I trembled with panic. I recognized that nurses and caregivers at long-term facilities and hospitals all over the world were sacrificing everything during the pandemic, but I was still furious that Sycamore Hill staff hadn't been more careful and had let this deadly virus run loose, endangering innocent residents. Stacy finally admitted that a staff member told her she had shared a cigarette with her cousin who had tested positive for COVID the week before.

The staff informed families that we couldn't visit

residents through a *closed* window for a couple of weeks because they didn't want to risk any exposure, and we could only FaceTime once a week because, as Stacy said, "if all families asked to FaceTime every day, we wouldn't be able to take care of our residents. And they're our number one priority right now." It felt like a prison sentence imposed on my mom, but I needed to accept these temporary rules to ensure everyone's safety. I still showed up with food for my mom once a week, only to be told "no" when I begged to see her through a window.

There were only about twenty-eight residents left at Sycamore Hill, and my mom was testing negative weekly. She got to walk around outside and in certain rooms where only four COVID-negative people were allowed at once. Then they started quarantining everyone in their rooms in the evenings when, in one of the nurse's words, "the staff was too busy with feedings, meds, and bathing to watch every resident's move so we need to keep people safe in their rooms." Also, as a response to the Department of Social Services breathing down Sycamore Hill's neck to follow stricter COVID-prevention protocols after the Thanksgiving outbreak, staff members were required to gear up in full-body PPE, double masks, gloves, and face shields. Luckily they seemed to take these protocols more seriously. According to Stacey, they had "everything under control."

I watched it all unfold with trepidation. I didn't plan on informing Sycamore Hill staff of my plans to bring my mom home permanently during Christmas week out of paranoia that they'd maliciously neglect her, because what was the point of caring for someone who was going to leave soon?

My mother was the most active resident at Sycamore Hill so the change in her behavior was striking when, a week later, she wouldn't get out of bed for two days. There were times my mom had stayed in bed for a day, no more than two, when she lived at home, so I didn't think much of it at first. The weather was cooling and turning gray and gloomy, and I thought she preferred to stay warm in bed.

"Your mom is just being lazy because we don't have activities anymore due to COVID restrictions," one of the med techs told me after I called multiple times on the morning of December 10. "Her schedule is off, and we've been quarantining everyone in their rooms on and off throughout the day. She just tested negative for COVID again." It didn't escape me how fucked up it was for the med tech to say my mom was "lazy" when she was the most ambulatory resident there. *You can't say that about a vulnerable eighty-two-year-old with advancing dementia!*

Stacy didn't notify a nurse after I called to tell her my mom was not feeling well. Out of desperation I called Lisa who didn't return my phone calls, either. So, I turned to calling the nursing staff.

"There are so many viruses going around, Sunny, she could have any of them," Vicky, an LVN, said cheerfully.

"You mean the coronavirus?!" I exclaimed. "She's been testing negative every week, she just tested negative yesterday!"

"No, I mean the common cold. If I feel there's any reason to send your mom to the hospital, you'll be the first person I call." It was amazing how circumstances and situations could seem much more credible when someone spoke with confidence and kindness.

I had taken for granted my mom's tenacity to survive

intractable, painful situations my entire life. Her obstinate will was reliable, a given. "My mom never wants to be a problem or burden so you must be her voice. Tell me now, do you think she needs to go to the hospital?" I asked for the tenth time that day.

"No, Sunny, her vitals are good. She's eating and drinking, she's going to the toilet on her own, and she's smiling."

"She's smiling because that's her nature, you have to see beyond that." Like most survivors of war, famine, and a persistent fear of imminent danger, my mom was stoic and had an unusually high tolerance for pain—dementia or not.

"Your mother doesn't even have a fever. She looks like she wants to stay cozy in bed," Vicky said.

Nobody had reached out to the resident doctor since my mom's change of condition. When I called the doctor's office myself, his assistant told me to get in touch with Carmen, the nurse practitioner who made rounds at Sycamore Hill. Carmen had more nursing education and experience than the LVNs at Sycamore Hill so I had more confidence in her. She ordered blood tests and a urinalysis because she suspected a UTI, which could cause fatigue in seniors. To be safe, Carmen started my mom on mild antibiotics. I had never hoped more for a UTI.

I called on the morning of the seventh day of my mom's "cold," only to be told by the receptionist that she was still sleeping. I asked to speak to Vicky to tell her to let my mom use her cell phone to call me.

"Umma, gwaenchanh-ayo?" I asked when Vicky called.

"Noo-gu-ya?" My mom asked who I was. Johnny had mentioned she hadn't recognized him, either, when he called the day before. He was traveling a lot for work but he still called Sycamore Hill a few times after I contacted him with my concerns. A few times, the staff members wouldn't let him talk to her because he wasn't her power of attorney, and their HIPAA excuses, again.

"My mom would never forget my brother or me. And why won't you let him talk to his own mother? What does patient privacy and not being my mom's power of attorney have anything to do with it? I'm her power of attorney and I insist you let her speak to her son."

"Sunny, your mother is resting and her vitals are still very normal. She was sleeping when you called, maybe she had a momentary lapse of memory. I have no idea why your brother can't speak to your mom, but I'll ask the receptionist to see what's going on."

"My mom sounded winded, almost like she had just walked up two flights of stairs. Her primary care physician believes she has asthma. I was going to get her screened earlier this year, but COVID hit, so . . ."

"Your mom's not out of breath, either. She was up walking around an hour ago and watching TV in the main room," Vicky interrupted me.

Something didn't add up. I was beginning to think Sycamore Hill was short-staffed, which would explain why they used HIPAA excuses and power of attorney requirements as ways to not help Mom answer the phone. Nausea pounded my body as I imagined her confusion and fear, isolated in her room.

I made up my mind. I would pick her up the next morning, December 21, 2020, a few days earlier than planned.

29

"What?!" I shouted when Yolanda, the wellness director, called around 8:15 a.m., just as I was getting ready to pick up my mom and bring her home. They were sending my mom to the ER for suspected COVID, after everything Vicky had said the previous evening to assure me.

"Sunny! Sunny! Your mom's blood oxygen level is 55. I was a COVID nurse, I know what it looks like," Yolanda shouted back, trying to establish authority.

"My mom tested negative two days ago!" I yelled so loudly that Abby ran into the room.

"I understand your frustration, and I'm sorry. But your mom's blood saturation is very low right now. I sent her to Juniper Pass Hospital as soon as I saw that she wasn't able to eat and was drooling her breakfast. She's under respiratory distress."

"How did you see that her blood oxygen level was that low? Vicky said she wasn't out of breath at all."

"I used a pulse oximeter." Yolanda's voice quivered.

"Doesn't the rest of the staff use one? They told me her vitals were within range all last week!"

Little did I know that Sycamore Hill's pulse oximeter had broken the first week after Mom got sick, preventing them from getting accurate updates on her vitals. They hadn't replaced it for an average cost of $19.99, a tool so essential and critical during COVID. They had blatantly lied to me.

"I don't know, but I have a personal one," Yolanda said flatly.

I hung up on Yolanda and called Carmen to see if she'd gotten any updates overnight. "Oh no Sunny, Juniper Pass is a small, terrible hospital. A lot of their doctors are newly graduated med students, which doesn't mean that they lack skill and experience, but I've just heard some bad stories about care . . . just tell Yolanda to redirect your mother to Pomona Valley Hospital. Nobody called me last night. I'm so sorry."

I didn't have time to learn about these bad stories, so I quickly called Yolanda, who said that she had no control over where they took patients, especially during COVID.

I was in shock and denial but still didn't think my mom had COVID. And realizing the severity of the situation, COVID or no COVID, my mom was being rushed to the ER during the height of COVID cases. A blood oxygen level as low as 55 was life-threatening—she should have been dead—making me vacillate from incredulity to a pure, chilling horror that my mom's life was at stake. I shook wretchedly during the hour-long drive to Juniper Pass Hospital while my teeth clenched so intensely that my jaws locked.

"Hi!" my mom said cheerfully, waving at Abby and me as we frantically ran up to the back of the ambulance truck where she was waiting to be admitted, next to the parking lot filled with makeshift testing stations and tents covering other waiting patients. My mom was awake and alert, with her saturation levels back up in the 90s due to the oxygen she had received during the ten-minute drive there. I bawled while massaging her feet and legs.

"Umma! I'm so sorry you're in so much pain. They told me you were okay! I was going to pick you up today, but it was too late!" I could barely get the words out from under the weight of devastation.

My mom looked confused, but by some grace, she knowingly nodded her head.

"Mom, can you talk? Naega nuguya?"

"Song, Sung Won," my mom said I was her father. I continued rubbing her feet.

"It's a six-hour wait for a room," one of the EMTs said, dozing off on the chair holding the emergency room doors open. "It would be a longer wait at a larger hospital like Pomona Valley," the second EMT chimed in. But I wanted my mom to be at Pomona Valley, which, I conjectured, would have the technologically advanced, powerful life-saving machines that Juniper Pass Hospital didn't.

Mom wiggled her feet and smiled as I adjusted her blanket to cover her body.

"Gomawoyo," she said while bowing her head after I handed her a small Styrofoam cup of water. *Thank you.*

She's still bright and knew the customs, I thought. *She's going to make it.*

As the EMTs wheeled my mom on her gurney down the ER hallway to get a chest X-ray in the radiology room, her late-onset chanting intensified into a keening cry. My mind went numb as I tried to catch a fading glimpse of her at the same time I attempted to understand the stress and unnecessary neglect that had unfolded in a matter of a week. How did it get to this? Mom had been singing and laughing two weeks earlier, and now she was fighting for her life at the worst hospital in San Bernardino County. I had done everything in my control to avoid this same issue of neglect at Golden View, yet both times my mom had fallen through the cracks. I was completely confounded by this turn of events. I pushed and fought to prevent this kind of disaster from happening, and in a sick twist of circumstances, my worst nightmares were becoming real. I couldn't believe the disturbing irony.

Watching, reading, and hearing the news for ten months about families being separated at hospitals or COVID patients having to say goodbye to their loved ones through FaceTime made the acids in my stomach churn as I wondered if we'd be another statistic. The accounts in the media instilled a terror in me that these outcomes could really happen to us now: TV footage of the fingers of barely conscious COVID patients delicately skimming the screen of an iPad, which inadequately represented the weeping faces of their families, while IV lines crisscrossed their bodies to connect to oxygen machines; harrowing accounts of families forced to wait outside of hospitals, devastatingly unable to be at the bedside of loved ones as they were dying within close reach; anguishing stories of hospitals running out of oxygen while doctors had to decide who got to live or die. These events went against the order of human nature and the universe, inverting the norms of end-of-life rituals that our loved ones deserved.

Everything was happening all at once, and I was completely incapable of grasping what I had spent months, years preparing myself for. My entire life had been spent controlling my mom's health, safety, and care, and I'd spent a massive amount of time and energy trying to perfect this attribute of control that was not perfect-able. My sense of reality, made clear and understandable by my mother, was crashing down on me.

Twenty minutes after my mom was taken for her X-ray,

a frenzied ER doctor came back outside to tell us, "The chest X-ray revealed bilateral COVID pneumonia."

A heavy weight in my throat prevented me from speaking and all I could do was continue trembling. I was furious Sycamore Hill lied to me about my mom's "common cold" and testing negative for COVID two days earlier. But still, something was off. I couldn't put my finger on it. I consistently heard and read about how deadly COVID pneumonia was especially for the elderly—deep down I believed if Mom indeed had COVID it would have taken her quickly. And on the heels of trusting Sycamore Hill I thought there was no way she could have gotten COVID given the new strict protocols in place there.

The EMTs brought my mom back outside on her gurney and hoisted her into the back of the paramedic truck again.

"What kind of test did you give her?" I asked, the anger and bitterness in my voice intensifying.

"We just gave her a rapid test, which came back negative, but we also did some more extensive COVID testing that will come back in three days."

I didn't care about any rapid test. It meant nothing to me. "We don't have time…I don't trust anyone right now. The entire health care system failed her, we all failed her. I want my mom to go to a bigger hospital or somewhere I can be with her. I'll take her home and take care of her myself, I don't care if we get COVID!"

Sycamore Hill said Mom was testing negative for COVID for weeks and didn't send her to the hospital sooner, but now that she was here in the hands of overworked and potentially underskilled staff, I just wanted her home. I was completely aware of my erratically changing feelings. Above all, what I needed was transparency, not more lies.

I felt my mind leave me and continued on with what I knew sounded like a fantasy, "I can help the hospice nurses monitor her antibiotics and other medication to make her feel safe and comfortable at my house. Hospice doesn't always mean end of life, oftentimes they help people recover in the comforts of home." I was parroting what I had overheard once at Sycamore Hill about their hospice services. "If we can't do this, what about transferring her to a skilled nursing facility where they're treating a lot of seniors with COVID and allowing families to visit, which is something hospitals are not doing at all." Carmen told me a couple of weeks earlier that some Southern California skilled nursing facilities had started treating senior residents and nonresidents with COVID because hospitals had reached their limits. These SNFs had all the same medical equipment, medications, and doctors and nurses that hospitals did, and they were also more amenable to allowing families visit their loved ones, which I desperately wanted.

"Let's get her oxygen levels back up first. But if I were you I'd keep her in a hospital. In fact, we have room for her now," the flustered ER doctor said as he ran back inside the building, leaving us alone in the paramedic truck with my mom.

Abby turned to me. "Sunny, kiss your mom goodbye. This is going to be the last time you'll see her," he said bluntly.

Born pessimistic, Abby always anticipated the worst-case scenario in every challenging situation he was confronted with. Pessimism was his defense mechanism, a preemptive strike against any negative forces: should something not go his way, he would have the time to process his disappointment by expecting or planning for the worst. Abby was convinced that Mom had COVID and would be lost in the hospital system. I couldn't fault him because, in spite of my skepticism, a part of me feared that, too. However, I was furious that he didn't have a goddamn filter to save me from his bleakness, that he was unable to think of the best-case scenario for my mom when she needed our support.

We were all confused and untethered from logic during COVID's rampage. I couldn't yet perceive or grieve the tragic impossibility of our predicament. No viable, strong options existed for what to do next, and I toiled on the burden of making the "correct" decision when there weren't any in sight. My emotional distress compromised me from making nonconflicting, unobscured, good decisions about whether to leave my mom at the hospital, take her home for hospice care, or send her to an SNF.

Paralyzed, I called Johnny so he could speak with Mom. She was delighted to hear his voice but couldn't talk. Waiting in the paramedic truck and trying to recover her breath had drained her of her earlier spurt of energy.

"Mom, can you hear me? Please be strong, you're going to be okay. I'll call you later," Johnny said groggily from just waking up. Still in denial of Mom's condition, it was unsurprising that he didn't comprehend the gravity of our situation. My mom wearily nodded her head, but I wasn't sure whether she had understood what Johnny said or whether she had just recognized a familiar voice.

"What the fuck was that, Johnny?!" I murderously growled after taking the phone away from my mom's ear. I walked into the parking lot where I could scream, even for a couple minutes. "Mom's really sick! How can you act like this is nothing?"

"You told me earlier that the facility said Mom was fine! But now she's at the ER? How did she get to this point?"

"I don't fucking know. I'm having a nervous breakdown and I know you're just as shocked. I'll call you later once I get an update." I hung up and ran back to my mom.

"Please be strong for me, Umma. I won't let anything happen to you." I'm not allowed to go in with you, but I'm going to be here the entire time. I love you. Saranghaeyo." I forced myself not to cry. "I'm so sorry this is happening to you. I'm so sorry, umma." The desperation in my voice yearned to hold on to her.

She grunted something incoherent and nodded. I could tell she was tiring out again so I told the EMT to give her more oxygen. They put the mask over her face and wheeled her into the ER. We waved to each other, but as soon as I lost sight of her down the hallway, I crouched down and wept.

Abby and I waited in the car in the hospital parking lot for seven hours. I called my mom's nurses every hour to see when they were going to start antibiotics, but they shot me down each time and told me they needed to hear from the doctor who was making his rounds.

My neck hurt from strain and stress and my organs and muscles felt choked from not eating. I was too scared to leave the hospital in fear that something would happen to my mom without my being within running distance of her. I felt helpless waiting for news and wanted as many options as possible to get her the best care, even if they weren't within reach. I called Cedars Sinai Hospital in LA to start a patient transfer, and as expected, they refused to accept her because they were at capacity. The same distressed ER doctor who had diagnosed my mom with COVID finally called me at 5 p.m. to say that my mom was being moved to a non-ICU, non-COVID room—they had found out she didn't have COVID after all. A pulmonologist finally ruled it out based on Mom's X-ray that the ER doctor misread, and I was not surprised that he didn't apologize for it either. I was livid, but I had also been right. How could we trust any of these doctors if they couldn't tell what COVID pneumonia looked like on an X-ray? Carmen was right —Juniper Pass Hospital was shit irrespective of the chaos of COVID.

Overcome with relief that Mom didn't have COVID, my thoughts still caromed wondering what kind of pneumonia she had: bacterial or viral? I'd always heard bacterial pneumonia was worse but treatable if caught early. But what the hell did I know? I was drowning in panic, aware that my mom's asthma would make the pneumonia even more resistant to treatment.

We drove back home around 5:30 p.m. I'd forgotten about the winter solstice and how darkness descended so prematurely. The residual proof of an early blazing sunset still electrified the horizon. The orange-red skyline shattered my spirit in innumerable pieces. I wanted my mother to see something that beautiful, then remark, "Oh my gosh, too many cars," on the jammed 10 freeway.

Dr. Lao, an evening doctor, called me at 7:30 p.m. "Your mother has a 70 percent chance of recovering. She has aspiration pneumonia. I can tell by the shadows on the right side of her lungs. I'm ruling out COVID because she has tested negative multiple times and the X-rays are consistent with aspiration pneumonia. We've administered Zosyn. My only concern is she came in already needing a moderate flow of oxygen. But her blood work is good and she's a feisty, tough lady."

My spirit was a vacuum, but I felt more buoyant with this glass-more-than-half-full outlook for recovery.

Dr. Lao continued, "Did the staff at Sycamore Hill tell you she wasn't swallowing?"

"I was in touch with the nurses and staff every day, sometimes up to twenty times a day, and they kept telling me she had a cold and was fine. They said she was eating and drinking, but obviously they were too incompetent to see that she wasn't swallowing!" I sobbed incorrigibly. "How did those idiots not see she wasn't swallowing?" I could barely speak.

"Your mother also came in with severe malnutrition and dehydration. She'd be in a better position if they had seen she wasn't swallowing earlier on. You need proper nutrition to fight pneumonia. Aspiration pneumonia can happen when particles from the stomach, vomit, or food get into the lungs and bacteria forms. Or even from a hiatal hernia or acid reflux when part of the stomach pushes up through the diaphragm, which causes fluids from the stomach to enter the lungs," Dr. Lao said.

I sat silenced at the words *hiatal hernia*, remembering her "incidental" one seen on an X-ray at her pulmonologist's office earlier in the year.

"My mom's pulmonologist saw a small one in January. Do you think that could have caused it? I told Sycamore Hill staff to be on the lookout for any abdominal pain, but they said nothing!" I exclaimed on the phone, delirious from a flurry of thoughts.

"I'm not completely sure. However, dysphagia, which is an inability to swallow, is very common in dementia patients as they forget how to swallow."

"She's never had dysphagia and ate very well when my family and I were with her," I said. There was no way of definitively knowing whether the hiatal hernia was the true cause of the aspiration pneumonia, but my sadness was strenuous for trusting her pulmonologist's assessment that it was nothing to worry about, that it didn't require surgery. It didn't matter anymore. Nothing did, except for my mom's recovery.

"If she had come into the hospital a week ago when Sycamore Hill confidently shrugged off my concerns and told me she had a cold, would she have been in a much stronger position to fight the pneumonia?" I asked masochistically, wanting and not wanting to know. There was no path to understanding and I was left with only my desultory thoughts.

"I can't say for certain, but if they had been trained to see she wasn't swallowing, which they should have been since your mother was in a memory care facility, she wouldn't be this dehydrated and malnourished. Did they tell you she was drooling?"

"Never. Except this morning before they sent her to the ER. She must not have been swallowing her food the entire time. I didn't know, oh my god." I felt like I was chasing my mom off the edge of a cliff.

"It's not your fault you were given such wrong information, or no information at all. Let's monitor her on the antibiotic. If it doesn't work in a couple days, we'll add another one. This combination may be more powerful. What happened to your family is not new, we see this all the time. They don't send residents to the hospital in time, or they don't tell families the truth when they should, even when you're as involved as you are," Dr. Lao said, trying to comfort me.

His efforts weren't helping. I rattled with more anger and self-loathing than ever for trusting Sycamore Hill. I was unable to comprehend how it was that memory care facilities lacked true memory care. Rage flowed through me like my spirit was being burned by poison realizing that my mom was unable to eat or drink, struggling to breathe, and fighting off pneumonia in an overburdened hospital during Christmas week while the staff at Sycamore Hill, too incompetent to know how sick she was, or more despicably, had withheld the truth, was obliviously enjoying their holiday.

Since the beginning of the pandemic, news reports of widespread neglect and abuse in nursing homes and care facilities dominated the news. COVID exposed severe staff shortages; coverups about the true amount of lives lost to COVID; the dumping of bodies in nursing home garages when morgues were at capacity; and the inappropriate use of seniors' finances to move assets, purchase goods, or make cash withdrawals. But the one glaring abuse that hit home for me was when Sycamore Hill eliminated all in-person visitation after their Thanksgiving outbreak, even through a *closed window*. Early in the pandemic state and federal officials reasonably ordered care facilities to do away with in-person visits to minimize COVID outbreaks, but I'm hard-pressed to say they required facilities to decline family visits through a closed window like they did with us. After experiencing the effects of these systemic horrors, I deeply believe Sycamore Hill exploited our fears to cover up their staff shortage and give them free rein to enjoy a "COVID holiday," where they didn't feel beholden to the demands of families since everything was behind closed doors, and windows. My mom was being protected to death.

My thoughts were in complete disarray. I was freezing and couldn't feel my legs. We forgot to turn on the heater when we got home and I just stared at the thermostat from the couch, unable to ask Abby for help.

30

I received a report the following morning that my mom had wiggled out of the soft restraints the nurses had put on her wrists overnight to prevent her from removing her mask, and that she pulled out all of the IV lines from her arms. Dementia was warping her cognitive abilities, making her do dangerous things to herself again. But she was fighting to get out, my only sign of hope.

Abby and I obsessed over my mom's white blood cell count to measure whether the antibiotics were working. The higher it got, the lower we felt. Because of the growing number of COVID cases at Juniper Pass Hospital, they enforced a new rule that nurses would only answer the phones at 1:30 p.m. and 11:30 p.m. to give status updates and reports on lab results. On mom's second day there her WBC count shot up to 14 from 8.4 the day before. I brought my iPad to the hospital that afternoon in hopes of communicating with her on FaceTime. She was barely conscious and the administrator couldn't get her to sit up. He tried to position her body to face the window where Abby and I stood waving our arms and screaming her name, desperately trying to get her attention, but her eyes were sealed shut. It didn't help that her roommate had the bed closest to the window, so she waved at us instead.

We stood outside my mom's window for two hours waiting for her to wake up, but thick, heavy sleep won. I set my alarm for 11:30 p.m. to call my mom's nurse, who told me she had removed the soft restraints and IV lines again, but this time she had gotten up to sit on the chair next to her bed. The nurse said her blood saturation level plummeted to 30 by the time anyone got to her.

"How did you let her oxygen level drop so low? Why wasn't anyone nearby? She needs a caregiver to be at her bedside and watch her all day!" I was in such a static state of stress for the past few weeks that by that evening, waves of nausea from insomnia made my body inert and buoyant while the corners of the room felt like they were falling beside me, spiraling into a wretched vertigo.

"We have a central monitor at the nurses' station. We see and hear everything. We always get to her on time," the nurse said. I heard the high-pitched beeping of life-preserving machines in the background.

"She's uncomfortable and her back hurts. She loves to walk and hasn't for days. I bet you anything she wants to go home or get up to use the bathroom. She can still go on her own. I know my mother the best. Can you get her to stand and walk around?" I sensed I was unsettling the nurse.

"I don't think she can stand, she'll fall. It's too dangerous," the nurse warned.

I called thirty minutes later. This time a different nurse held the phone next to my mom's ear. She was out of breath but happy to hear a familiar voice. I couldn't believe how indomitable her spirit was.

"Umma, you're coming to my house soon, okay? Please stay strong for me." I tried to stay calm.

"Okay, okay," my mom said with exhausted enthusiasm. I could tell she recognized my voice. She couldn't speak anymore, but hearing her gave me hope, even with the crescendoing beeps of machines in the background.

"Umma, saranghaeyo. I'm so sorry for everything," I lamented. I didn't want to scare my mom so I didn't cry, but my heartache was formidable.

The nurse took back the phone and rushed, "I have to go but I'll make sure a caregiver sits with your mom. Oh my god, it's already 12:30 a.m."

The following few days at the hospital were full of the same hand-wringing outside my mom's window, desperately calling hospitals and SNFs in LA to check whether they could accept my mom, just to be rejected each time. My hopes were deflating. A Juniper Pass social worker had also called some neighboring and LA County SNFs, but there was a shortage of beds. I texted family and friends and talked to Johnny who, by then, understood the seriousness of our situation and was looking into flying or driving to see Mom from Arizona.

By the fifth day my mom's WBC count jumped up to 18.6. Abby and I arrived at the hospital early that morning, Christmas Day, to speak with a new doctor who was filling in for Dr. Lao while he was off for a few days.

"My mom's WBC is increasing, are the antibiotics working?" I asked the young doctor in front of the reception area. "I want to bring her home. I don't like that I can only get status updates twice a day. She'll respond to me because I'm her daughter. She'll recover if she's with her family at my house." Hospice treatment seemed more attractive than ever. I knew the risks and that I wasn't going to be able to provide the same level of medical care for my mom at home, but I was feeling the burn of betrayal and neglect from health care systems. I wanted to restore my mom's dignity, to advocate for her by her side. I didn't think about the fact that hospice care required the availability of hospice nurses, staff, medication, and equipment, and with the pandemic raging, I had no idea if these options were even available. Abby would have done anything for Mom and supported any decision I made.

"Her WBC isn't that bad actually. I've seen much higher. I don't think it's a good idea to take her home just yet when she's still on antibiotics. She still needs a moderate to high flow of oxygen. I'm going to ask the staff to move her bed closer to the window so you can see her better. Her roommate was just discharged. I'll have them add Vancomycin, the second antibiotic, tonight."

I was envious of the roommate's family.

"Can I go in and sit with her for a little bit?" I pleaded, tears streaming from my swollen eyes, the same puffy eyes my mom got after a cry.

"Yes, for about five minutes. We can't risk exposure." It was Christmas and the doctor was merciful.

I didn't care if I got COVID.

I wore head-to-toe PPE before entering the hospital: a cap, gown, gloves, and two masks. A certified nursing assistant asked if my mom had a UTI since she had been admitted with antibiotics to treat one. I told her I didn't know but that her urinalysis eventually came back contaminated from Sycamore Hill. Those idiots couldn't even get a clean catch.

"Merry Christmas, umma. Sun Yongee-ya. I'm right here. Don't be afraid. You're going to come home with me soon. I'm never going to leave you. I'm sorry for all this suffering," I said in her ears. My misery focused on a negative life review: the wars, famine, physical abuse, infidelity, tendinopathy, and disappointment she must have felt for Johnny and me, but was too adoring to ever bring up. She was unresponsive and all I could focus on was the rushing of oxygen going into her lungs from the non-rebreather mask. I touched her arms marked by ominous dark blue bruises from intimidating IV tributaries. The discoloration looked menacing, and I couldn't tell if it was bruises or cyanosis.

When I was ushered back outside after ten minutes, the staff had already moved my mom's bed next to the window. There was a heartbreaking three feet between her bed and Abby and me standing outside the window. Juniper Pass was a small one-story hospital with about one hundred beds. My mom's window was easily accessible from the parking lot as it was the third room on the right that overlooked the courtyard, which had a sad threadbare Christmas tree with a few flimsily hung lights. Outside her window was a barren garden with scattered camellia trees and a few bushes that provided privacy from the courtyard. We were sandwiched between one of the bushes and the window. There was no awning above, and our open umbrella barely fit to block the heavy rain in late December.

The callous irony didn't escape me that just a couple of weeks ago I had been excited to bring Mom home for Christmas, but now I was separated from her by the walls of a cold, institutional building while she fought for her life. I was unable to chase the words to describe the unfathomable.

A family of seven was standing outside a window about sixty feet from us, shouting and crying their own goodbyes to a loved one, oblivious to the rain while clutching their forgotten, closed umbrellas. A few hours later, we saw other groups of people huddling together, doing a similar thing. I heard wailing in a myriad of languages from wives, husbands, children, grandchildren; COVID was dragging all of us down its dark hole. Some of us got to be with our loved ones from outside a hospital window, but I knew many other families didn't have this opportunity. It was one of the greatest traumas of the pandemic.

Abby and I decided to camp outside my mom's bedroom for as long as we could. A peculiar aspect of Abby was that he could temper his pessimism by reaching inward for a sprout of hope in almost any situation. It was like he needed to publicize his outrage, then keep his optimism private. He might have thought the worst for my mom's outcome the day she was admitted to the ER, but by the next day he was fiercely fighting for her life, supporting any of my decisions to bring her home or send her to an SNF. Mom and Abby were smitten with each other, and I knew he would have sacrificed his own health to save hers by losing sleep, skipping meals, or waiting for long stretches of time outside a hospital in the freezing rain.

We brought director's chairs whose legs drowned in the puddles, as well as warm coats and sleeping bags for the frigid evenings. When we ate, we subsisted on bruised bananas, stale pastries, nuts and berries, and the occasional hot meal. I fell asleep around 7:30 p.m. with the sleeping bag over my head, but was startled awake when I sensed someone in her room. A CNA was changing her adult diaper. My mom was asleep, but she was still trying to pull at the IV lines, so the CNA shoved her hands away. I banged on the window and shouted at her not to be aggressive.

"I'm not being aggressive, she's trying to pull out her IV lines!" the CNA yelled.

"You're being too rough with her! You don't need to jerk the bed either. Can't you see she's sleeping and you're moving her too much. She tries to pull out the IV lines every time you wake her up. She has dementia!" I shouted.

I reported the CNA to her supervisor, who replaced her with someone gentler. I shuddered to think how my mom had been neglected by Sycamore Hill staff. With hospitals likely in triage, my mom faced a mountain of carelessness given her age and dementia, floating in and out of consciousness.

"You should put lotion on your hands," Abby said indifferently, momentarily dissociating from our shitty reality. I looked down at my dry, scaly hands replete with bulging veins. They looked like my mom's, but more aged. When I was twenty-one I remembered thinking it was ironic that my hands were parched and wrinkled from reading books, writing papers, starving myself, or doing nothing at all, hardly surviving in the time of war or performing unrelenting manual labor like my mother, while her hands remained soft and translucent, delicate like rice paper, softly blurred by arthritis and tendinopathy.

As I was guarding my mother through the window, I broke down seeing her small frame, alone, petite, and powerful. The horror of the dark, ominous bruises all over my mom's pale arms from circuitous IV and PICC lines overwhelmed me with quiet panic attacks that I couldn't inhale because the air felt like one massive boulder. She couldn't see or hear me screaming, "Umma!" through the thick glass.

By then my mom had stopped wiggling out of the soft restraints. Her feistiness, the only sign of hope, was diminishing.

31

Johnny told me he was going to do the five-hour drive from Arizona to the hospital.

"I'll try to come down soon, but keep me posted if she improves," Johnny said, like he had other options.

"So you won't come even if she gets better? This is serious. Don't you want to see her anyway?"

"It's not that, I just can't take time off last minute."

I hung up on him. Up until the very end Johnny was never going to match action with reality. He was always going to exist in denial and take my mom's health for granted.

Along with not wiggling out of her restraints anymore, Mom stopped trying to get out of bed to walk around, the one thing she loved to do. She was now confined to the bed with no autonomy to leave, which had been one of the things that marked her curiousness and love of life. Her legs flailed involuntarily, which shook me entirely. The one thing she still did was remove her oxygen mask, after which her saturation levels would dip into the 80s, then 60s, then 50s. The mask looked uncomfortable, like a miniature, malevolent shell. A couple of times my mom heard me shouting or banging on the window and tried to look over, but the effort tired her out and she fell asleep mid turn. I looked down at the sides of my clenched fists and saw dark-blue bruises. I implored the staff again to get a sitter to stay with her as they promised.

"Your mother is two steps away from intubation. Did you want her to be intubated? It's not anything you need to think about now, but if you decide to do it, she'll also need to have a feeding tube inserted so she can get her nutrients that way." The respiratory therapist said when he finally came to the window.

"What are the risks?"

"It's really hard for eighty-year-olds to wean off of intubation, but you can discuss it with the doctor. Your mother hasn't been eating or drinking much. She's getting fluids and electrolytes intravenously, but that's not enough to help her fight the infection." The RT hesitated to say more and was trying his best not to upset me. "She's on a high-flow nasal cannula now and the next step would be a BIPAP mask. After that is intubation. The good news is if her breathing improves, we can take her off the BIPAP and put her back on a normal mask."

Abby and I stood under the sprinkles that were quickly turning into showers. I looked up at the open sky; no building architect could have predicted a need for an awning to be precisely where we were standing to shield separated families who were camping outside this hospital's windows during stormy weather. My intractable, rapid-fire thoughts were blurring into infinity, making the days bleed into each other. It was the longest Christmas Day I'd ever had.

There was a tall camellia tree right outside my mom's window. I stared at it all day. The rain came down hard, but during a reprieve, the sunlight poked through the tree and illuminated one pink camellia facing my mom's room. It endured the beating rain and stood triumphant with its perfect spiraling petals, fluttering and folding. It reminded me of Mom's love of pink carnations and roses. She would have loved this camellia flower, too. The woolly clouds intermittently rolled in to mute the sun, but the saturation of the flower remained dauntless. I willed the flower to stretch closer to the window so it could be delightful to my mom.

I was on the phone for two days with hospice companies trying to move my mom home. I called ten companies on Christmas Day, realizing that the death industry didn't take holiday breaks because each one of them was open for business, and each one of them declined my mom's case. One of the hospice coordinators told me, "It's a huge risk. There'd be no way to resuscitate your mother and do an emergency intubation in the ambulance. And you live an hour away, it's dangerous." My mind scattered to find hope, but I settled with guarded optimism that my mom was going to respond better with the second antibiotic.

At 9:30 p.m., an ebullient CNA came to the window where Abby and I stood. "Please go home. You must be starving and cold. I'll take good care of your mother. I promise to check in on her regularly. I feel for all the families who can't be with their loved ones right now."

"My mom is here due to untimely medical attention and neglect at a memory care facility. I don't trust anyone anymore," I said bluntly.

"You're welcome to stay, and I know you don't have to trust me, but I do care about everyone here. I'll do my best to take care of her. You can return early tomorrow morning."

"Please promise me you'll sit with her if she wakes up to remove the mask. She'll die if . . ."

The caregiver smiled warmly. "You have my word."

The caregiver kept her word, but only for a temporary ten-hour period, between the last time I saw her and when I returned the following morning on December 26 to camp outside Mom's window. The burden once again fell on me to advocate for her and chase down the nurses and staff. The double antibiotic combination seemed to be working after only one course, as her WBC count dropped a bit the next day. But she was still exhausted and oxygen-starved because she wasn't inhaling properly. Every time she woke up she'd involuntarily flail her legs in pain and disorientation. And to her that meant removing the agent of pain, which was the mask. I saw that distress of not being able to move, get up, breathe, live with dignity. When she removed the mask I'd pound on the window to get the nurse's attention. They'd reapply the mask while her levels dropped below 40 sometimes, then the cycle would repeat itself. I volunteered again to sit with her, but the staff refused. I told them I'd take full responsibility and sign waivers if I got COVID. They still refused.

After getting a pain reliever, Mom calmed down and fell back asleep, but her oxygen levels still coasted in the low 80s: 85, 83, 80, sometimes 78. I asked the RT if she needed more oxygen, but he said she was on the maximum setting, and the next step would be a BIPAP mask. I called the doctor who was filling in for Dr. Lao and she recommended that the RT apply the BIPAP mask to see how my mom would respond.

The RT held up a note on his phone through the window for us to read: "The BIPAP mask is extremely uncomfortable. It's tight on the face so she will try to take it off, but this time we can't put her in restraints overnight because if she vomits and nobody is here, she'll need to be able to quickly remove it. It's dangerous to put anyone in restraints with a BIPAP."

The hospital staff and I now had a system to write notes on our phones so we didn't need to shout, which was the only improvement in the situation. The rain had stopped earlier in the day and the sun was shining on the pink camellia.

Thank god Mom was on the ground floor of the hospital, I thought. I didn't know what I would have done if I hadn't been able to stay outside her bedroom to be her advocate. I felt an overwhelming sense of empathy for families whose loved ones had been relegated to the highest floor of a large hospital.

"Let's try the BIPAP and if it doesn't work I'll talk to the doctor." I was stung by *if it doesn't work.*

The BIPAP mask was dreadful. It looked like a hard plastic carapace that smothered my mom's small face, with an elephant trunk appendage that she pulled at immediately. A strap went across her forehead to secure it in with a firm vise grip. Her oxygen levels remained in the 90s with it on, but I saw that the discomfort was unbearable. I wanted everything to stop.

I called more hospice companies. One company finally agreed to drive my mom to my house so they sent a nurse to meet with the hospital administrator and nurses to assess her needs. After four hours of waiting, the hospice nurse told me they couldn't accept my mom because the risk was too high driving her to LA on a 100 percent BIPAP mask setting.

"I told your supervisor my mom's oxygen requirements. Why did you come here then? You just wasted crucial time when I could have looked for other hospices." I lost it in front of everyone.

"I'm sorry, my supervisor isn't a medical professional and she must have misunderstood. Our home devices can only go up to a 50 percent BIPAP setting, maximum. And our ambulances don't have the capacity for the highest setting. I wish I could have spoken to you first." She paused. "Your mother was admitted with aspiration pneumonia along with malnutrition, dehydration, *and* sepsis. Did you know that? The doctors should have told you when she was first admitted."

I stared at her, dumbfounded, as she continued, "The point of hospice is to provide comfort care. Some hospices will administer antibiotics, but most of them don't recommend it because it can be hard on the kidneys and extremely painful, going against the purpose of palliative care. I know you want to help your mother, but you have to consider her level of comfort first." The nurse swung her backpack over her shoulders to leave.

I was appalled. I had known about my mom's dehydration and malnutrition but not sepsis, which none of the doctors had mentioned. A million thoughts ricocheted in my head, unable to be pacified. All the could-haves, should-haves, what-ifs led up to a single thought: had the hospital let me stay with my mom, I was certain she would have been recovering by now. I had no doubt of that. I had no medical proof to back that up, only trust and faith in our bond.

The hospital finally got an overnight sitter to stay with Mom. She was stable, so Abby and I went home to eat dinner and call more hospice companies.

I set another alarm to wake me up to call the hospital at 11:30 p.m. I heard a concatenation of shouting and machines beeping and blaring in the background before a beleaguered nurse finally picked up the phone. The nurse said three COVID patients had died within minutes of one another and the staff was running wild.

"Where's my mom?!" I screamed so loudly my neighbor's bedroom light flicked on.

"She's in her room sleeping, she's fine. Her oxygen is good, in the mid-90s. I need to get off the phone. Please call later!" the frantic nurse yelled.

I called thirty minutes later to speak with another nurse who said my mom was still stable and sleeping, with a caregiver sitting next to her bed.

On the morning of December 27, her WBC count had dropped from 18.1 to 11. I finally struck luck with a reputable hospice company who was willing to drive my mom home from the hospital. They delivered a bed, table, and BIPAP machine to our house by 9 a.m. I didn't request that they also treat my mom with antibiotics in fear that it would be a deal-breaker; I planned on springing the topic on them when Mom was home. The truth was I wanted to bring Mom home to cure her, not for end-of-life palliative care like the previous nurse had suggested.

After the hospice equipment was delivered, Abby and I left for the hospital and got there by 10:30 a.m. Dr. Lao was back from his break so I left him a message to call me back. I wanted to know what he thought about her chance of recovery now but was too afraid to ask. Though I'd only talked to him three days ago, it seemed like we'd since gone through hell and back, and I wasn't sure what was up or down and whether the 70 percent chance of recovery still held true.

We set up camp outside my mom's window again. I looked in to see her coloring was nearly gray. Her wrist injury, strokes, and dementia never stole the cotton-candy pink from her cheeks. I had never seen her that pale. My skin felt fragile, pulled taut in every direction, like I was leaving to create a protective force field around her.

By midmorning a tall elderly Indian pulmonologist stopped by my mom's room to say what I was already sensing. "Your mother isn't inhaling, she's very tired," she said as she stroked my mom's back and smiled at her in pity. I saw that a lot in doctors: the supercilious pity was there, along with a dearth of compassion.

"Can you come outside to speak to me?" I begged the pulmonologist from outside the hospital window.

"I have to see other patients so I can't." We were just another frightened family who was watching a loved one suffer through a window. The pulmonologist assessed my mom for what seemed like three minutes. "Your mother started on a moderate flow of oxygen, and now she's on the maximum BIPAP setting. She can't take the *in* breath." She said the same thing in a different way, which infuriated me. It was like she was trying to soften the blow with condescending semantics. I'd never seen this doctor before, and she hadn't been updated with my mom's improved WBC count—the layperson's benchmark by which recovery is measured. The pulmonologist shot me the same wry smile she had given to my mother and walked away.

Dr. Lao called me back four hours later. "I heard you want to take your mom home. Hospices are set up for palliative care. Most of them don't administer the strong antibiotics your mother needs. They actually prefer not to do that. Their goal is to keep your mom comfortable, and to provide her the respect and dignity of spending time at home with family. You can do whatever you want, but I encourage you to keep her here and see how she does with the BIPAP mask. If you take her home today, you'll need to sign a form that says you're taking her against our will."

I had already lost sensitivity to the cold outside, but my rain boots, sleeping bag, and thick, blanket-lined Carhartt coat couldn't thaw the throbbing internal chills. I didn't want to hear another science- and data-backed assertion. *Mom is different*, I thought. *She will live.*

"I'll coach my mom to inhale. She's very strong, she'll recover. It's cruel to separate families, especially since she has dementia. She has so much more working against her! If she dies it will be due to our separation. Please let me stay with her all day. She's tired, let me help her," I bawled through my pleas.

"I know for a fact we can't do that. I'm so sorry, Sunny. All hospitals have the same restrictions right now. Did you still want to intubate?"

"I don't know. Why is it so hard for seniors to wean off intubation? And if she's intubated and successfully fights off the pneumonia, what are her chances for a good, pain-free recovery in the long run?"

"It's possible, but in my experience many seniors can't get off intubation. Even people in their sixties lose their fight. It's hard for them to breathe on their own because they're not as strong, they get used to a respirator breathing for them. And yes, the recovery is an uphill climb as well. I'm not saying she can't do it, but it's difficult. Months of physical therapy. She'll probably need to be on a puréed food diet for the rest of her life."

I nearly dropped the phone in the puddle I was standing in. My proud, stubborn, feisty, joyful mother would never want to eat puréed food, even with dementia. If her sixty-five-year-old self had seen her eighty-two-year-old frail body in adult diapers pinned down to a bed with an elephant trunk mask, she'd have chosen death. I remembered when my mom had asked me rhetorically, *how long does he want to live?* after my father pressured us to give him money so he could fly to Mexico to start holistic treatment on his stage 4 liver cancer. She would have accepted her fate. My mother loved crunchy kimchi, chewy and salty stir-fried squid, crispy apples, pungent doenjang jjigae, fish and chips, onion rings, and rice cakes stippled with red and black beans. She cherished her chewy, sweet white rice, which was indissoluble from her identity. I couldn't imagine in my most tormenting nightmares seeing her hunched over in a wheelchair drooling her puréed food because she couldn't swallow anymore. I suddenly saw my mom's eyes, and something in me shifted.

It had always been my mother who gave me advice and support even into my late thirties, right before dementia struck. When my mom was hell-bent on doing things her way I deferred to her because her temper and will were intimidating. I saw her ferociousness and tenacity when she always had to have the last word during my parents' fights no matter how hard my dad's beatings tried to silence her. She observed the same bullheadedness in me when I started to gain my own autonomy. I'd never imagined I'd ever be confronted with making an impossible life decision like this for her—a decision that resisted language—when she couldn't make her own choices anymore. In this precise moment I was hit with the harsh truth that our mutual codependency was no more, that it hadn't existed for nearly ten years.

I was forty-eight and wanted Mom back, before

dementia had taken away her grit. I needed her to tell me what to do.

I stood outside the bedroom window. Bereft that nobody was by her side to encourage and show her how to inhale because she didn't know how to anymore, to stroke her back to ease her anxiety, or to calmly whisper, "Everything is going to be okay." I needed to know what she was thinking now. Was she scared, lonely, sad? Was she conscious? I wondered if she thought I had abandoned her. I hope she knew I was standing only three feet away from her, separated by glass, grateful to be her daughter. I ran around the perimeter of her wing chasing down hospital staff, begging them to keep my mom alive.

"We're doing the best we can. We have about six patients per nurse," one of the nurses exclaimed.

"Bullshit, you're lying to me!" I left my mind.

32

A new caregiver arrived at 5 p.m. on December 27. His name was Aaron. He was a kind, gentle Filipino man who sat at my mom's bedside and arranged the IV lines, rubbed her arms and feet, and palpated her hands to check if they were cold. We wrote notes on our phones to stay updated. I wanted to be Aaron, I wanted to breathe the same air as my mom. When my mom struggled with the BIPAP mask, he requested a smaller one that would better fit her face.

Aaron ate his lunch by the kitchen sink near the foot of her bed, and when my mom moaned, he ran to her side and stroked her back. I was not the type of person who loved freely, but I loved Aaron right then and there. I loved him for treating my mom like a human being, with respect and dignity, compassion and sympathy; with love, during a senseless and loveless tragedy. He was me when I was forced to stay away.

"Your mom's blood pressure is a little high, but her arms and legs still feel warm," Aaron wrote on the notepad of his phone. "She just needs to eat, but she doesn't want to."

Language and reason failed to explain how my mom had been smiling and cracking jokes in the back of an ambulance a week before and was now struggling to fight for her life. The rain returned by 7:30 p.m. I didn't notice I had a missed call from Dr. Lao. Aaron said my mom was stable and resting. The oxygen machine read 92.

"You should go home, it's pouring outside. I'll be here with your mom all night. Get some food and rest. I'll be here tomorrow morning, too," Aaron informed me. He looked tired; I had no idea how much rest he got in between his twelve-hour shifts.

"Thank you, Aaron!" I shouted through the window with tears streaming down my face. "I don't know what I'd do without you. You're my lifeline. You've been so kind . . ." I stopped myself from almost saying, "I love you."

I called Dr. Lao back on the way home to tell him I didn't want my mom to be intubated. The list of the hardest things I'd ever done in my life was becoming longer and more unbelievable. I would have done anything to save my mom's life, but not at her expense. She had had enough.

As we walked up to the house I'd forgotten about the medical equipment in our living room. I looked at the bed with its austere, institutional brown metal frame and the silhouette of the wiry springs trying to tear though the mattress and started screaming. I scared Molly, who hid under our bed for the rest of the evening.

"Sunny," Abby said, his eyes drooping from fatigue, "try to see this equipment as a sign of hope. Try thinking about it as a chance to be with your mom for the amount of time she wants to be here. You never know what can happen. She can be with us for days, weeks, months . . . I don't know."

Abby's pessimism loosened. He could drive me batshit crazy with his doom and gloom, but in that second, he wanted to believe what he had said out of love for my mother.

We got to the hospital by eight the morning of December 28. We sped on the freeway, but the drive was still gloomy and long. The entire week at the hospital had been full of days where the bright winter sun lowered too soon and nighttime was a warning. When we set up our chairs outside my mom's window, I caught Aaron arranging her blanket and feeling her feet and arms for temperature changes. I knocked on the window, and he waved with a thumb's up.

"Her blood pressure is still good, but she feels a little cold since it's cold in here. I'm going to adjust the temperature. She keeps trying to take off her mask and when I put it back on, it takes about twenty minutes for her to calm down and for her oxygen levels to stabilize. So the nurse just gave her a sedative," Aaron said through the window. We had ditched the notes because Mom was sleeping through the medication. She wore a grimace on her face, which looked paler and ashier. But her skin was still supple. I looked at Mom's fair legs covered in the varicose veins she always complained about, but at eighty-two, they still looked young and graceful.

I checked in with the pink camellia. It was droopy from the overnight rain but still hanging strong. Defiant.

The oxygen machine read 90. I put my ear to the window and actually heard my mom's breathing made shriller by the high flow of oxygen gushing through the BIPAP mask. It sounded like muted screaming. I wanted to unzip my face and release a primal, guttural lamentation.

The day moved slower than any of the previous days at the hospital. Her WBC was down to 9. The infection was clearing, but she was oxygen-starved, still struggling to inhale. Aaron was heartbreakingly attentive and watched my mom's every move like a hawk surveilling its eyas, while gently encouraging her to breathe. He kept Mom's arms warm by wrapping them in the blanket she kept throwing off. Aaron stepped out for lunch just as I saw the dark-pink grooves on her cheeks and chin from the suctions that sealed the sides of the mask to her face.

Aaron returned a half hour later and told me through the window that the same condescending pulmonologist with the wry smile had recommended comfort care the day before.

"Did she not tell you?" Aaron loud whispered, wide-eyed, just as shocked as I was. He didn't need to shout; I could read his lips. I knew what he was saying.

"That pulmonologist could have told me to my face when she saw me! Fucking coward!" I saw Aaron's gold cross shimmering around his neck and, in my head, heard my mom suck her teeth and admonish me, *Shodey-a, you cannot talk like that to Christian person.*

"I'm sorry, Aaron." I looked down at the sizable puddle at my feet, but didn't flinch when it engulfed my slip-on Vans and ankle socks. I wasn't in my right mind and couldn't dress appropriately.

"No, I'm sorry. You're right, that's messed up. I'm totally reporting her dumb ass."

Dr. Lao called me two hours after I had paged him, at around 3 p.m. Edging out my frenzied words, Dr. Lao's tone was sober.

"Your mother is not doing very well, Sunny. I recommend comfort care, *without antibiotics*. I'm so sorry for this change of condition. Even if the antibiotics were working right now, the problem is she's not inhaling on her own. You can take all the time you need to decide if you want to wean her off the high-flow BIPAP setting, but I'm not sure she'll make it overnight. I'm sorry for this terrible news."

They were impossible words. The extreme dehydration and malnutrition, sepsis, and oxygen starvation that Sycamore Hill had failed to see was causing my mom's organs to fail. Never in my most vile, wretched thoughts could I have imagined an assisted living facility obliterating the benefits of hundreds of doctors' appointments and health screenings and all of our efforts to keep my mom healthy over the years. Never in my most despicable nightmares would I have dreamt of them taking my umma away from me.

"Why isn't she able to inhale when her infection is clearing?" Abby asked Dr. Lao. I'd never heard him so sober.

"It takes about six months, at least, for the lungs to heal completely from pneumonia. Your mother has asthma and dementia to complicate her recovery . . ." Dr. Lao started to rattle off a list of complications that was drowned by my inability to comprehend words.

"Why didn't anyone tell me this earlier in the week? You and your colleagues just let her suffering drag on when you knew she had a poor prognosis earlier on. I could have brought her home to be surrounded by family, not here where I can't even sit with her. If this were your mother, would you just let her go like this?" A pressure in my chest heaved to help me breathe through the sobs. I felt Abby's hands trying to pull away the phone.

"Because the antibiotics were working and we wanted to see how she'd respond, but now we see that she's still extremely oxygen-starved. And to answer a question no family should ever have to ask, yes—I would let my mother go to end her suffering, out of compassion. It's a devastating decision, but one you make out of love," Dr. Lao said without any hesitation. It didn't sound like Dr. Lao took any breaths while he was talking. His measured cadence made each word drag on like infinity.

"We scheduled hospice to come tomorrow. What should I do?"

"It's completely up to you if you want to take your mother home, but please understand the risks are high. If she makes it home, I'm not sure how much time she'll have. Four hours, a couple of days, maybe even a week, maybe even longer? Nobody truly knows, but please see it from her perspective. She may end up suffering more."

"I'll call you back," I said tersely. I had had enough.

"I'm so sorry." Dr. Lao hung up.

At a small, dismal hospital in San Bernardino County, I now had to make the most consequential, important decision of my life. I replayed my mom's life, expressions, and mannerisms, but they squirmed in my mind because I couldn't comfortably situate these memories at Juniper Pass Hospital. I feared that her beauty was going to be somehow obscured by this singular, defining moment. That no matter how much I'd try to concentrate on the positive aspects of Mom's legacy, this viscerally unfair decision and merciless misfortune would try to muddy it. I would fight it, but who would win in the midst of loss this unnameable? My mom was the only person who was true to me, who allowed the world to make sense to me. I was faced with the disintegration of truth.

Abby and I hadn't eaten for a full day. The sideways rain drowned the silence as we drove to find a restaurant in a food desert. We stopped at the first strip mall we saw and walked into a dreary Thai restaurant that offered takeout. We ate our green curry and white rice quietly in the car. It was delicious. I focused on the chewy, sweet white rice. I saw how even one grain glistened by itself. I wished my mom was with us so I could point that out to her. I didn't want to accept it, but nearing the edge of unnecessary, senseless tragedy, this Thai food was an affirmation.

33

I wanted to postpone the decision, to delay it out of existence, but we rushed back in case of another change of condition.

Slumped over in the car, tears seared my face. I wailed like my dad and his sisters had done for their father after he died in Korea. I had thought it was just histrionics when I was eleven because they cried on a set schedule when everyone was there to watch, but who was I to judge their unfettered grieving? My jaw hurt from bruxism. Every muscle and tendon contracted. Nerve endings burned above my eyebrows.

Abby and I were distracted by nothing but our invariable mumbling: *she can't suffer anymore.* Abby was an atheist, but came from a family of reform Jews who believed death was an affirmation of life. Mom deserved to die with dignity with family by her side. I didn't want to lose her overnight, without me, if I left her at the hospital. But if I continued with our plans for hospice the next day, I'd never be able to live with myself knowing I was the cause of her death if she passed away in a cold, soulless ambulance.

I looked at my phone: 4:30 p.m. I called Dr. Lao. "Could you call my brother, Johnny, to explain to him the change in my mom's condition? I can't. . ."

"Yes, of course. I'll call him right now."

Johnny called me twenty minutes later. "The doctor explained everything. How the hell did we get to this point?" I heard him whimper, then drift away into the background where he cried. He came back to the phone. "I was going to drive up there in the next day or two, thinking we still had time. I don't want Mom to suffer anymore. I'll still try to drive up, but I can't handle this right now. Call me when you're in the room with her." This was the first time I'd ever heard Johnny cry unabashedly. He finally understood Mom's unconditional love, something he had always taken for granted, but the devastation of hearing her struggle for her life immobilized him from making any plans at all. He hung up before I could ask him if he thought we were doing the right thing. But we both knew.

Abby and I knocked on the side entrance door, which was two doors down from Mom's room. Her nurse came out to tell me she'd call me in before they started the morphine drip, presumably before Mom lost all consciousness. I stumbled back to the car. Abby and I sat motionless, listening to the pitter-patter of rain. I used to think it was banal when people told me their past losses reminded them of plot lines and scenes in movies. I didn't believe cinematography and screenwriting could ever accurately or realistically reflect the ruthlessness of tragedy. But the cinematic density of the somber gray clouds and rain mirrored my heartbreak.

The nurse called me a little before 6 p.m. I picked up immediately, hoping they had a change of plans, but she told me they were ready to start the morphine drip. As I approached the side door, the nurse handed me full body PPE. The robe wouldn't fit over my oversized coat, so I haphazardly draped it over the front. A suffocating tension formed inside my chest. Someone new was in the bed closest to the door, but I immediately dismissed her from my thoughts and struggled to find any point of reference that could help me rationalize the irrational. My body buzzed. The flicker of red, yellow, green, and blue lights reflecting off large life-preserving machines made the keening of my mom's oxygen machine louder and brighter.

Then I saw her pale, still body. The pressurized oxygen flowing into the BIPAP mask made her breathing shrill, much more confrontational and murderous in person. I wanted to crawl into bed with her, spoon her like I had done the last time she was at my house—exactly four months ago in August, the day before I admitted Mom to Sycamore Hill—to make up for Thanksgiving and Christmas 2019 when I hadn't because I was too afraid I'd miss her too much after she was gone. I hated myself for having thought that, for selfishly protecting myself from sorrow. It was only now in the upheaval of desperation when absolutely nothing else mattered that I truly realized my colossal regret for not doing it each time she stayed over; if not for me, then for her.

I called Johnny and put the phone next to my mom's ear. I heard him crying uncontrollably. "Mommy, I love you!" Hailing her like a child, to spark a memory. *Mommy*. My mom lifted her head. Life seeped out of me.

"Johnny, Mom responded to your voice, she's trying to get up!" I squealed.

"She's always loved me even when I never deserved it," Johnny said sobbing, choking on his words.

I put the phone back to Mom's ear again so Johnny could finish speaking to her, but after only seconds, she lost consciousness again. I told him I'd call him back. I couldn't help but absorb Johnny's desperation, fear, and loneliness through the phone that I suddenly became consumed by the most overwhelming sense of compassion for him. He couldn't say goodbye to his own mother in person. In the midst of all the ricocheting thoughts and noisy, chaotic machines, I only knew one truth that held my brother and me together and that was my mom, but now this truth was transitioning.

It was bewildering to see no change in her skin. It remained preternaturally supple when everything around her was transforming unjustly. Even her alabaster glow defied the bruises on her arms. Her back and legs were still the same: fair, delicate, extraordinary. I touched her hands, arms, legs, and feet. They were cold. Her fingernails were long, longer than I had ever kept them. I always trimmed her nails short so germs and bacteria wouldn't get trapped underneath. If I had had nail clippers, I would have trimmed them short and filed them smooth right then and there. I wanted to groom her the way my aunt groomed her dying father in Korea. I wanted to apply lotion all over her body, but I didn't have any. I looked around the room for some, but there was nothing except a bottle of hand sanitizer. I saw the fading cellulitis rashes on her calves and wished we could go back in time to her last ER visit in August when she had to be retreated for the skin infection. I would have found a way to keep her at home with us. I would have installed interior door locks so Mom couldn't wander out, with no regard to potential fire hazards or safety concerns. I would have enthusiastically quit my job and been her full-time caregiver. I would have made Abby stay with a friend until his contract was over so he wouldn't have risked bringing COVID home.

"Umma, jibae gacha." *Let's go home*, I said to my mom. I wanted to keep her in the moment, focus on what gave her peace, which was her home in Rancho. She tried to lift her head again, but was too weak. For a fugitive moment I felt emboldened that, even during the suffering of pneumonia, she still knew Rancho. But Mom's crushing exhaustion sucked all the oxygen out of the room. She couldn't open her eyes. I felt myself panting and taking shorter and shorter breaths. I opened her left eye and saw she couldn't focus. I couldn't tell whether her pupils were dilated or whether her dark-brown eyes had turned ink black.

It was just Mom and me in the room. I didn't notice that the nurse had already started the morphine drip fifteen minutes earlier, and that Abby was standing at the window.

"It's going to take an hour or more for your mother to feel comfortable from the morphine. Our safety protocols require you to wait outside," the nurse said. "I'll call you back in so you can be with your mother again." I could only focus on the nurse's bloodshot eyes.

I walked carefully in the pouring rain to the car thinking about how to reverse what had been started. I felt the Thai food clambering up my throat, but I forced myself not to vomit. I took huge gulps of water, which was the only thing we had brought that day. I covered myself in the sleeping bag and shivered in panic. My throat clenched, and I stopped inhaling. I couldn't control my twitching arms and legs, which had taken a barbaric life of their own. When Aunt Min Jee died, I had held my mom in my arms when I was fourteen. She couldn't control her involuntary muscle spasms, either. I was unmoored, like my mother, so many years ago in the throes of mourning. I lost the muscle control that grieving inflicts on people to mark them as a surviving family member who will have to carry on living with indistinct purpose.

It was about 7 p.m. when I saw the same restricted number that the nurse had used an hour before. This time, I waited to answer. She told me they were ready.

"I can't do it, this can't be happening! I can't pull the plug on Mom, please, Abby!" I screamed.

"I hate that we feel like we have no choice, but she wouldn't want to live like this, we know this." Abby said, crying into the sleeping bag on my lap. I didn't know anything.

Abby walked me to the door where the nurse was waiting and kissed me on the forehead. I saw him head over to the corner outside my mom's room where we had camped for three days. I was still wearing the PPE that I had forgotten to take off. Aaron was standing outside my mom's room.

"Pray for your mom, Sunny. I'm praying for her," Aaron said with tears in his eyes. I wanted to hug him, but knew I couldn't.

"Thank you for being so kind and loving to my mom, Aaron. You did exactly what I would have done. Maybe she thought you were her son? I'm never going to forget you." I couldn't speak anymore.

"You love your mother deeply, which tells me how much she loves you, too. I know this is extremely difficult, but this is true love. You have to trust that." Aaron turned and walked down the hallway. It was the last time I saw him.

I entered my mom's room again and saw the nurse with the bloodshot eyes reappear with the RT. He was taller in person.

"Is the BIPAP mask really that uncomfortable?" I asked, trying to negotiate my way out of our hell.

"Yes. And your mother isn't inhaling. She may feel like

she's suffocating or drowning."

"When you remove the mask, will she feel like she's gasping for air?" I asked, in complete disbelief at the words coming out of my mouth.

"No, because she's deeply sedated. We know she's not in pain because she's not grimacing. She may open her mouth like a fish, but she won't be gasping for air." And with that the RT broke down in tears. "I'm sorry, I know how hard this is for you, and to say these things is very difficult for me, too. I've seen you guys outside the window for days. I've been working with your mom on and off for a week. . ."

I called Johnny a final time and held the phone to my mom's ear. I wanted to give him the privacy he deserved but couldn't. After a couple minutes, the only thing I heard him say was, "Mom, I love you. I'm sorry I'm not there. You're the best mother in the world, and I'm sorry I was a terrible son. I love you so much." My mom didn't lift her head this time.

"Are you done, Johnny?" I asked when I couldn't hear him anymore.

"I feel horrible for not being there. I can't take this." Johnny stopped to bawl uncontrollably. I couldn't help but recognize in this single devastating moment the effects his childhood trauma had had on the way he dealt with his adult life in the phrase, *I can't take this.* Four words in the most desolating and distressing time of our lives explained his escapes into gambling and now his struggles to realize her mortality. "Please tell her again I love her." Johnny hung up.

Abby looked at me from the window and nodded. I softly sang "You Are My Sunshine" in her ear seven times in a row. Seven was always her favorite number. I remembered Renee holding up Aunt Soo Jin's music box that played "Für Elise" when she was dying at home. I yearned for the intimacy of home and family for my mom. She deserved that comfort and familiarity, the absence of which was the greatest violation. The morphine relaxed the sound of the murderous screaming from the mask. I didn't know if my mom was conscious or not. She didn't stir, and her face looked strangely calm when I sang to her. I hadn't noticed it earlier, but when I bent down closer to study her face, I saw bits of food in her teeth obscured by the mask. They had probably been there since she was at Sycamore Hill, only a week old, because she hadn't eaten at the hospital. I wanted to brush her teeth but knew it was impossible. My stomach was turning over itself, churning acids, thrashing the green curry. I felt the food clambering up again, but I forced myself to keep swallowing until the sensation went away.

I spoke calmly and slowly to my mom to push time away. Language fails at a time like this. The words *saranghaeyo; I love you; thank you for being my beautiful, wonderful mother; thank you for my life;* and *thank you for your light* surrender their meanings near the crucial, decisive moment when you're about to lose someone you can't live without. I said these profoundly insufficient words and others to my mother, scornful that they didn't carry the magnitude of what I meant and felt. These words were not whole or adequate in describing my life with my umma.

I tried to reposition the IV lines that were taking my place in her bed so I could lie next to her, but they consumed her. Instead, I bent down to rearrange her fallen side swipe with shocks of silver and the warmest browns. I whispered more things to her. I moved her hair away from her face and kissed her forehead. Her adorable bob that was just above her shoulders in April was now two inches past them. It had been nine months since her last haircut, in March. Diane always admired Mom's hair, saying how elegant and stunning it was to see it glinting under the sun. Her hair was always healthy and commanding. I studied it, smelled it, touched it. I wiped her face clean of all the weeks of suffering and touched her arms and legs, knowing it would be the last time. I stared at her entire body to lock it into forever memory. I spent twenty minutes scanning and memorizing her face and body, oblong fingernails, wrists, feet, nose, stomach, knees.

The nurse and RT came in.

"How are you, Sunny?" the nurse asked.

I didn't respond.

My mom started slouching toward the left side of the bed, and I just watched her willing her to wake up and say something. I looked out the window to see Abby's hands covering his face.

"I'm going to replace the BIPAP mask with a high-flow nasal cannula," the RT whispered. "Take all the time you need. She's not in pain." The RT and nurse turned to leave.

I saw the deep, heinous grooves that the BIPAP mask left on her cheeks, chin, and nose. The nose she was proud of because it had become microscopically aquiline with age. I visualized my mom gently pulling at the bridge to contour it with her right thumb and index finger while watching TV. The mask had left a violent indentation on the subtle slope, and I couldn't tell if it had crushed her nose. I held my mom's hands tighter and lowered my face close to hers. The expression on her face was relaxed, relieved from the morphine, relieved that the pain of the BIPAP mask was finally over. Her expression turned blank when she tried to inhale, so I pressed the high-flow nasal cannula mask more firmly on her face, covering any gaps. She couldn't inhale. I turned around to look at the clock: 7:14.

"Umma, jibae gacha. Let's go home. I love you, I love you, I love you, I love you, I love you." I stroked her back and held her hand. I remained intently connected to her, briefly focusing on the mole on her left temple that she impetuously sliced off with a razor blade so many years ago, to throw myself in the past. I memorized her earlobes where two symmetrical piercings once held her beloved diamond stud earrings. I stared at her eyelashes and longed for our life together again with an intensity so tremendous, I felt like I was sliding over the edge of lunacy pulled by the heaviness of incontrovertible loss. I finally held my mom's face with both hands. It was lamentably soft. I saw her lips mouth an *O* shape like the RT had said, not like a fish but like the way a newborn infant does for reasons we will never know. She didn't gasp for air. She was drifting, gently. But I felt the earth rumble. Her eyes rolled back, and I was taken by an ocean of despair and finality. The oxygen machine beeped and flared colors in my periphery. I remembered the serenity on my mom's face fifteen years ago after waking up from the twilight anesthesia administered before her colonoscopy, the relief of not hearing bad news and the excitement for living because everyday contained an unknown small promise. This memory startled me with its blazing brilliance. I maddeningly wondered if she had thought she'd suddenly wake up one morning during this hellish week with the same feeling of hope —that, in her silent patience, the world would return to order.

I glanced up at Abby who was watching us from outside the window, then looked at Mom again before she exhaled a punctured sigh so startling I jumped back and strenuously gasped for air. A minute later, another one. A couple minutes later, the last. My hand on her forehead. I looked at the clock.

34

The death certificate from Hollywood Forever Cemetery contains a typo for my address and also says my mom died at 19:55 on December 28, 2020. She would have turned eighty-three in eleven days. The doctor perfunctorily marked her time of death as the time the pronouncement was made—the quiet pronouncement I heard while I watched her, waiting for her. But I know the exact time I witnessed her last breath: 7:18 p.m., the indelible time she left. I envisioned the world before and after death, the conclusion of things, an existence without my mother as her consciousness departed with the moon. I ached a pristine sadness for the longing born of nostalgia and for everything I would never come to experience.

I sometimes replay how quickly she left after we removed the BIPAP mask. It must have been less than three minutes. She was that oxygen-deprived. I don't know why it's important for me to emphasize to strangers that my mom didn't die of COVID or remind my family and friends that she was swept away with the tsunami. When one of my friends texted me to suggest contacting FEMA to see whether I qualified for aid toward COVID funeral costs, I texted back, "I told you my mom DID NOT have COVID!" I haven't heard from this friend since.

I used to dread the commute to Rancho, but nostalgia is ironic these days that I wish I could do it again and again to see her surrounded by tall sycamore and lemon trees, star jasmine plants, and benches to rest on. I miss the petrichor of that parched place. There's a stigma associated with grieving that stems from being labelled as overly sentimental about one's own sorrow, so I learned to dodge acquaintances I hadn't seen in a while whenever I ran into them on the street. But if I'm caught, I don't bring up the loss of my mother when they cheerfully ask, "How've you been?" The magnitude of my anguish doesn't fit into a banal ten-minute conversation that, if I did bare my sorrow, would be received with sympathy and discomfort, but ultimately forgotten as they moved toward their next errand. People don't do death, and they sure as hell don't do dementia. I can't even wrap my head around trying to explain my mom's passing due to the neglect and incompetence of the people I trusted to take care of her. Her death was preventable, but our society, which is in denial of death, tends to discreetly blame the *victim* for dying: *if you're taking care of yourself, you shouldn't get sick and die.* And survivors blame themselves for living through something that should have been prevented.

My first bereavement counselor was a Japanese American Vietnam War veteran named Carl, who said I repeated the events that led to my mom's death in a linear, inventory-list style like my life depended on obsessing over the details. But logic and reason are fleeting during times like this. Carl understood that grieving is a maudlin enterprise that feels like an eternity, making it easy for guilt and regret to prevail. He told me things I already knew, that my guilt was exacerbated by forceful feelings of shame that's endemic in my Asian upbringing: "I've seen that Asian shame surfaces when a person feels like they haven't lived up to his or her own expectations of a community. To live up to others' expectations creates harmony, but when you think you haven't, you become immersed in feelings of pronounced unworthiness," he'd say. But I let him remind me over and over because it made me feel less walled off.

Carl said it took him years to untangle his feelings of self-loathing and unworthiness when he couldn't save his friends' lives. He compared my behavior to that of the vets he worked with because "Humans are not supposed to kill or be neglected and abused." It didn't make sense to avoid looking at photos of Mom or visiting Korean grocery stores for a full year after her death, because that was synonymous with our meanderings. Going without her felt like trying to stop water. "Complicated grieving," Carl said, because my mother's dementia "blocked the conduit for communication." We had both been prisoners of incoherence when her memories slipped into evanescence many years ago.

In response, I told Carl that just like my mother had recounted her trauma from wars, the only trauma I had was the kind that did not seek pity but meaning and justice, in whatever form that took. I'm completely aware that eighty-year-olds die, but so do children, teenagers, and twenty-year-olds when they're sick and not given timely medical attention. My vision blurred when I heard well-meaning people tell me *it was her time to go.*

The day after my mom passed away, I made an official complaint to the Community Care Licensing division of the Department of Social Services so they could open an investigation on the neglect, untimely medical attention, and unlawful death of my mom. I also reported Sycamore Hill to the long-term care ombudsman's office, which documented all of these abuses. Two weeks later, a representative from the ombudsman's office picked up narrative charting that the nurses and med techs took during the week my mom was sick.

Sycamore Hill staff had initially refused to hand over these notes when I requested them after Mom passed away. On the evenings of December 15 and 16, 2020, a full week before she was rushed to the ER, she had vomited twice, and nobody informed me even though I talked to the LVN, Vicky, on those days to ask how she was doing. I wept so strenuously for hours after reading the notes that my entire body jerked in different directions, like it was thrashing to chase down old time.

The ombudsman also said there was a severe caregiver shortage at the same time because staff members had quit in droves due to COVID concerns, while management didn't inform families. I had already suspected this only a couple days before my mom was sent to the ER, when Johnny told me the receptionist wouldn't let him talk to Mom. The HIPAA and power of attorney excuses made absolutely no sense aside from the fact that Sycamore Hill lacked the staff to help her get to the phone. Stacy and the entire staff had lied to me about this, too. I can only describe this feeling of discovering urgent information *after* my mom passed away as the revelation of events leading up to a loved one's murder.

When my mom called me on Thanksgiving 2015 to tell me she had thrown up, I rushed her to the ER, after which she was admitted for three nights because she was moderately dehydrated. At the age of sixty-seven she still recovered slowly and uncomfortably after receiving timely medical attention. Had anyone at Sycamore Hill told me she had vomited during a period of time when medical attention was critical, life and death, I would have rushed my mother to the hospital myself. Her elasticity and love of life would have carried her through. Without any doubt in my mind, I know she'd be here now if they had just told me anything.

Assisted living and nursing home care is a multibillion-dollar business. The only thing the administrators and owners of these facilities care about is money. I strongly believe the staff at Sycamore Hill knew my mom was sick, but refused to send her to a hospital or even a skilled nursing facility because they realized she wasn't going to return. Sycamore Hill would lose their head count and money. That the vulnerable are acceptable collateral damage during a human catastrophe is untenable.

It's the way she left that unmoors me.

After my father died in 2008, my new age neighbor, Gino, who was a regular at the Bodhi Tree Bookstore in West Hollywood, as well as a disbarred lawyer with a heart of gold, told me to call my dad into my dreams.

"When people transition, it's confusing and jarring at first because they're not in their bodies anymore. It's like the excitement you feel on the first day of school when you don't know where you're going or where your next class is. Call your father into your dreams, but give it some time, and he'll visit you when he's ready," Gino advised in a perfectly reasonable tone of voice. So, I did. I grieved our estranged relationship and had nothing to lose.

Within three weeks, my father appeared in my dream, which to this day is still vivid to me: he was hovering over my bed as I was waking up, wearing a full head of dyed black hair and a purple robe. He sat tall, his stomach swollen by ascites, the way it looked when he died.

"Dad! Are you okay?" I shouted. He said nothing but returned a Buddha smile, then nodded and faded away. I woke up in high spirits and told Gino later that morning.

"The purple chakra is the crown chakra. It represents strength, dignity, and spirituality. It's the highest chakra," Gino said with conviction and excitement.

"I don't know about that," I giggled. "He wasn't the most enlightened of people."

"Well, he did something right. He must have been conscious enough in his life to be bathed in purple. That's quite remarkable."

"I'm not sure I'd go that far, but he did the best he could."

"Don't we all?" Gino smiled.

I didn't know whether I could take Gino's new age mysticism, but I was pleased with his assessment and that he thought my father was so gifted.

I feverishly called my mom into my dreams every night after she passed away. I needed that direct connection I got from that clear dream with my father. I didn't care whether there was any validity to the purple robe, crown chakra, or to what Gino espoused. If my father flowed like a celestial presence in my dreams, what was my mom capable of?

COVID restrictions in LA started to relax around April 2021 so I planned my mom's memorial service the Friday before Mother's Day weekend. It took me nearly four months to write a thirty-seven-minute-long eulogy. The memorial service was held at First Presbyterian Church of Hollywood on May 7, 2021. My mom was Presbyterian so I wanted her service to be in line with her faith. Twelve people showed up, which was more than I expected during this time. My cousin Sophia flew in from Santa Cruz, Johnny from Arizona, and the rest were local: Steven (my oldest cousin), Julie (my younger cousin), Jason (Julie's son), Jason's girlfriend, Aunt Helen, Paul (her son), Aunt Yun Hee, Aunt Chan Mi, Abby, and me. Seven people attended via Zoom: my cousins Renee, Shelley, Josie, and Melissa, as well as Dennis (Uncle Terry's son and Melissa and Renee's stepbrother), Caren (Dennis's wife), and my friend Leigha. Diane, my mom's caregiver, had two deaths in her family around this time so she couldn't attend. My mom's other sisters, Aunt Seo Yun (who lived in Texas and was afraid to fly during COVID) and Aunt Young Soon (who was bedridden), also couldn't attend.

It was a beautiful service, and I was surprised my long eulogy was a hit. I thought everyone was going to kill me for the length, but they all said the memories moved them in specific ways that spoke directly to their grief. I talked about my mom's superb cooking, intimidating work ethic, expensive taste, as well as love of music and old movies. And her unassailable love of life. I brought up Mom's idiosyncrasies and OCD walk, along with her raging temper and depression when we were young. I described Mom's strong will and tenacity that had guided her survival of two wars, domestic violence, and professional and personal heartbreaks. I also spoke of Johnny's devotion to Mom during COVID.

I saved a key takeaway for some members of my family near the end of the eulogy, those who had not stayed in touch with my mom: "Some immediate family members stopped calling due to their ignorance and fear of dementia, or because they didn't know how to relate to someone they feared they'd lost. To them, my mom was gone, but the secrets of her essence were still there. She was a vital human being whose joys, sufferings, and internal experiences still survive in us. My mom was many truths to me, and one indisputable truth was that if she had never had dementia, but one of her family members did, she would have been there for them without any doubt in my mind."

After my eulogy, the pastor opened the service to others who wanted to share their memories of Mom. Abby spoke of her curiosity and sweetness even during the absolute worst of dementia. Aunt Helen said how thoughtful and considerate Mom was, always saying thank you and buying gifts for her after big holiday dinners at her house. Julie remembered how my mom used to shout, "Johnny cry!" after hearing "Boys Don't Cry" by The Cure. Then Johnny got up to speak and my jaw dropped to my feet.

"In Virginia, after my dad beat the crap out of my mom, she came home from the hospital and pulled me aside and asked if it was okay to divorce him. I begged her not to. I was scared and said we needed a father. I feel like it's my fault she went through more abuse over the years because she stayed with him. Oh, Mom!" Crying uncontrollably, he paused for a few seconds, then said, "I promise you, we will never know anyone like her again."

Of all the times Johnny's forty-year-old childhood trauma could have come gushing out, he had chosen my mom's memorial service, and it was perfect. It was the therapy he had always needed yet shunned, and we were all ears and sobs. Johnny was detached and mechanical during the throes of his gambling addiction; a numb, poker-faced, taciturn brother who didn't seem to care about anything else besides his next trip to a green felt table. But the volatile ingredients of his latent humanity finally erupted in front of all of us.

I used to blame my dad and Johnny for my mom's dementia, thinking they had given her the stress and hypertension that led to her strokes, which, later in life, paved a way for an anomaly in her neural circuitry to give life to this brutal disease. After my dad died, Johnny became the sole object of my blame. When grieving has me on my knees, I still struggle with this thought, just not as much. Maybe because my resentment of him dissipated when he took such thoughtful and thorough care of Mom during her last year at home. Or maybe because I'm getting nowhere by punishing the pain out of him.

Near the end of Mom's life, after accepting that dementia was bigger than all of us, I forgave Johnny because I realized that gambling was a temporary escape from his own pain, just like anorexia had been for me. I don't believe anybody chooses to be addicted. It took me many years of hard work to understand that Johnny didn't choose to gamble away Mom's and his money—he didn't know how to unravel his trauma. In our conversations after Mom passed away, Johnny has sprinkled in, "I wasn't in my right head," whenever he refers to his "dark days." I don't know if that means he's currently seeking ways to heal, or recognizes he needs to. I've learned I can't pressure him, that this decision is ultimately his own.

I often think about Johnny's raw speech because it surfaces my own life's regrets in different ways, before dementia entered our lives. I regret not living abroad or going to New York for graduate school in my twenties because I was constantly worried about my mom's health and happiness. I felt tethered and beholden to her not by any pressure she imposed on me, but because I felt it was my lifelong purpose based on an instinct to survive a toxic family. This stifling devotion made me implode with what-ifs and thoughts of a loving, yet imperfect mother–daughter relationship that soon revealed its cracks.

I was frustrated with my mom when she was in her late fifties and early sixties for being antisocial, drifting away from family and friends. Impatient with her lack of agency to address her mental health, I took it on for her even when she resisted. In my twenties and thirties I sometimes fell into my father's cynical trappings of assuming my mom was manipulating me to stay with her by seeming depressed and lonely, by projecting her doubts onto me. But my mom actually encouraged me to see the world, it had been my own uncertainties of embarking on directionless adventures that stopped me. It was easier to let go of my desires and support her instead, even if it left me with a displaced resentment at the time, as well as a self-reproach for the insecurities I felt she influenced. At the end, I wanted to be near. Our relationship was made whole and magnificent with its flaws and imperfections. My mom and I navigated our lives around each other through our stumbles and challenges by prioritizing what mattered the most: our love above all else.

On our drive back home from my father's memorial service in 2008, my mom told me she also wanted "crimination." I brought my mom's cremated remains to her memorial service and set them on a table draped in white linen, overflowing with lilies and chamomile flowers.

We ate lunch at Kang Ho Dong Baekjeong, a popular restaurant in K-Town that my Korean-food-snob family loved. As I was looking around at my fractured, dysfunctional family, symbolically scattered at different tables because we couldn't get a large communal one, I remembered Renee's snicker about my sheltered existence in Orange County, codependent with my mom. I resented Renee for saying that when we were teenagers, even though I knew it came out of her own sadness of losing her mother. For some reason I replayed this comment in my head as I was mixing my bibimbap and became buoyed with a sense of radiating gratitude. The reminder of our porous mutual codependency blending with the memories of mixing dolsot bibimbap together was conflicting: after all these years, I was smugly overjoyed that Renee regarded Mom and me as infrangible, but the heartache of my mother leaving our relationship to move on in death as I moved on in life was unbearable.

The kimchi tasted like Mom's: cold, crunchy, crispy, spicy, and a little sweet. I took the check when it arrived, before my aunts or cousins could try to pay. As I walked up to the cashier, Julie came up behind me and slipped her hand through mine to grab the check. I sensed a Twister-style wrestling match about to ensue, the same one I had witnessed growing up when my mom and her younger sisters fought to pay the bill. Julie was three years younger, so I pulled the "I'm the oldest, I'm paying" card, laughing maniacally while we enacted tradition.

"No! We want to treat you!" Julie cackled as she wrapped both arms around me like she was giving me a cuddly back hug; instead, she was really trying to finagle her way into loosening my grip of the check. I jerked out of her hold, but she was nimble and managed to slide the check from my hand. I got creative and weaved my leg through Julie's so she couldn't walk. I even sucked my teeth like my mom did. But instead of stopping, she just hopped to the front of the restaurant, making me hop right behind her. By this time the entire restaurant was watching as we chortled, twisted, and violated personal space. I pulled her arm holding the ruffled, torn check the way I had seen my mother do to her sisters—knees bent, hips tilted posteriorly, haunches back—and yelled at the cashier, "I'm the oldest, I'm paying!"

"The oldest wins!" the cashier said. He wasn't messing with tradition.

I reached around and pulled the check from her hand and slammed it down next to the register with cash.

As everyone was leaving, Aunts Yun Hee and Chan Mi sheepishly came up to me to say goodbye. Their guilt was palpable. I didn't want to start an argument so I just smiled and walked away. I often link attention with love. Mom paid attention to my dad, Johnny, and me. She spent her entire life paying attention to her parents and siblings out of duty, respect, to redeem herself. I wonder what happened along the way that made my mom's sisters stop paying attention to her.

I remember the attention she gave to minutiae: the way she'd put the food she knew I wasn't going to eat into to-go boxes at Korean restaurants *before* we ate; the way she painstakingly arranged the cascading leaves of our money plants dangling in their knit holders above our couch; the way she carefully pulled out the meat from my kimchi jjigae; and the way she palpated the tops of nearly every plastic-wrapped Styrofoam plate of rice cakes, searching for the spongelike spring of freshness.

This was her love.

35

I fell into a deep, protracted depression the days following my mom's memorial service. I felt the love and support of my friends and family, but I couldn't bring her back. My mother's daily challenges and obstacles living with dementia taught me about patience, to live in the moment, to notice the genius of nature as well as its ordinariness. Her memory slipped away, but she was immersed in life's tiny things—the way the sunlight came through the window or the way it hit the trees. Or how nice the weather was and how warm the sun felt on her. She was an idealist misfit who kept her dreams close. Mom sought beauty in every single aspect and chose to embody lightness, humor, and infinite curiosity. Dementia lost when it tried to fracture our bond, we became defiantly indissoluble.

It's in the process of going back that helps to stop the struggle, to stop pushing back the wave. Sometimes in the quiet darkness right before dawn, memories that carry powerful verisimilitude help me capture a part of my mother's essence that places me in a liminal state of intense joy and isolation. Focusing on how my mom died, scraping the wound, felt vital like air because her death was her, too. And in recalling every detail, I feel like I'm resuscitating my mother. It helps me to see her in every aspect. Her essence immortalized in my heart, mind, and muscle—a paltry alternative, but the best one available to me.

A week before the memorial service, I had a dream that my mom, Johnny, and I were swimming like dolphins down rapids, but the current was exceptionally gentle. We had our human forms but moved gracefully. Johnny was holding my mom's left arm and I was behind both of them holding Johnny's right leg. Somewhere along the river I swam up to face him and pointed to my mom, then pointed up, signaling to let her come up for air. Johnny let go and Mom floated upward, lifting her face to the open air, and she inhaled the world.

I want to be her.

Cited Works

1. *Finding Dispersed Families.* Directed by Park Hee-ung. Aired originally on June 30 to November 14, 1983, on the Korean Broadcasting System (KBS).

2. Acoff, Vester and Rogers, Christina. " "She Had Dreams In Life": A Remembrance Of Latasha Harlins." *StoryCorps.* May 3, 2022. https://storycorps.org/stories/she-had-dreams-in-life-a-remembrance-of-latasha-harlins/

3. Ford, Andrea and Wilkinson, Tracy. "Grocer Is Convicted in Teen Killing: Verdict: Jury finds Korean woman guilty of voluntary manslaughter in the fatal shooting of a black girl." *Los Angeles Times.* Oct. 12, 1991. https://www.latimes.com/archives/la-xpm-1991-10-12-mn-152-story.html

4. Clifford, Frank and Wilkinson, Tracy. "Korean Grocer Who Killed Black Teen Gets Probation." *Los Angeles Times.* Nov. 16, 1991. https://www.latimes.com/archives/la-xpm-1991-11-16-mn-1402-story.html

5. Serrano, Richard A. and Wilkinson, Tracy. "All 4 in King Beating Acquitted : Violence Follows Verdicts; Guard Called Out : Trial: Governor deploys troops at mayor's request after arson, looting erupt. Ventura County jury apparently was not convinced that videotape told the whole story." *Los Angeles Times.* April 30, 1992. https://www.latimes.com/archives/la-xpm-1992-04-30-mn-1891-story.html

6. Kang, Inkoo. "Growing Up In Koreatown - And Watching It Burn." *MTV News.* April 27, 2017. https://web.archive.org/web/20170501071829/http://www.mtv.com/news/3005922/strangers-in-town

Acknowledgements

Encouragement for this book came from family and friends after hearing my very long eulogy during my mom's memorial service. Thank you to those who saw something blossom in the eruption of laughter and tears. An excerpt of this book was taken from my essay, "Umma," published by *Entropy* magazine in November 2021.

Immense gratitude to my editor, Kimberley Lim, whose close reading and guidance helped to keep my writing open and honest. Her candor and curiosity inspired me at every stage.

Deep thanks to Kyoko Takahashi for her impeccable cover design and illustration, which captured what I could not put into words. I'm honored that this vivid, moving design came to life through Kyoko's vision. Special thanks also to Pamela Olecki for her invaluable support with last-minute design updates before launch.

Thank you to some big hearts, Sara Russell and Celeste Jacobi, who held me up along the way.

To Abby Antweil, thank you for all you are.

Sunny Pak is a writer and essayist based in Los Angeles. *Umma, at the Edge of Memory* is her first book.

@sunnypak
sunny-pak.com

www.ingramcontent.com/pod-product-compliance
Lightning Source LLC
Chambersburg PA
CBHW020857150726
48196CB00048B/1075

* 9 7 9 8 2 1 8 7 7 6 4 0 4 *